I Still Believe

Hazel McBride

MUM

Without you, none of this would have been possible.

IN THE BEGINNING

Killer Whale. Free Willy. Shamu. The Blackfish.
They have had many different names over the years and have been
represented in many different ways, but regardless of how you
came to know them, they undoubtedly left an impression.
You fell in love with the gentle giant Keiko in the movie *Free
Willy* and were rooting for Jesse and 'Willy's' other caretakers in
their fight to return him to his family. Or perhaps you were one of
thousands of people who sat on the hard metal benches of Shamu
Stadium and cheered as you watched man and killer whale leap
together from the water, in a show of deep relationship and trust.
Maybe the first time you connected with killer whales was through
their portrayal in *Blackfish* which made you angry or confused
about the truth of their lives under human care and ignited a desire
to do more for the animals' well-being.
There is an uncanny ability among cetaceans (such as dolphins and
killer whales) that draws humans to them. They are able to spark
an organic connection with us, even if we are only exposed to them
for the briefest of moments.
Perhaps it is their very mysteriousness that creates our fascination.
They are essentially an air breathing mammal that has adapted to
live in one of the harshest and unforgiving environments in the
world. The ocean.
They appear to experience deep emotions similar to humans and
we crave the ability to communicate with them to truly understand
what it is they are thinking or feeling.
Humans have been drawn to killer whales for hundreds of years.

For the Native Americans, the orca symbolizes family, communication and protection. Some tribes believe that orcas are closely related to humans and that when a human drowns at sea, they are then taken down to the deep of the ocean by an orca and henceforth, transformed into an orca themselves. Other tribes consider the orca to be a particular symbol of power and consider an orca sighting to be a great omen.

The aboriginal people of British Columbia believe that the orca is the guardian of the ocean.

Spiritual teachings like these are proof of the longevity of belief across cultures that the killer whale has been sacred to humans for generations.

Before the 1960s (aside from myths and legends), orcas were viewed as monstrous predators that were feared by humans and regularly hunted by fishermen. Their ability to outsmart their prey and work as a team to maximise the efficiency of their hunting techniques not only made them more of a nightmare for fishermen watching their catch disappear down the gullets of a pod of hungry orcas, it made them a terrifyingly intelligent predator.

Six decades of captivity has seen an enormous change in the way we view these extraordinary animals.

After the early capture and display of orcas in aquariums and marine parks, the public were introduced to an undiscovered side of the animals.

They remained a powerful apex predator, but one with the ability to form close bonds with humans. Instead of being solely represented as a ruthless killer, they were shown to have the ability to experience emotion on a much more profound level.

As a result of this, the public fell in love with the killer whale and spent decades visiting marine parks across the globe in order to see its majesty in person.

Trainers were hailed as 'superstars' and seemed closer to Gods than mere mortals as they bravely dove into the water with the largest predator in the ocean. Each spectator who paid for their ticket watched in awe as whale and trainer leaped from the water in perfect synchronization, a miraculous partnership between man and beast.

However this period of seemingly blissful harmony between humans and killer whales was relatively short-lived. The ethical argument against the keeping of killer whales in captivity has long been in the forefront of people's minds.

In fact, only four years after the live captures began off the coast of the United States of America in 1968, the government passed the Marine Mammal Protection Act in 1972.

This act effectively outlawed the practice of capturing killer whales off the coast of the US. However the practice continued in the waters surrounding Iceland until all live captures were ultimately banned in the western world in the 1980's.

Since this date no marine park in Western Europe or the United States has captured killer whales, or other cetaceans, from the wild. Through successfully breeding orcas in captivity, there has been no need for live captures.

By studying the animals in a captive setting, researchers were better able to control variables and thus gain more significant data. This was then applied to aid scientists researching orcas in their natural environment.

For three decades animal rights activists protesting captivity were simply background noise.

Trainers continued to form deeper relationships with the animals in their care and began to unravel and understand the complexities of orca social structure and the full extent of their individual personalities.

Generations of marine park visitors found within themselves a deeper respect for killer whales, and by extension, all marine life. However the tragic and unforeseen events that would occur towards the end of 2009 and the beginning of 2010 would be the catalyst that animal rights activists needed to bring their argument into the forefront of the public's mind.

 The two fatal accidents that occurred between trainer and killer whale at Loro Parque, Tenerife and in SeaWorld of Orlando sparked a landslide of media coverage and raised never-ending amounts of questions, culminating in the 2013 film, *Blackfish*.

This loosely-based documentary managed to convince millions of people that captivity was driving killer whales insane and causing them to attack their trainers.

Since its release, activists have been gaining public and governmental support for their cause and becoming ever more present on social media platforms, gaining thousands of followers. Trainers like myself have slipped from being people admired for their abilities to connect with killer whales, to being despised for keeping them 'prisoner' in concrete pools.

The dream job I envisioned for myself quite simply no longer exists.

Working with killer whales in the modern world requires a very different type of person than it did thirty years ago.

Unfortunately nowadays, our reality is full of controversy.

When I was younger I must have watched my *Free Willy* VHS so often, I'm surprised the tape never wore through. I would sit, enthralled, as I watched the young orphan boy named Jesse develop a bond with this enormous animal that, despite his size, seemed as cuddly as a teddy bear. I would go to bed dreaming that I was in Jesse's place, that it was *me* Willy had chosen and I would be able to rub his tongue and bring him tasty salmon treats.

I even used to force my younger cousins to play Willy when we would spend Sunday mornings at the local swimming pool. I would kneel on the cold stone tiles and splash the chlorinated water to get them to come over to me so I could pretend to feed them a fish and ask them to do tricks for me.

I would put the tape into our bulky VHS player and sit with my heart pounding, even though I already knew the ending, crossing my fingers in the hope that Willy would make it to the ocean without getting caught by the corporate villains who wanted to kill him for the insurance money.

I still remember the strangest vivid details from the movie.

The way the huge salmon was wrapped in crunchy white paper, like the type you got from the fish and chip shop. Or how the stolen cake the runaways were eating with their bare hands at the beginning of the movie looked so tasty I always wished I could have a piece. And of course the novice harmonica playing from *Willy's* young friend Jesse.

Fast forward fifteen years and I was sat backstage at Loro Parque, listening to a colleague butcher whatever five-note song he was attempting to blow through the battered old harmonica he had found. Regardless of the poor quality playing, the whales actually seemed to really like it. Well, they liked it better than the screeching recorder we tried afterwards at least. Perhaps it reflects more on the musical abilities of the trainers than the instrument of choice.

When the movie finally finished I would even watch the end credits, four minutes of visually stunning footage of orcas breaking the surface of a flat calm ocean at sunset to the crooning of Michael Jackson's *Will You be There.*

That was the first time I felt a connection with killer whales.

When I was eight years old I sat in Shamu Stadium for the first time watching trainers swim in the water alongside the killer whales and I felt my mouth drop open in wonder that such a thing was possible.

The Shamu Adventure was the show presented to the audience when I visited in 2001. The trainers wore red and black wetsuits, a striking colour contrast with the bright white of the whales. I watched as Jack Hannah, a leader and spokesman of animal conservation from the Columbus Zoo and Aquarium, spoke to us about the importance of conserving the natural environment from the large screens on either side of the pool.

A trainer then stepped out from behind the screen and began telling us about the importance of captive killer whales as ambassadors for the rest of their species in the wild, and how we could all do our part to conserve the orcas' natural environment.

During the show I watched trainers perform behaviours I could never have imagined in my wildest dreams- the rockethop, the hydrohop, a fast swim ride, a stand-on.

I may know the names of those waterwork behaviours now but back then, little eight year old me was already dreaming of being able to dive off the rostrum of a whale and surf on its back.

Little did I know that I would never get that opportunity.

Looking back it almost seems as if I started out in my career at exactly the wrong time.

One of the major catalysts that sparked public outcry against the keeping of killer whales in captivity was the death of Dawn Brancheau, which occurred while I was just starting my bachelor's degree in Psychology at University.

The second major catalyst that accelerated the change in public opinion was the release of the movie Blackfish, which happened while I was completing my second internship, just before I graduated.

These two major events set a ball rolling that never really stopped. Therefore, just as I was beginning my career as a marine mammal trainer, with the firm intention of becoming a killer whale trainer in the future, I knew that I was diving head first into a maelstrom of controversy.

The movie *Blackfish* is clever and it never fails to provoke an emotional response from anyone who watches it. When I watched it for the first time it made me furious because I knew it had the potential to become a very powerful movie, and I was scared.

I was scared of what it would have the ability to do, of how it would plant the seeds of doubt in millions of people's minds and completely change the way people viewed trainers and the lives of the animals we care for.

I watched it for a second time only three days later, determined this time to remain objective. What I realised was that the majority of the movie is loosely based in truth, but that the producers manipulated and twisted that truth to fit their own agenda.

The 'truth' that is portrayed within the movie is either outdated, exaggerated or fabricated. With the majority of the commentary a far cry from what I, and other trainers, experience with the whales every single day.

It doesn't really matter what it was that inspired you to care about killer whales, all that matters is that it happened.

Perhaps it was a movie like *Flipper* or *Free Willy* that first showed you cetaceans' ability to experience emotion and develop connections with humans.

Or for you, like me, it was also the Shamu Adventure show and its message of conservation inspired you to do your part to protect the killer whales' natural environment.

Possibly it didn't happen until years later when you watched the Believe show and felt moved by the powerful imagery and message it conveyed to the audience.

Or maybe it was *Blackfish* that led you to seriously question the ethics surrounding the keeping of such large and intelligent animals in zoological settings.

Regardless of what your opinion is or where it came from, we are all in the same boat.

We are all people who care about killer whales.

The modern day controversy surrounding the keeping of killer whales in captivity and the plight facing their wild counterparts is not as black and white as the animals themselves.

I think that when we all take a step back and decide to stop fighting each other and realise that we all want the same thing, what is best for the animals, then we can finally start helping killer whales everywhere.

*

I am not a veteran trainer who has spent thirty years working in the water with killer whales.

I am not a manager of a facility or a marine biologist or an accredited researcher. I am just a girl who spends my days working around and loving killer whales for a living.

The only way to achieve an impossible dream is single-minded determination and resigning yourself to the fact that the road to your dream may not always be a smooth one.

Mine definitely had its fair share of pot-holes and road blocks along the way.

Against all the odds I managed to make my dream a reality.

It doesn't matter what I went through to get here, all that matters now is the difference I can make to change our world of marine mammal care for the better. I love my job, I love the whales more than almost anything else in the world, and I truly believe in what I do every day when I zip up my wetsuit.

And I don't want this world to go anywhere.

That is why it is so important to me to share with you, the reader, my story and my experiences.

I want everyone, everywhere, to have a better understanding of what it is like to be a trainer, who these animals are, what their lives are really like and where their future lies.

Because their future is in our hands.

I am a killer whale trainer and I still Believe.

CHAPTER ONE – THE SPARK

So how exactly does a young girl from a very small countryside village in Scotland one day decide that she wants to become a killer whale trainer?

As unexpected and unconventional as it may have seemed to everyone around me, it sometimes feels like my entire childhood and adolescence was priming me for the job.

The village I grew up in was very small.

Nestled among lush green hills overlooking the sprawling city of Glasgow, there is a classic main street featuring a butchers and a bakers but minus the candlestick makers. Two small primary schools, a swimming pool, church, town hall and library all within less than a mile radius. There was one modest housing development estate down the hill from the main street where the majority of my family lived- three sets of aunts and uncles and a horde of cousins.

The flat I grew up in was directly on the main street, a great location for people-watching or for a full-blown catch up from passing neighbours or friends through the kitchen window. I've seen my Mum passing tea and biscuits through that window to our local painter and it wasn't unusual to ask someone to drop a letter off for you as they passed the post box up the street. In a freezing Scottish winter you do whatever you can to avoid leaving a cosily heated home.

The village encompassed a sense of old-world community, dependence on the land and good old fashioned fun.

I know my childhood wasn't perfect but it came pretty close.

Knowing now what it is like to live a long way from home, family and everything familiar, I really appreciate the fact that while I was growing up I had everyone important near me.

I remember fondly the times I spent with my Gran, sitting at a slightly sticky table in the café across the road from the church, licking the melted butter off of my toast while she had tea with her friends. We would take long walks through the village together, often because she would grow far too impatient to wait for the bus and would tell me that we could walk there faster. Inevitably halfway to our destination the bus would pass us by.

I was raised by a single mother.

A beautifully selfless woman who worked permanent nightshift as a psychiatric nurse for over thirty years. She is the hardest working woman I know and my absolute rock.

There is no way that I would be where I am today if it wasn't for her.

Considering the fact that she spent the majority of her nights restraining patients in the middle of psychotic episodes, ultimately resulting in two slipped disks and irreversible nerve damage in her spine, she did an incredible job of never letting the strain show. Just taking care of me she must have been exhausted.

Not being able to go to bed until she had dropped me off at school and then religiously waking up less than six hours later to take me to whatever after-school club she had worked extra shifts to be able to sign me up for.

Despite her undeniable exhaustion and lack of time she was an incredibly hands-on mum. Always there to help me with my homework, patiently waiting as I spelled things out for her or struggled over my sums, she would sit in her special chair beside my bed and read me my bedtime stories, barely showing her exasperation when I pointed out that she had skipped a page.

Now that I am older I appreciate how tough it must have been for her, but she never once let me see how much she must have struggled.

The majority of clothes that she wore when I was growing up were threadbare and washed out. I'm pretty sure she wore her shoes down until there was practically no sole left on them before buying herself a new pair, and she never allowed herself luxuries.

Any clothes that were bought were strictly practical. Trainers, jumpers and jeans, no accessories except a sturdy handbag and the one gold necklace that had been a gift from a friend ten years ago. When I was young I just accepted that's the way my mum was, assuming she just didn't want to fuss over her appearance.

I never questioned the fact that maybe it was through necessity and not through choice.

In my young brain I just never put two and two together, the fact that I was never left wanting but my mum never seemed to want anything for herself.

Because whatever it was that she had, she immediately gave to me. I always had nice new clothes, the latest Barbie doll and snazzy light up trainers that must have cost a fortune. I was enrolled in dance classes, violin classes, swimming classes and told that the world was my oyster.

She wanted to give me the very best that she had, even if that meant she had to go without.

I smile when I think of the times we would spend together when she was off work, playing board games on the living room floor listening to old Phil Collins or Billy Joel CDs on the stereo. How she would be just as involved in my imaginary play as I was, inventing endless stories along with me for my Polly Pockets and Barbies.

She would take me on 'mystery tours' which sounded incredibly exciting when I was six but was really just a fancy name for what happened before Google Maps existed when you got lost, ending up at a completely different destination to the one you had planned.

Despite being the only parent and working all the hours God sent in order to keep our heads above water, she was always volunteering to chaperone school day trips, baking for the jumble sales and organising raffle prizes for the school charity events.

An impossibly kind and generous woman who would bend over backwards in order to help her loved ones, but with a fiery temper that let you know that you never wanted to get on her bad side. It's impressive when you see a woman standing at only five foot three put a grown man in his place with the smallest look.

That kind of inner fire was necessary for three decades working in psychiatry and unfortunately I was especially skilled at getting on the wrong side of her, especially in my ungrateful, attitude-filled teenage years.

Oh the fights we used to have!

Even my gran would tell us that the whole problem was that we were far too alike and that neither of us had anyone else to argue with.

We would, and still do on occasion, spat and squabble like sisters instead of mother and daughter. But the best by-product of a single mother and only daughter relationship is that you become inseparable.

She is my best friend, my travel buddy, my shoulder to cry on and my biggest champion.

I only wish that we could spend more time together nowadays, a geographical impossibility given the fact that we live in different countries.

While my Mum was at work I would be looked after by my Gran. I would curl up next to my gran's cat Judy on a sun-warmed patch of carpet beneath the high living room window and happily munch on thick ham sandwiches slathered with butter.

I would sleep on the floor in my gran's room beside her bed on a blow up mattress when my mum was working, usually I would fall asleep holding her hand and when I woke up in the morning her hand would still be dangling over one side of the bed. I can still picture the way it looked, she had deep grooves on her fingernails that caught the light.

The two of us would spend the frequent Scottish downpours buried in books, my gran's neatly curled grey hair peeking out over the top of her latest novel and my own hair wildly escaping out of its pigtail. We would dash to the library before or after mass to grab up to six new titles and cosy up in our respective armchairs with the fire on and read in silence for hours.

On the rare days when it was not raining (I won't go so far as to say sunny since the sun only comes out in Scotland for about two weeks of the year) we would go on long walks together.

We would wander the country lanes with my gran pointing out the new lambs in the fields either side of us, and I would pick wildflowers to take back to my mum when she woke up late in the afternoon.

It was all very Enid-Blyton.

Even though I came from a small town, my mum wanted more for me.

She wanted to expose me to all the possibilities that were on offer and miraculously she managed to make me feel like anything was possible.

Despite the fact that she was supporting us both on a basic nurse's salary which did not stretch very far, she worked all the overtime that was on offer to be able to take us on a trip to Orlando when I was eight years old.

In this way throughout my entire life my mum consistently showed me that anything was possible with enough hard work and determination. A principle that I still live by to this day. If you want something badly enough, you will find a way to make it happen.

The trip was heavily focused on Disney World.

I was eight and I was obsessed with Disney Princesses, especially Pocahontas.

On our first day we went to the Magic Kingdom and because we were resort guests we were able to get into the park an hour before the general public. I'm pretty sure we were one of the first people into the park that morning, as we took advantage of the 'extra magic hours' during the May off-season.

I remember walking onto Main Street USA and being greeted with a ginormous snow globe that seemed to be moving down the street as if by magic. My mouth dropped open and I looked up almost in slow motion and there was Pinocchio inside the snow globe.

And he was waving at me.

Waving. At. Me.

Apparently they were filming an early morning parade for a promotional video, part of the Millennium celebration, but that instant sense of magic set the tone for the rest of the holiday. I was already a very imaginative child. I believed in Santa Claus until I was eleven (I will still argue his existence with anyone who dares tell me he isn't real to this day) and spent my downtime playing imaginary games involving fairies and pixies and magic wizards. I'm pretty sure my mum needed a whole second holiday after our two weeks in Orlando just to recover from it.

We were on our feet all day, every day.

From eight in the morning I was awake and hurrying down to the breakfast hall to stuff my face with the delicious American buttermilk pancakes. Then it was straight onto the bus that would take us to our park of choice for the day and we would not stop until it was time for lunch.

Character-spotting, water-rides, crazy rollercoasters in the dark, you name the attraction and we did it. Almost every night we stayed in the park to watch the fireworks meaning that we weren't on the bus back to the hotel until just before midnight each night. I remember the feeling of complete exhaustion and falling asleep on my mum's knee only to be rudely jerked awake by the harsh lights and groaning of other tired children as we finally arrived back at the hotel.

Luckily, she decided that one day away from Disney wouldn't be the worst thing in the world and so she reserved one day to take us to SeaWorld Orlando.

After a week of Disney parks I was ready and excited to see what kind of magic this place held inside.

When the gates finally opened, my mum and I rushed straight to Dolphin Cove because we had heard that if you were quick you could buy some fish to feed to the dolphins.

We got into the queue and purchased a soggy paper cone filled with exactly seven capelin each.

We approached the edge of the pool, me being so small I had to balance on my stomach to be able to see over, and saw the dolphins waiting for us. Their grey faces bright and alert, black eyes darting to and fro, ready for their morning snack.

I am extremely proud of my mum and the amount of care and respect she took while feeding the animals herself and while teaching me how to feed them.

She payed attention to the briefing videos playing in the background, and made me read the signs that told us how to properly give the dolphins a fish. No dangling the whole cone over the edge, no baiting the dolphins by teasing them with the fish and no sharp movements to try and touch them, being careful of their unprotected eyes.

She placed our fish on the back of the wall and waited for me to get a good grip on my first slippery capelin. I placed my left hand in the correct position to be able to potentially touch the dolphin's lower jaw and I held that single capelin out over the water like a beacon. Obviously it didn't take long for one of them to become interested.

I have seen a lot of children come in to do dolphin interaction programs or dolphin feeding sessions like this where they nervously take the fish, listen to their parents telling them to hold the fish out and then squeal and toss the fish away when the dolphin approaches, quickly leaping back from the wall.

It is understandable, a dolphin is a very large animal and completely different to any animal a child will have seen up close until that moment. Not to mention that the first time that child saw the dolphin up close they were coming at them with their mouth open displaying four rows of gleaming sharp white teeth.

I was not one of those children.

I mentioned already my love of reading as a child, I was never far away from a story and the stories I loved reading most were about animals. One of my all-time favourite series' as a child was about the daughter of a marine biologist who travelled all around the world with her parents, studying and building relationships with dolphins and whales.

I was desperate for that to be me.

I remember holding out those seven capelin, waiting for the dolphins to come over and when they slid their little grey faces into my left hand, I dropped my capelin into their gaping mouths with a plop and then they swam away in search of another easy snack.

Once I had finished my supply of dolphin treats I turned around and immediately begged my mum to get us another cone full.

Even though those cones cost seven dollars each (that is one dollar per fish!) My mum could see how happy it made me and so she left me watching the dolphins and rushed off to see if there were any cones left at the stall.

When she came back, I eagerly grabbed my newly filled cone and as soon as she passed it to me, the dolphins started crowding around. The animals knew that the majority of people by this point had already finished their fish and I was one of the last options. This time because there were so many of them, between feeding each capelin I put my hands flat out on the surface of the water, just like the instructional video had said, and waited for a dolphin to swim by. Unfortunately because I was so short, even with my arms stretched to their limit and the rough stone wall scratching my chest and stomach, the dolphins were still swimming too far away for me to reach. I think a couple of times I may have tried to make some desperate grabbing motions, and I need to thank my mum again for swiftly telling me off.

But she was right.

I watched the people who seemed to become crazed around the dolphin pool, making silly whistling noises and trying to splash the water to get the animals to come over, and I knew I didn't want to be like them.

Dolphin feeding pools like this have thankfully gone out of fashion.

Yes it is an easy way for a park to allow guests to get up close with the animals and it is more affordable for the masses than paying a fortune for a structured dolphin encounter, but it is also difficult to police.

Even though the fish used during the 'dolphin feeding times' was nothing more than a snack to supplement the diet of each animal, some animals can become easily frustrated by guests teasing them with the fish. It would be the same as meeting a dog you don't know for the first time and waving a piece of tasty chicken in front of his face but refusing to give it to him until you had petted him. If someone I didn't know walked up to me and offered me a strawberry glazed donut from Dunkin' Donuts (my treat of choice) but then slapped my hand away every time I tried to reach for it, I would not have a good attitude towards that person.

That's not to say that it was all bad, there are a lot of people like my mum who were very aware that the rules and regulations were there for a reason and no matter how much they wanted to touch a dolphin they respected the animals and their space.

I know for a fact that in that moment my mum was more excited to meet the dolphins than I was.

My mum harboured a fascination and love for bottlenose dolphins that has lasted a lifetime. When she was younger and coming from a background of very limited means, she knew that my gran would never have been able to offer her something like this. My gran was too busy supporting her family on the salary of a cleaner after the untimely death of my grandad while she was still pregnant with her eighth child. So when my mum was younger she wrote into TV shows and entered competitions to try and win her dream experience of swimming with dolphins.

When my Mum didn't let me have all fourteen capelin to myself, it was obvious how desperately she wanted to have her special moment with a dolphin. A woman who, up until that point in my life had never given me less than everything she had, refused to let me feed all of the fish to the dolphin because this was a moment she had dreamed about since her own childhood.

I think I had gotten halfway through the cone before she took me off the wall and asked me to switch with her, passing me the disposable camera to try and capture her first moment with the dolphins. I wish I was able to remember her facial expression the first time she touched their silky smooth skin. We are so spoiled these days with smartphones and high-tech cameras that we take for granted the ability to capture any moment we want to remember in perfect HD quality. I can't even remember if I took the picture properly, I think maybe I cut off half of her head by accident.

I like to brag to my mum that I made both of her childhood dreams come true.

Thanks to my job I have been able to offer her a lot of dolphin encounters. She has done a structured dolphin swim with me as her trainer, a natural swim and snorkel with the dolphins at one of the facilities I interned at (and I will never forget the elation on her face when she came out of that lagoon) and multiple dolphin meet and greets. We won't talk about the times I've forced her to have her picture taken with sea lions, she never seems to be able to get over the wet-dog mixed with herring smell.

For her second life-long dream, thanks to my incredibly loud voice and inability to get embarrassed, when we went to see Donny Osmond perform in Las Vegas I screamed his name so loudly and frequently that he finally came over to us and gave my mum a kiss on the cheek. She was mortified and immediately swiped at me with her handbag before blushing a deep crimson, but I am the reason she was kissed by her childhood crush.

1000 daughter points to me.

After we had finished feeding the dolphins at Dolphin Cove we had some time to kill before the first dolphin show and so we geared up to get on the water ride Atlantis. Water rides with big drops have always been my favourite and I was super excited to get on it. I remember balancing at the top of the ride, waiting for the drop and then feeling that whoosh in my stomach as we shot down the chute to the bottom to get absolutely drenched. Luckily for two Scottish people, as it was the only way to survive the Floridian humidity.

Within thirty minutes we were already dry and sitting in the stands for the dolphin show. I almost wrenched my arm out of its socket when they asked for a volunteer, unfortunately they didn't pick me but I did run down to the glass to get soaked again, this time in freezing cold salt water.

As a special treat, just before lunchtime, my Mum had booked us onto the behind the scenes tour which back then included going behind the scenes at Shamu Stadium. I honestly don't remember much about the rest of the tour even though I know we saw a lot of different departments, except one moment where we were in the shark tunnel and one shark started slithering up the glass right beside me and it completely freaked me out.

It was dark and I wasn't expecting it, and I may or may not have screamed.

But I remember our time backstage at Shamu very clearly.

The trainer had lined our small group up behind the yellow safety line adjacent to the back holding pool and began to talk to the group. I'm sure at this point the trainer began explaining killer whale anatomy, training techniques, and other things similar to what I myself now explain to guests on a daily basis.

However I wasn't listening to a word, all I could see were the whales.

I stood there as if hypnotized, their black backs glistening as they glided through the water, skin so smooth I would have done anything to see if it really felt as soft as it looked.

I am pretty sure I was also making some fairly ridiculous and definitely embarrassing 'whale noises' in some childish effort to communicate with them.

We stood there for a while before the trainer said that the children could go a little closer if they wished, right up to the yellow line. Hearing this, my mum immediately grabbed me by the back of my t-shirt.

Not because she was afraid of the whales, which is what I'm sure the trainer thought, but instead because she knew that I had absolutely no fear of them whatsoever.

It was much to my disappointment that she had such an uncanny ability to read my mind. Because both of us knew at that moment, and as my Mum kindly explained to the trainer after her questioning look, was that if I was allowed to go any closer I would probably have made up my mind to jump right into the pool with them.

Which would have been a really terrible decision for a whole number of reasons.

Basically I was the rogue kid that all trainers hate to have in a whale encounter because you always have to have one eye on them at all times, just in case they decide to make a break for it.

But I had seen Free Willy repeatedly, I was a strong swimmer for my age and I loved animals. So of course I was convinced that there could be nothing better than jumping into a pool full of orcas.

After the tour was over we made our way into the massive Shamu Stadium and watched the Shamu Adventure show.

For me, the magic that had encompassed our whole holiday which had begun at Walt Disney World was continuing in ways I didn't even know was possible. I had read books about humans and animals having connections and relationships but in my head I always thought they were just stories. Like my imaginary games they were made in your head and they stayed there.

But right here in front of my very eyes I was watching trainers swimming in the water with the killer whales.

A trainer and whale appeared from nowhere in the middle of the pool, her lying on the whale's stomach, both looking like they were kicking back relaxing. Another girl was unbelievably surfing the back of a whale and not falling off. A man was flying through the air, seemingly suspended by magic after being flung from the water by his whale in a spray of salt.

The impossible was possible after all.

When the show ended, the trainers let all of the whales out into the front pool and I sat there transfixed, the grooves from the metal bench digging into the backs of my thighs, watching the whales swim together through the glass windows.

I sat there for so long that we ended up being asked to leave the stadium so they could begin cleaning and my Mum had to practically drag me away, apologising to the cleaners.

Something had sparked inside me that day.

The most magical holiday of my life unfortunately came to an end as I sat on a British Airways flight heading back to dreary Glasgow with my hands clutching my new Disney Atlantis Kida doll and my head full of impossible dreams.

CHAPTER TWO - WATERBABY

In the years that followed, money became even tighter with my introduction to the world of competitive swimming. Soon all of my mum's money was going towards club fees, new swimsuits and competition race entrances.

I'm pretty sure we went five years without going on holiday.

She made a lot of sacrifices for me.

Even though at my most committed to the sport I was training upwards of twenty hours in the pool per week, she would always come and watch me. For my morning practices I was on my own since she was either still at work, or wisely choosing to stay in her nice warm bed instead of heading out into the drizzling fog at five in the morning. But for two hours every single evening she would be standing vigilantly at the window watching me pull and haul myself up and down the lane.

It was boring enough for me and I was the one swimming, but she faithfully stood there night after night. Most often she was driving me crazy telling me that my sets were too slow or that my turns were sloppy, but she was always there. When I was competing she would sit on those incredibly uncomfortable plastic chairs in the sweltering heat and chlorinated humidity of a public swimming pool for more than eight hours a day just to cheer me on.

The first moment she said she realised I was a water baby was when she took me on holiday aged three to Minorca, a small island off the coast of Spain.

I have photos of me doggy paddling my way around the kiddie pool, frilly Minnie Mouse swim suit and wide brimmed hat bobbing along, adamant that I absolutely did not need armbands.

I still have memories from that same holiday where I would wait until my poor Mother had finally laid her head back on the sun lounger to try and relax, something she sorely needed considering she was alone on holiday with a three year old, so I could seize my opportunity to sprint towards the 'big pool'. Being just a toddler I thought there was nothing more fun in the whole world than to run, giggling, burning the soles of my feet on the hot tiles, towards the deep water of the adult pool.

With no fear I would take a deep breath and fill my little lungs with as much air as possible and launch myself into the blue.

I remember feeling how much colder the adult pool temperature was than the kiddie pool.

I would wait there under the water, no doubt imagining I was the Little Mermaid, until my Mum inevitably jumped in to 'rescue' me.

She enrolled me in swimming lessons at the village pool the week we came back.

My village only has one public swimming pool, it is old and more than slightly run down, but it has character.

For eighteen years of my life not a week went by where I didn't swim in it.

That pool shaped who I am as a person.

I've been up and down it so much that my body instinctively knows where the wall is and prepares me for my tumble turn. I know where the cracked tiles are on the floor and how many wooden beams criss-cross the ceiling. I know how many strokes it will take me to get from one side to the other and which shower in the ladies changing room never runs completely hot because of a damaged water pipe.

From ages three through five I was enrolled in swimming lessons, completing all levels in record time and graduated, begging my mum to allow me to enrol in the local swimming club. As its youngest member at age six I started training once a week, every Sunday evening, in the development squad of the club.

I remember the cosy feeling of finishing my 'training' session with a towel wrapped around my sopping wet hair that I absolutely refused to get cut even though I could almost sit on it, and stepping out into the biting cold and pitch darkness of a cold winters night. Allowing my Mum to bundle me into the car for the two minute drive home, knowing that she already had something delicious waiting in the oven for our dinner.

I won my first competition aged just eight years old but the real races started happening for me when I was around twelve or thirteen.

As I got older, competitive swimming became my life. Unfortunately, considering my swimming commitments increased dramatically at around the same year that I went to high school, I sacrificed all of my friendships with anyone outside of swimming in the process.

Having to continually cancel plans or decline invites to birthday parties or sleepovers because I had to wake up at six on a Saturday morning to train, meant that my peers quickly stopped inviting me anywhere.

I soon turned to books throughout my adolescence in order to find some escape.

When I wasn't training or at school, I was disappearing into the fantasy worlds and magic stories that I loved so much. Phillip Pullman, JK Rowling and JRR Tolkien soon became my best friends, taking me on adventures I didn't have the time to go on in real life.

This isn't to say that I didn't have any friends, in fact I had several incredibly close friends who were also swimmers who I either trained with every day or saw at competitions practically every weekend.

A lot of the people I know from my swimming days I still keep in touch with today.

I must have been about thirteen, changing my swimsuit for a race at the Scottish Nationals, when one of my best friends came running around the corner to excitedly tell me that she had just had her first kiss in the cubicle behind me.

Six months later during a daring game of spin-the bottle at a warm-weather training camp in Cyprus she was one of the spectators of my first kiss.

Just last year I sat on a ribbon wrapped chair, my thighs sweating in a long dress on an uncharacteristically hot June day in Troon, trying not to cry as I watched her have her first kiss as a married woman.

The friendships that you form as a competitive athlete, regardless of the sport, become unbreakable.

Once you have seen that person at five in the morning every morning for a year, or held their hand as they sobbed over a failed race they had trained so hard for, or exchanged pained grimaces as your coach forces you through yet another set of two minute planks, you know you have a friend for life.

I find the same thing happens with marine mammal trainers.

When you work with people who have the same mentality as you, who are with you during the freezing hours of a night-watch for a pregnant dolphin, up at six in the morning to do fish kitchen and volunteering to stay late at work in order to monitor a sick animal. Those bonds are not easily broken either.

Having such an immense commitment in your life completely changes everything and my teenage years were dominated by swimming.

I started training up to twenty six hours a week with competitions taking up ten hours each weekend day.

Don't get me wrong I hated training. I honestly do not know a single competitive swimmer who enjoys it. Swim training is boring. We don't get to listen to music to pump ourselves up and keep us motivated during the session, we don't have an endless amount of drills to keep the session variable and we certainly don't have a team of people helping us out.

In swimming it is just you, the black line on the tiled floor and a lane rope.

But we train to win races.

The same principle can be applied to aspiring trainers. If you don't train right then you aren't going to win the race.

For every race won there are hundreds of hours of training put in and multiple failed events.

In order to become a trainer you need to put in the hours of volunteering and interning and still expect to get knocked down along the way before something finally works out.

Those without the determination and commitment required to endure that, will never win the race.

You just have to ask yourself, how badly do you want it?

I was addicted to the rush of the competition.

Walking into an amateur swim meet is mayhem.

Hundreds of socially restricted teenagers gathered together in one leisure centre for the weekend. Everyone hyped up with adrenaline and wearing swimsuits that cover less skin than the average underpants and you end up with an insanely charged atmosphere. Every single competitive swimmer has a residual fear of the competition warm up.

You are basically putting about six hundred teenagers with excess amounts of pent-up competitive energy into a pool that's maximum capacity should be about two hundred individuals.

There are arms flailing around and legs jutting out in all directions so you end up swimming up and down the lane like you're dodging bullets in the matrix.

If you don't have the guts and dominance to quite literally swim over people to create space for yourself, then you will spend the hour you are supposed to be warming up helplessly floundering with only your cap and goggles visible at the surface, stuck at the end of the lane trying to merge into the traffic.

If you do finally manage to get a decent warm up, you then get to sit down on the hard plastic chairs by the side of the pool and wait for three hours until it is time for your race.

I was a good backstroker, and I had a lot of potential, but I struggled in my later years with confidence issues. I had a horrible pattern of letting the pressure get to me and completely failing during really important races.

Physically, I was doing everything I could and more to prepare my body but it was my mind that was letting me down.

Psychologically, I was failing every test that was put in front of me.

My first appearance at the British Nationals was not only a fluke but a spectacular flop.

I had qualified for the 200m backstroke as one of the youngest in my age group by racing at a low-profile swim meet in Ayrshire, shaving more than 22 seconds off my previous personal best. Highly unexpected.

I got to the British Nationals having only just turned fourteen and was immediately overwhelmed by the scale of the competition. Everything was so much bigger, brighter and louder. I went from being a big fish in a small pond to a very tiny fish in a lake the size of Loch Ness overnight. Needless to say I completely choked under the pressure and ended up finishing the race nowhere near my personal best time.

The funny thing about that race was that at the time I felt like I was racing as hard as I could, but when I think back, I was barely out of breath when I hit the wall.

I had been swimming against myself the whole time, my mental block was stopping me from performing to the best of my ability.

I had failed my first test in the big leagues and it was all my own fault.

I had taken a look around when I arrived and everyone else seemed so much bigger, so much faster, and so much more deserving of a medal or a place in the final than I did. As a result of this, there had not been even the slightest chance in my mind that I was going to succeed in the pool that day.

As a direct result I had given up before I had even pulled on my swimsuit.

This is exactly the kind of self-doubt that kills people's drive to achieve their dreams before they even get going. We need to start by believing in ourselves, and believing that we have the ability to make anything happen if we have enough determination and drive. Whenever I think back to races I won versus races I lost, the difference was always psychological.

It didn't matter if I had been eating right or training enough hours, if my head wasn't in the game and I didn't believe that I could win then I wouldn't. And for my first outing at the British Nationals, my race was over before it had even begun.

It was an important lesson that took me years, and a change in coaching, to learn.

In the middle of my swimming career I started floundering psychologically.

For so many years I had been on a steady incline, but suddenly thanks to my confidence issues and lack of proper coaching, I was drowning in the current of my competitors.

Luckily a young coach by the name of Jimmy Orr, a man who embodies every Scottish stereotype known to mankind, decided he could take me on and turn my career around.

He used psychology in every single training session.

Making sure his swimmers were motivated, confident, mindful and passionate about what they were trying to achieve. He knew all of our strengths and weaknesses and most importantly, our motivators.

For some reason, anger and a desire to prove people wrong, is my greatest motivator.

So Jimmy, with his face flushing as red as his hair, can of Irn Bru clutched in one hand, swim meet schedule rolled up in the other, would cleverly and subtly find ways to make me mad as hell before races.

In actual fact he went on to win Great British Coach of the Year just a few years ago and has successfully coached several athletes to Olympic careers.

The last race of my own career was bittersweet and I didn't know that it would be my last race before I swam it.

It was my second time competing in the Inter-County International Championships for the West of Scotland team and I knew that this year my team counted me as one of their top athletes.

Based on a points system, athletes compete to gain the most points for their team and the team with the most points at the end of the meet wins the championship.

Almost one thousand highly-competitive, socially-backwards teenagers are gathered together inside the enormous Ponds-Forge swimming pool, Sheffield.

I sat in the hard plastic chair, damp in my tracksuit, trying not to let my nerves show.

I was waiting in the marshalling area with forty other girls in my age group, all of us eager for the gold. In the harsh lights that reflected off the unnaturally blue water and ugly tiled floor, it was impossible to know what time of the day or night it was.

The only time that mattered was the one taken from the stopwatch. My lucky fastskin was already cutting into my shoulders, no doubt leaving deep red welts, even though I had left it until the last possible moment before sliding the straps up. A seamless, hydrodynamic, water-repellent scrap of £300 material that takes fifteen minutes to squeeze into but is designed to help you win races.

My coach had begged me to wear another racing suit. Given this one's age it probably had no streamlining advantages left except the fact that it was two sizes too small and fit me like a second skin.

When I appeared out of the changing rooms after the warm-up to sit with the West of Scotland team the Scottish coach had rolled his eyes and asked me to change into a newer suit. Instead of doing just that, I sat down beside him and dumped my bag on the wet floor, shrugging on my team tracksuit.

I bit into my first cereal bar of the day and flicked my wet hair off my neck

My competition may have believed in the psychological edge given to an athlete wearing a brand-new tech suit, but the edge I needed was going to come from the suit that had been with me when I had broken Scottish records and won some of my most important gold medals.

Even if it was a few years out of date.

Ignoring the advice of the Scotland coach but secure in the knowledge that Jimmy would be in full support of my decision, I went to sit with the rest of my team. Forty socially-deprived teenagers who had been let loose with no parents for a weekend.

Looking back, I pity the coaches' job as chaperones.

The previous day we had all spent six hours on a stagecoach being bussed down to Sheffield from Glasgow.

When we stopped at a service station after a few hours to grab some lunch, all of the 'newbies' were given a challenge. A dare if you will, to be carried out within sight of a 'senior' athlete inside the service station before we got back onto the bus as an initiation game.

The year before when I had been competing for the first time, my dare had been to sing my order at Burger King.

The 'seniors' got a big surprise when I ordered my chicken nuggets and chips to the tune of Christina Aguilera's 'Survivor', my voice carrying through to the WHSmiths on the other end of the hall. My last notes ended with a round of applause from the other customers as I stowed my Evian water bottle, which I had been using as a microphone, back in my bag.

I had just been relieved to escape the humiliation of the infamous 'Banana Push-up'. I'll spare you the details but it's no surprise that it was born out of the brain of a sexually frustrated teenage swimmer.

The dares aren't only used to humiliate new team members but also to make them feel like a part of the team before we start competing.

For some of the older athletes, the competition is a lot more important. Setting new personal bests and having the team finish in a good position can open doors to elite training camps or even to the Commonwealth Games.

Sitting on my chair that morning I was waiting to compete in my best event, the 100m backstroke, and I knew that I was in with a real chance of winning.

Trying to surreptitiously extract my racing suit from my butt crack as the girls in the heat before mine were called up by the runner, I started eyeing up my competition.

There were only a couple of girls that I had known previously from other important competitions in Scotland, but because I rarely competed on the English circuit, except for in international events like this one, there were a lot of unfamiliar faces.

Unfamiliar was not something I liked.

I liked to look at who was in my heat, know what their best time was and either feel secure in the knowledge that I could beat it, or know how much time I would have to shave off my own personal best in order to be faster.

I saw some of the other girls looking at me in the same way and allowed myself a small internal smile. Even though I didn't know who they were, they didn't know who I was either.

And that was an advantage I could use.

I stood up and scraped my long dark hair up into a severe high bun, drawing the eyes of the majority of my competition.

Jimmy had coached me well, and he understood how psychology could tip the scales in an athletes favour. By psyching-out the competition you can win a race before it had even begun and by never allowing yourself to become psyched-out by any other athlete, you retain your advantage over them.

By standing up and moving around while everyone else was sitting calmly made me stand out.

With my hair tied up securely I then pulled on my swim cap. Brand-new for the team meet, thick latex sparkling silver with a proud purple lion-rampant emblazoned over the words 'Scotland West', also in purple. I knew I was the only Scottish girl representing my team in the final.

This made me stand out even more and I saw some of the other girls exchange looks out of the corner of my eye. It was working.

I stayed standing and started stretching out my muscles, making sure everything was warmed up for the race. The actual swimming warm up had taken place hours ago and since then I had done nothing but sit in the stands with my team, drawing war-paint on ourselves in the spirit of the unique competition.

The runner finally came to collect us from the marshalling area to line us up in order before we were allowed to approach the starting blocks. Going into the race I was lying in fifth position on a time of 1.06.64, the fastest girl had a time of 1.05.37 and even though that may not seem like a lot of time, in the world of competitive swimming, milliseconds can separate a gold medal from last place. I pulled my swim cap tighter around my ears to muffle the sound of the screams and cheers echoing off the walls as team mates cheered each other on. I walked the breadth of the pool until I reached my lane and stood behind the timekeeper's chair, watching the heat before me start.

"Take your marks. Beep!"

The robotic voice announced the start of the race, followed by the loaded silence of the pause, and finally the starting beep. My competitors were off.

I took a few deep breaths to calm my nerves and reminded myself that I was prepared for this. I slid out of my flip flops and placed them in the plastic bin before me, my bare feet hitting the cool damp floor. I peeled off my tracksuit and dumped it on top of my flip flops, letting the humid atmosphere engulf my exposed skin. I adjusted the straps on my fastskin suit for the hundredth time, running my index finger over the ridged indentations they had left behind in the fleshy part of my shoulders. Rolling them first backwards and then forwards, I felt the tight straps stretch as my muscles flexed.

I took one more deep breath as the heat before me ended and pulled on my dark tinted prescription goggles. Blind as a bat, I had gone through the majority of my swimming career squinting at whiteboards to try and interpret what set I was supposed to be doing from the already illegible scrawl. Speedo had recently started manufacturing racing goggles that allowed prescription adjusted lenses, for a hefty price tag.

Although the goggles I wore were still not as small as some worn by other athletes, they were the best I could get. Streamlining is everything to a swimmer, to minimise drag some people even went so far as to have goggles without rubber, which is used to protect the sensitive skin around the eyes, and so small that they covered only the eye socket itself.

Testing the slack in my goggles to make sure they were securely fitted around my head and would not slip off or fill with water during take-off (every swimmers nightmare), I snuck a glance up at the big screen behind me and saw that the fastest time for the previous heat had been 1.06.89, slower than my personal best. Another breath to tame the butterflies in my stomach.

Our heat was announced and I stepped up to the starting block. I padded across the immaculately clean tiles and looked up from my starting block to the enormous cavern of the Ponds Forge. The same pool that had broken me the first time I had raced in it at the British Nationals aged fourteen was going to make me.

Backstroke being my best event, I started the majority of my important races in the water. Alongside me in their respective lanes, nine other girls were poised beside their own starting blocks waiting for the signal to jump in.

Three sharp, piercing whistle blasts and we all jumped into the frigid pool.

As I sank to the bottom and the water cooled my heated skin, the bubbles from my exhalation on entry tickling my face, the world went silent. The butterflies stopped their incessant flapping in my stomach and I steeled myself for the race.

I surfaced slowly, my nose and mouth still submerged and I heard the long single warning whistle blow, telling us to take our positions. I pulled my swim cap securely over my ears one last time and reached up above me to grab onto the metal bar.

A few milliseconds to flex my grip and test my hold and then I was suspended, balanced on a knife edge with a blank mind, waiting for the starting beep.

"Take your marks."

My whole body tensed, my arms pulling me almost clean out of the water, curled tight like a spring. My feet flush with the touchpad on the wall, knees bent and muscles quivering with anticipation.

"Beep!"

I launched myself off the wall, arching my back so I entered the water fingertips first. With my whole body underwater I started frantically butterfly kicking. A good start can win you a race and using the propulsion from a good take-off and strong butterfly kick can put you, quite literally, head and shoulders above the rest. Adrenaline pumping and fresh muscles make the start of the race the most promising and the most enjoyable. The fire to win is burning in your heart and in your mind, but not yet in your lungs.

I surfaced, my arms slicing through the glassy surface of the pool like a hot knife through butter, shoulders rolling my body from side to side and my legs kicking like crazy behind me. My arms soon sent the calm surface of the water churning as I cupped my hands to push myself further and propelled my arms harder to move myself faster.

Blue, Red and White flags appeared in my vision above me meaning the wall was coming and it was time to turn. One, two, three strokes and flip forward, one frontcrawl stroke to propel me down and my legs flipped over my head and it was back to butterfly kick off the wall. Adrenaline was still pumping madly through my system allowing me to undulate my hips, knees locked together and arms pressed tight to my ears in the streamline position. Up to the surface again, pushing my arms as fast as they would go, snatches of the cheering crowd made their way into my ears as the water surged around me. The harsh light strips on the ceiling seared their way onto my retinas as I stared above me.

I completed the second turn, back at the wall where I started and as I turned over I knew that the next time I hit the same spot the race would be over.

As I raced down the third length I noticed that my body was still feeling good. Having raced the 100m backstroke more times than I could count, I knew from experience this was the moment where I usually started to struggle. The muscle cramping would begin and I would have to grit my teeth and push through. But my muscles still felt like elastic bands pulled taut, waiting for release. I was sucking in air like a man rescued from drowning but the burning in my lungs that I usually experienced, a combination of mild asthma and exertion, was minimal. In that moment I felt like laughing, if only I had trained as hard my entire career as I had been for the last month, I would have had better times and won more races.

Coming off of the third turn I noticed the burning in my lungs intensify and my need for oxygen increased, I could no longer stay underwater doing lengthy butterfly kicks.

I was up to the surface just past the flags.

It was the last length, the final push.

I gritted my teeth and asked my body to push as hard as it ever had before, lactic acid starting to build up in my legs, stinging its way from my calves up the back of my thighs. My arms started to feel like lead weights but still I kept swinging them around my head. I tried to take a sneaky look out the corner of my eyes with my limited goggle-vision to see what position I was in and if I was doing as well as I thought I was, but all I could see was the spray of water created by my own flailing limbs.

Suddenly the flags flew above me and I took one last deep breath and threw myself against the wall with all the strength I had left. My fingers sunk into the yellow flesh of the touchpad, immediately recording my time and I returned to reality.

The crowd was screaming, the atmosphere electric as I gathered myself together enough to hold onto the metal bar of the starting block with a shaking arm and peer through my steamed-up goggles at the screen.

I managed to pick out my name from the list however before I could look across to see my time, they switched the order of the board to display the results in descending order.

My name was at the top.

1.05.04

My jaw dropped and my eyes welled up with tears. Not only had I won my event, my best event, at one of the most important competitions of my career, but I had won it with a personal best. I had been trying to get my 100m backstroke time under the 1.06 mark for over a year at that point and it had seemed that no matter what I tried I was cursed to never go any faster.

I just could not get under 1.06.

But that day, with my body feeling like it could carry me for miles and not get tired, I flew through the water and blew the competition away.

I turned around, still dumbstruck, floating at the end of my lane and looked up into the spectator stands at the Scottish coach who was repeatedly punching the air in victory. Just behind him was another coach who knew me very well, the mother of my ex-boyfriend, who was beaming at me in complete understanding, knowing how hard I had worked to get to this moment.

I dunked my sweltering face, beaming red with exertion, under the water to cool it off and to wipe away my tears as I swam from lane to lane to get to the edge of the pool. I was met by the majority of the other girls in my heat who were also collecting their clothes, shoes and water bottles from the bins. Luckily for most swimmers, as soon as the race is over we are a relatively sociable bunch and I was met with genuinely warm smiles and I was able to exchange congratulations with some of them.

Arms and legs shaking with fatigue I gathered up my belongings and made my way unsteadily behind the curtain to the cool-down pool.

I eased myself into the water and pushed off the wall in a slow and steady recovery rhythm drowning the biggest smile in the water. I was elated, I had managed to finally break my personal best time, had helped push my team into second place. I had won an incredibly difficult race in a swimming pool that had previously brought me nothing but bad luck and bad races. I was only disappointed that I couldn't get a gold medal for my individual efforts.

I had finally passed the test. I finally knew how to believe in myself enough to make miracles happen.

At 8pm the next evening, every race had been swum and Scotland West had finished in bronze medal position, the best ranking they had ever achieved in the competition.

The whole team piled down the stairs and onto the enlarged podium, all of us fighting to have a place on top of it for the official photograph.

As I stood there surrounded by people who had been a part of my life almost every weekend for the past ten years, finally victorious in smashing my 1.06 time to pieces, I made my decision to stop swimming competitively.

At eighteen years of age I had spent more than a decade dedicated to twelve training sessions a week, eaten more nutri-grain bars than any human being ever should and absorbed so much chlorine into my skin that it was coming out of my pores.

I was faced with a choice. Keep pulling myself out of bed at ridiculous times in the morning every day to keep company with a lane rope and make the Commonwealth Games team the following year, or go to University.

It was time for a change.

CHAPTER THREE – THE SWIM TEST

The decision to leave the world of competitive swimming was not an easy one, even though by that point I had realised that I desperately wanted to become a marine mammal trainer. When something has been such a large part of your life for so many years, especially those critical adolescent years, you don't know how you will be without it.

Turns out that I got a lot more sleep and was stuck with the appetite of an athlete for life.

I am very lucky that my background in swimming set me up very well for my transition to the world of marine mammal training.

I'm pretty sure every aspiring trainer reading this book has the fear about The Swim Test.

Almost every facility will have some type of swim test that trainers need to pass, either as an extension of the interview process or within a probation period.

When I was researching as much as possible into the job, I would find myself freaking out after deep-diving into online chat forums of other aspiring trainers talking about how insanely difficult swim tests were. There were people who had been able to do a 'mock' swim test as part of an internship and others who had actually gone for a job interview. And we were all hanging on every word they said, sucking them dry of information like hungry leeches, desperate for the answer to successfully completing a swim test. Those online chat forums are a death trap, you are always going to end up reading things that make you feel worse about your level of experience. There will always be one girl on there who has done five internships, has somehow been allowed to assist in training a behaviour and has done sessions on her own with a dolphin. Another guy will probably be bragging about how he got to use a real whistle bridge at his internship while he was acting as a B point trainer (cue a bunch of false congratulations loaded with envy from everyone else on the forum), and there will always be someone trying to make a swim test sound like The Hardest Thing Ever.

Do you realise what they are doing?

They are psyching you out!

Don't get sucked into this mentality and fail the test before it has even begun.

Even I wasn't immune to it. Even knowing that I was a very strong swimmer, I was seriously questioning my abilities. Those people who were able to pass a swim test made themselves sound like they needed superhuman powers in order to complete it. Horror stories of people bursting their eardrums, getting disoriented under the water so they ended up swimming double the length they were required to or even passing out during the underwater breath hold. They made it sound impossible.

I knew I was a strong swimmer, but I had asthma, so maybe my underwater swim wouldn't be good enough because I couldn't hold my breath for very long. I had never been in a pool deep enough in order to see if I could even get to the depth required of swim tests.

I considered so many options in order to help myself train for The Future Swim Test.

In reality I did none of them.

My first plan was to ask my mum to drive me an hour and a half away to Edinburgh, where they had a diving pool that reached ten meters, so I could practice diving down.

Understandably my mum said no.

My other plan was to enrol myself on a lengthy and expensive free diving course in order to train myself in correct breath holding techniques.

That didn't happen either.

When I got the job on the orca team at Loro Parque, I was given one month to complete the swim test or I would no longer have a job. Quite a terrifying thought considering I had just relocated my entire life across the world to Tenerife.

When I started working there, the requirements for the swim test were to free dive to the bottom of the show pool at twelve meters with no mask or goggles, then swim frontcrawl from the stage to the slide out at the other side of the pool as fast as possible, finishing with an exit from the glass.

Luckily I had that one month in which to practice.

The first time I dived into the orca pool, the freezing temperature of the water hit me like a knife in the chest. I had only been tasked with touching the bottom of the medical pool, a measly four meters, but suddenly my lungs felt six times smaller and I was left gasping for air.

I treaded water at the surface and waited for my respiratory system to calm down. Even in a thick wetsuit the cold penetrated everywhere. The orca pools at Loro Parque are kept at a chilly twelve degrees Celsius, that's fifty three degrees Fahrenheit.

Orcas can live quite comfortably in a variety of water temperatures, from the freezing Antarctic to the warm Mediterranean, but unfortunately humans aren't designed with a layer of insulating blubber.

On a hot summers day it is lovely to jump into the pool (when there are no animals in it obviously) and let the freezing water get into your wetsuit. Because the temperature is so low, the cold sticks to your wetsuit, meaning that even in the hot Tenerife sun you can walk around staying nice and cool.

Once I managed to get my breathing under control, even though I still couldn't fill my lungs to capacity, I took a deep breath and surface dove to the bottom.

Now the cold wasn't the only problem.

I was used to swimming in a swimsuit and goggles, meaning I had relatively little drag or buoyancy and was always able to see where I was going. Now my underwater world became blurry and out of focus and as I stroked closer to the bottom, I worried that I was going to misjudge the distance and smack my face into it.

Not only was it more difficult to see, it was harder to get myself down. The combined buoyancy of a wetsuit and salt water meant that I had to use a lot more energy than usual to pull myself deeper. I might have been a freshwater baby, but I was in the ocean now. Luckily the medical pool at Loro Parque has a rising floor and so the gaps in the slats in the bottom provided enough of a reference for me to stop before I smashed my face into it.

All of the whales at Loro Parque are trained to calmly float at the surface of the water and allow themselves to be raised up by the false bottom. Not only does it give a great opportunity for trainers and vets to give the whales a close-up physical examination, but also allows us to give them rubdowns across their whole body, something they find incredibly reinforcing.

Who wouldn't? Everybody loves a full-body massage.

A few days later I started practicing in the two back pools which had a depth of eight meters, meaning that for the first time in my life while free diving, I was going to have to equalise my ears underwater. So in the few spare minutes of the day when there was time to clear away toys from playtimes and take a break from training sessions, the whales were gated to a different pool to make time for me to practice.

I had completed my SCUBA Padi certification a couple of years previously in Scotland and had never particularly enjoyed scuba diving, finding the gear restrictive and claustrophobic. I much prefer to free dive with a snorkel and fins. So I knew how to equalize my ears at pressure but that didn't mean I was any good at it.

During my scuba course my ears had been a big problem. I was the slowest on my course to descend to the bottom of the frigid lake we trained in because I was highly susceptible to 'squeezes'. A 'squeeze' is when pocket of air gets trapped in the sinuses of your face, your head or even your teeth and when that air expands as it becomes more pressurized it creates an incredible amount of pain.

A couple of years into my job at Loro Parque, I was diving to clean the show pool in the morning. We had just purchased new brushes which were an excellent addition as they allowed us to clean faster and more efficiently than before.

Even though orca pools have a great filtration system that clears out almost all of the liquid faecal matter that cetaceans pass, some of it does sink down to the bottom of the pool before the filters catch it. This means that divers need to scrub the floor and walls to make sure the filters will get it the second time around.

At Loro Parque there is a whole separate team of dedicated and proficient divers whose job it was to dive and clean the pools each day. However very occasionally they would find themselves short staffed which resulted in us trainers lending a hand. Unfortunately for me that morning, I miscalculated the amount of weight I was carrying on me at the time. The new brush apparatus being heavier than the previous model, combined with the fact that I had lost 10kg in weight since my last dive, meant that I should have adjusted my weight belt accordingly.

I did not.

So hoisting on my usual amount of weight onto my weight belt which was now far too heavy for my smaller frame, I clutched the new brush in both hands and jumped into the water.

I sank like a stone the twelve meters to the bottom.

I had descended too far too quickly for it to be safe and ended up in hospital.

Unbeknownst to me at the time of the dive I had been in the beginning stages of sinusitis and the dive had made my symptoms worse. However because I arrived at the hospital after a scuba diving incident, the first thing they did was put me into a hyperbaric chamber.

This meant that I was put 'down' to pressure and brought back 'up' again.

I was in the chamber for the minimum required time of three hours. All I was allowed to do was sit still, wrapped in a scratchy blanket and stare at the white wall in front of me, breathing periodically into an oxygen mask. I wasn't even allowed to wear my glasses because metal couldn't be inside the chamber. I passed those three hours in a blurry, pain streaked, shivering haze which seemed like it would never end.

The last five minutes of the 'ascent' took thirty five minutes because I kept screaming for them to stop as every millibar of pressure they took away caused me even more pain.
I've never felt anything like it.
I came out of the chamber with a serious nosebleed and my head pounding so badly I thought it would explode. I had the doctor urgently asking me where the pain was in Spanish and my mum anxiously asking me what was wrong in English and I could barely even open my mouth to reply in any language it was so painful.
It turns out that having two exposures to pressure was too much for my sinuses when combined with the infection and had caused some of them to rupture.
For a week afterwards I was bedbound, and suffered a recurrence several months later when I caught a cold and mucus became trapped in my now messed-up sinuses. Luckily a strong prescription of steroids cleared it up and simultaneously cured my 10kg weight loss by increasing my appetite to intolerable levels so I started eating everything in sight.
These days I just have to take a lot of care while free diving and completing my swim test, especially if the water is cold.
On a standard day I will need to equalise between five and six times to comfortably reach twelve meters. Most people equalise twice or three times.
Strangely enough, the problem is often not when I'm going down, only when I'm coming back up. If I come up from a free dive too quickly I can feel my sinuses moving around, adjusting to the pressure and if it is really bad, I get shooting pains from the backs of my eyes through the top of my head and down to my neck.
Sometimes I can hear the whistling noise as the air rushes through them.
It isn't strange to find me holding on to the glass of the show pool, halfway up from my free dive, waiting for my sinuses to stabilize.
However equalising was not to be my only difficulty when re-training my competitive swimmers brain for an orca swim test.
I had absolutely no idea how to dive vertically.
My swimming background did me absolutely no favours whatsoever here.
I had been trained my whole life to dive as far and as flat as possible to give me maximum efficiency for speed. Now I needed to learn to dive short but deep.

My first few attempts were pathetic.

Even underwater I needed to constantly adjust my position in order to stay vertical. If you want to hold your breath for as little time as possible then the best plan is to swim straight down and straight back up. However the majority of people will end up swimming diagonally, as it is a natural instinct to want to look where you are going. So by searching for the floor we put our neck out of alignment and because our body will always follow our head, we descend diagonally.

There is nothing wrong with this, it just takes longer.

Vertically still isn't my favourite way to dive as the water does get up your nose and into your head and then for the rest of the day whenever you bend over salt water will pour out of your nose.

I've had it happen at dinner with non-trainers the night after a swim test day. I dropped my fork on the ground under the table at the restaurant and as I came back up I was leaking salt water from both nostrils. Attractive.

The first time I touched the bottom of the show pool at Loro Parque, after training in the back pools for a week, I was following another trainer. It is so much easier to stay relaxed and calm when you can see someone else in front of you down there.

Passing a swim test for the first time gives you such an overwhelming sense of relief and euphoria that it will easily carry you through the rest of the week. Until the moment you realise you work with killer whales and the swim test is a monthly or quarterly occurrence, you don't ever get to escape from it.

When I switched facilities after two years at Loro Parque and started working at Marineland, Antibes, the unknown began to psych me out again. Even though I had been completing the Loro Parque swim test monthly, I was worried about how my sinuses would cope with a longer required underwater breath hold as the show pool at Marineland was much bigger.

I was sceptical about it beforehand due to the expense, however I would now highly recommend a free diving course for anyone who wants to become more relaxed about holding their breath underwater. Before the course my maximum breath hold was one minute forty five seconds, already the longest out of the five of us on the course, but at the end of that day I held my breath for three minutes four seconds.

Thanks to the free diving course, swim test day now no longer causes me anxiety. Now swimming to the bottom of the pool is just something that we do every other month to make sure we are in good physical condition. No problem.

Due to my sinus issues, I prefer to do the 'V' swim test.

I start my dive from stage, free dive to the bottom of the pool diagonally and touch the deepest part in the middle, then ascend diagonally upwards towards the glass at the opposite end of the pool. This ticks off the depth and length portions of the swim test by completing both at the same time in a V shape.

Not all trainers attempt this simply because it requires a much longer breath hold than doing the two separately.

But, as I have said numerous times, it is all psychological.

I know trainers who have followed me down attempting the V, only to shoot straight back up to the surface once they had touched the bottom. Not because they actually had no air left, but because they associated touching the bottom with having no air left.

The swim test at Marineland is very different to the Loro Parque swim test.

It involves swimming both the depth and breadth of the pool while holding your breath, so that is 11m down and 55m across. Then you need to pull yourself up onto the net that runs along the surface of the pool which involves reaching up above your head and pulling your whole bodyweight up and out of the water.

Basically like doing a pull up and then instead of lowering back down, you end up turning yourself on your wrists and hauling yourself out of the pool.

I most certainly do not do this gracefully.

In fact I'm pretty sure that I emerge from the water and flop across the net like a half-drowned seal.

It may sound silly to practice exiting the pool at several different points but it is actually the hardest part of the swim test for me and arguably the most important.

If you do ever fall into the water then your immediate goal is to get back out again as quickly and safely as possible, and in this way the swim test makes sure you are prepared for any eventuality.

If we ever did fall into the water there is no way of knowing what a whale will do. Personally, I do not believe that they would attempt to attack us simply because we slipped into their environment. We come so close to these whales on a daily basis by kissing them, hugging them and rubbing them down. If any of them did want to attack us, like the majority of activists want people to believe, then the whales have plenty of opportunities to do so without us getting into the water at all.

So if they do not become aggressive towards us when we are in such close contact with them while remaining on dry land. Why would they suddenly change their behaviour towards us just because we get into the water?

In reality it is impossible to know what a whale would do if a trainer fell into the water. It would depend on the mood of the whale at the time, how many other whales are also in the pool, and the reaction of the trainer in question.

It is completely possible that the whales will simply ignore the trainer. Or more likely, they will swim over out of curiosity in which case the trainer could simply decide to give the whale a rubdown before pointing the whale to another trainer and exiting the water.

One of the most likely problems that could arise from falling into the water with a killer whale in an unstructured session is excitement on the whales' part.

Killer whales are incredibly social mammals, viewing trainers as an extension of their own family pod. A trainer falling into the water with a young and excitable whale could quickly find themselves in a potentially dangerous situation simply because there is an animal weighing thousands of kilograms swimming very quickly beside their own body.

An accidental knock by a tail fluke could be very damaging.

This is why it is important to be prepared for any eventual in-water situation.

During the swim test, once you have completed all of your exits, your arms feel like lead and you have more than likely pulled a muscle in one or both shoulders (a word of wisdom - always stretch before a swim test) then you have to swim the length of the pool twice at the surface.

When comparing the Marineland swim test to the Loro Parque swim test, due to the amount of upper body strength required for the Marineland swim test, I find it much more difficult. However they both prepare you well for any situation you might face if you fell into the water, as both tests are adapted depending how the pools are constructed and how the facilities work.

All of the pool surfaces at Loro Parque are flush to water level, rendering it unnecessary to practice difficult exits. The pools at Marineland are on varying levels, meaning that it is helpful to know the quickest and safest ways to exit the pool at all times.

Loro Parque trainers have a small scuba tank which is attached to a belt which is worn at all times around the waist. It is there as an extra safety measure, designed to give the trainer around five minutes of air should they ever find themselves in a potentially life-threatening situation. Therefore, Loro Parque adapted their swim test to ensure all of the trainers are comfortable and relaxed when using the apparatus.

Marineland do not use the belts (but do still have many air tanks dotted around the pools) and so it is more effective to practice apnoea to ensure trainers have good breath holding techniques.

Passing the swim test is a big milestone in any animal department but on an orca team it is a key element to getting on your way to counting as one of the team 'officially'.

On an orca team, safety is the number one priority.

Meaning that there needs to be a minimum number of trainers around the pool at all times and this number varies depending on how many trainers are needed to run a hypothetical emergency situation.

At Loro Parque the number is seven, at Marineland it is five. This is calculated based on the minimum number of people it would realistically take to run a security operation around the pool in an emergency situation. In a theoretical situation, where a trainer has an accident in the water then trainers will potentially be required to pull a net, take control of other animals, call for the emergency services or rescue the trainer in the water.

In this way, by passing the swim test and passing other security milestones like pulling nets in all of the pools or getting cleared on your safety belt formation, you are proving to the team that you are a valuable asset to them.

The best advice I have about swim tests is just to relax.

Before attempting any underwater practice do NOT hyperventilate, you will only succeed in passing out. Instead practice controlled slow breathing, fill your lungs with air and slowly let it back out until you can feel your heart rate slow down. Do not try to swim fast. This will only cause you to use up more energy, instead work on your technique so you are swimming efficiently. Use all of the propulsion you can get and use every inch of your glide.

Let your mind go blank and instead of focusing on how much air you have in your lungs, focus on how many strokes you have completed and slowly up that number one at a time as you get better at it.

'Slow and steady wins this race' said the tortoise to the hare.

You don't need to pay for any expensive courses in order to pass a swim test, just get down to your local pool and practice swimming underwater around the perimeter- just warn the lifeguard first!

And remember – it is all psychological.

CHAPTER FOUR – BEGINNING TO BELIEVE

Even though the years I competed took a large financial and mental toll on my mum with the sheer amount of time that was required, she was behind me 100% of the way. Even after I made the decision to stop swimming in order to focus on my university degree she stood by my decision because she trusted that I knew what was best for myself.
I think that is one of the things I admire most about my mum.
I have a lot of friends who are also only children (I think we somehow gravitate towards one another) and I've noticed that a lot of them have very strained relationships with their parents as a direct result of the pressure their parents put them under to achieve. Because they have only one child, that child has to succeed in absolutely everything that they do and be the best possible reflection of their parents.
I know this can also be true for children with siblings of course, however when you are the only child you do feel a heavier weight of responsibility to not let your parents down.
I never want to be a disappointment to my mum, and thankfully even in instances where I did end up failing, she was the one who was supporting me and building me back up again.

So after ten years of working endless overtime in order to buy me new expensive racing suits and extortionate club fees while driving me up and down the country to competitions, she still supported me when I chose to leave it all behind.

I think it's something that happens with all of us, when we grow up we start to realise exactly how much our parents sacrificed for us.

I wish I could repay my mum for everything she has done for me, undoubtedly I owe everything I have and everything I am to her.

But unfortunately I decided to become a marine mammal trainer so she will just need to keep being satisfied with a scarf from Primark and some Superdrug bubble bath on Christmas Day.

I have already mentioned how there were very few things that my Mum ever talked about wanting for herself. But anyone who knew my Mum, knew that the one thing she wanted more than anything else in the world was to swim with a dolphin.

After scrimping and saving for years, even with all of the swimming expense, she finally had enough money to take us to Orlando again and this time she told me that she had reserved us a place to swim with the dolphins at Discovery Cove.

I was fourteen at the time and still remembered the magic from our first trip to Orlando and was excited to return. Because I was a little older, there was less focus on Disney and because it was a lot cheaper, we stayed on International Drive.

The morning of Discovery Cove Day came and we excitedly bundled into the small minivan that would take us across the road from our meeting point at SeaWorld. I remember the butterflies flapping incessantly in my stomach, my body full of jitters.

I could barely sit still as we waited for the last stragglers to load into the van.

After a quick drive, we hopped out of the air conditioned minivan into the thick Florida air and I stopped dead in my tracks when I saw the insanely large queue snaking out from the main entrance and down the path towards the parking lot.

Even though I knew that my mum had reserved our swim already I had the irrational fear that for some reason because there were so many people in front of me there wouldn't be any dolphins left for us to swim with by the time we finally got in.

This is a perfect example of how my brain continues to work to this day.

Thank you anxiety.

After a short wait time by Orlando standards we soon filed into the cavernous lobby that was the gateway to Discovery Cove.

If you have ever visited you will know that it is a park that oozes peace and tranquillity. Nestled among the palm trees and white sand beaches, you could be mistaken for thinking that you were on a Caribbean island rather than in the middle of one of Florida's biggest cities.

While the woman checking us in struggled to understand my mum's thick Scottish accent, I gazed around me, completely entranced by the giant wooden dolphin statue that hung from the ceiling. Depicting three dolphins surfing the waves, I let my mind drift off and imagine how it would feel to finally be allowed into the water with such wonderful animals.

The woman behind the desk asked my mum what time we wanted to swim as there were some late afternoon slots available. Before she could even draw breath to answer I blurted out

"As soon as we can"

The check-in lady smiled knowingly and proceeded to book us into a swim slot in forty-five minutes.

Snapped out of my daydream by the prospect of being able to swim with a dolphin in less than an hour, I impatiently waited as our passes were printed.

Patience does not happen to be a virtue I possess. Those fifteen minutes may as well have been fifteen hours considering how desperate I was to be given my pass and be allowed out of the doors at the far end of the hall.

Eventually the wait came to an end and we left the busy air-conditioned entrance hall with our passes slung around our necks. We hastily made our way down the winding path through the luscious green foliage and emerged onto a pristine white sand beach.

And there were the dolphin lagoons.

With the sun still low in the sky, it reflected beautifully off of the water, each puff of breath from the dolphin's exhales catching the sun's rays, making a cloud of light above each grey back as it arched up to the surface.

I looked up at my mums face and I honestly don't think that I had ever seen her so happy. She couldn't take her eyes off them.

There is something magical about seeing someone's dream become a reality. I have been lucky enough in my line of work for this to happen regularly. Whether it was through running dolphin interaction programs and watching people have similar experiences to my mum's, or through introducing people to a killer whale for the first time.

It is a privilege to be able to be a part of someone else's dream as it becomes reality. That is where the spark lives, you can see it in people's eyes. Once people are exposed to these animals and that spark is ignited within them, they will be so much more likely to leave with a passion to do their part in helping to protect those animals through conservation.

Even though it was hard to tear ourselves away from the beach front and the dolphin lagoons, we knew that we couldn't be late for our educational briefing so we quickly laid out our towels and headed back up the beach towards the locker rooms.

Our attempts to smear the 'dolphin friendly' sunscreen, which had the consistency of halfway dried cement, onto our faces left us looking like we had lost a battle with a paint roller but we zipped ourselves into the little wetsuit vests that smelled strongly of damp and marched off into the briefing booth.

I have to admit, I have absolutely no idea what was said in that video. All I was thinking about was how soon I could get into the water.

I have seen this happen on numerous occasions.

While I was an intern at one facility in Florida, it was my job to give the educational briefing to the guests and as you were there explaining dolphin anatomy and the correct way to touch the dolphins, you could see that half of your audience was lost to you. They were either staring off in the direction of the dolphins, staring at the clock behind you counting the minutes until the briefing was over, or had their eyes glazed over entirely.

I owe a special thank you to all of the people who actually paid attention in my briefings. The American's who struggled through my Scottish accent before I learned how to dull it down. A special shout out goes to one family from Arkansas, who did their best not to laugh at me when I asked them what state that was in.

Once the briefing video was finished we were paired up with our trainers who led us down to meet our dolphins. The water was pleasantly cool as eight of us filed down into the shallow end of the lagoon and stood there in a single-file line, full of expectation. Suddenly, right before our trainers' hands, a little grey head popped up.

My heart started pounding, I had never been so close to a dolphin before.

It took everything in me not to break away from the group and dive down into the water. Unlike most guests that I have seen or spoken to, I wasn't desperate to touch, feed or 'ride' the animal.

I was desperate to get into their world.

I wanted to take a deep breath and dive.

I wanted to use my powerful swimmers body to actively swim *with* the dolphins, to feel them looping around me, see them surrounding me on all sides and feel like one of the pod.

Thankfully I would be lucky enough to get that experience years later.

The trainer introduced our dolphin as Dixie, who was the dominant female of the lagoon we were swimming in. After explaining a little more about Dixie's family, pointing out her baby who was with another trainer just to the left of us, she asked us to hold our hands out flat on the surface of the water.

All of a sudden Dixie was sliding under our hands.

It was like nothing I had ever felt before, smooth and soft but not at all slimy. I have heard it likened to velvet, newly shaved legs, a wet hot dog or even a peeled hard-boiled egg (that last one is actually pretty accurate).

As Dixie swam out of my hands and into my mum's, I turned to my side and couldn't believe the look on her face.

She just couldn't contain her smile.

It shocked me that I had become so used to seeing my mum tired, pale and overworked that I was so unaccustomed to seeing her smile like that.

From that second, maybe five minutes into our dolphin swim, it was no longer about me.

This was my mum's childhood dream coming to life.

This had to be her moment.

I tried to keep my touches as short as possible so that my mum would get more time stroking Dixie. I wanted my mum to go first for the kisses and for the fish feeding. More importantly I wanted her to go first for the deep water swim so that I could see her face. I treaded water as Dixie appeared beside my mum, I watched as she grasped onto her fins and I swear in that moment, looking at my mums face was like looking at the sun.

There is something that happens to people when they are so incredibly, joyously happy, it radiates from within and lights up everything around them.

Then it was my turn.

I was trying to remember the position that the trainer had explained to us, one hand on the pec fin and one on the dorsal fin, I was desperate not to mess it up.

Dixie appeared beside me and ever so patiently, waited until I got my hands into the right places. Then she started swimming gently towards the shallow area of the lagoon. Her peduncle propelling her tail flukes up and down ever so gently, we barely made a wave at the surface of the water.

And then it was over.

I stood up and returned to my mum who had already re-joined the rest of our group, but I hadn't had enough.

I had thought that this dolphin swim would satisfy the urge I felt, the urge that had been growing ever more incessant with every step I had taken closer to the water. I had thought that once I had made a physical connection with a dolphin and shared the same space as them, that I would be able to count it as an amazing once in a lifetime experience and move on.

It had the opposite effect. I was a drug addict, hooked after the first hit.

It simply wasn't enough and I needed more.

Looking back, I can see exactly what issues I had with the swim program.

I was a very strong swimmer who wanted to feel at one with the animals, but instead

I was allowed to 'ride' along with Dixie in a very slow and sedate surface swim that was nothing like the energetic and powerful underwater fantasy I had in my mind.

Running dolphin interaction programs can be difficult.

I worked at a similar kind of facility in the Caribbean for a year, bringing guests into the water and sparking connections. Being able to see such joy on people's faces every single day was a privilege but it was also very hard work.

You are never guaranteed to get respectful guests in the water with you and sometimes you feel like you are talking to a brick wall. Even though it is an amazing job, a dream job, it is still a lot of work.

I know what it is like to run dolphin interaction programs continuously for months on end. I have said the words over and over again until they don't even sound like words any more. I have ran so many swim programs in a row that I have forgotten which dolphins I was working and told the guests the wrong names. We have all been there.

But any time when I felt myself growing impatient with a guest who wasn't understanding the correct position to hold onto the animal correctly, or when I heard myself adopt the repetitive monologue that I used to explain dolphin anatomy in almost every program, I would catch myself and think back to my own first dolphin swim and to my mum's reaction.

To my mum, that program was her life's dream.

When you think about it like that you can usually put whatever is bugging you, out of your head. Whether it's the fact that you only got three hours sleep the night before, or that your roommate left the bins overflowing and cockroaches had gotten into it, or that you were so hungry because your boss had put you into late lunch yet again even though he knew that you hated it because you have serious hanger issues.

You need to put all of that to one side and remember that maybe, even if it is only one person out of ten in your swim program, it is the best moment of a guests life.

When I exited the water after that first dolphin swim I felt like my world had shifted.

My emotions were mixed and I was confused by it.

I could see from my mum's seer uncontained joy that she had experienced the same satisfying dream-achievement as most people.

For forty years she had wanted to swim with a dolphin and now she had finally been able to do it and it had been incredible. Best moment of her life. End of story.

We walked up the beach and unzipped the wetsuit jackets, unwilling to let them shield our pale vitamin D-deficient Scottish skin from the sun a moment longer.

I shoved my head under the freezing freshwater shower, attempted to scrape away the thick streaks of sunscreen from my face and tried to understand why I felt disappointed.

I couldn't say to my mum that I felt disappointed, that would make me sound like a spoiled brat. I had enjoyed every minute of the swim program and Dixie was such a sweet animal that it had been incredible to be allowed so close to her.

I didn't know why but I just needed more.

I never said anything about that to my mum at the time, I just continued having a truly incredible day with her exploring the reefs, stroking stingrays and laughing at her complete inability to breathe through a snorkel.

As we left Discovery Cove that day I was aware that a desire to potentially work with dolphins one day was growing inside of me.

A couple of days later we visited SeaWorld, I was desperate to see the killer whale show again and we rushed to Shamu Stadium for the first show of the day.

This time the show was different, it was no longer the Shamu Adventure, it was 'Believe'.

A show centred around the relationship between trainer and whale, with a message of 'anything is possible if you believe'. The message of the show was so powerful, truly showcasing the strong relationships between animal and trainer, and the waterwork in the show was so jaw-droppingly impressive that it simultaneously made my heart race and my eyes sting with tears.

'Believe' is still the epitome of what it means to be an orca trainer to me. Every moment of the show was specifically designed to demonstrate the trust and connection between trainer and animal and the mutual respect that plays a massive part in our day-to-day jobs.

The black and white wetsuits mirrored the orcas camouflage so perfectly, you almost couldn't tell where the animal ended and where the trainer began. The emotive music that repeated the inspirational message, the use of imagery to demonstrate how future generations becoming inspired by these very animals can make a difference to marine life everywhere.

To have been able to watch that show live in person was a gift.

Even when I watch that show back on DVD these days, I am still blown away by the level of talent, training and little spark of magic that it managed to capture.

And the rest was history.

I may not have fully understood all of the emotions that were going through me at the time but from that moment on, whenever someone asked me what I wanted to be when I grew up, my answer was always

"Killer whale trainer"

People's responses were always one of either three things

"What?"

"Yeah right"

"How do you even do that?"

That pretty much sums up what it is like getting into this field. Especially coming from the UK where there are no captive cetaceans to gain experience with. I quickly realised that I needed to figure out how to make this happen by myself.

It was just me and my google search bar.

I scrolled through so many different facilities websites. I joined Facebook groups. I even stalked trainers online.

Eventually I somehow came to the conclusion that I needed to know every single captive killer whale's name and family history because when the time came for me to go for a job interview, they would be incredibly impressed at the fact that I already 'knew' the animals and they would have no choice but to hire me.

I was incredibly naïve. Passionate. But naïve.

When I first started out on this journey I was flippantly telling everyone who asked that of course one day I was going to be a killer whale trainer, even though I still had absolutely no idea how I was going to make it happen. I gave no thought to the very real possibility that I was most likely going to fail.

That didn't seem to matter to me because I could feel it in my gut, I knew it was going to happen one day. Because I knew that I was never going to stop trying to make it happen.

I had managed to find out somewhere online that in order to be considered for a job opening then a degree in a related field of study was required, the preferred degrees being psychology, marine biology or zoology.

I was swaying heavily towards studying zoology. Nothing sounded better to me than being allowed to read books about and study animals all day long. But my mum managed to talk me around to studying psychology, just in case the 'training thing' never worked out then I would still have something to fall back on.

Smart woman my mum.

Because that is the thing that people don't realise.

This job is so highly competitive and there are so few spaces available that the majority of people don't have the commitment that it takes to see it through to the end. The majority of people who do make it all the way, often end up leaving the job after only a few years because they realise that even though it is amazing, it is incredibly hard work that takes so much sacrifice.

People become disheartened by the unpredictable work schedule, the late nights, the fact that we can never take holidays off. The job starts to take its toll on their bodies until they physically cannot do it any longer, or they simply grow tired of being so far away from their families.

The care and life of our animals are, quite literally, in our hands. Their quality of life depends on how well we are doing our job. Their physical condition depends on how multifaceted and variable we can be with our sessions. Their mental stimulation depends on the complexity and resourcefulness of our training processes. Their emotional well-being depends on how creative we can become with enrichment.

And that is why trainers are so dedicated to their jobs, because the animals are everything to us, they come first to the exclusion of almost everyone and everything else.

Not everyone has this level of commitment but for the majority of us it is the passion for our animals that allows us to keep going and keep sacrificing.

Yes we work long hours, often from very early in the morning until late at night, including weekends and holidays. You might as well never try to make plans with a trainer on Christmas Day, Easter, New Year's Eve or any other holiday because yes we will be working, and we will probably have an extra show which means extra hours.

More often than not these long hours will be spent in horrible weather conditions, the result of having a job that keeps you wet and outdoors. There is nothing worse than it being a chilly 6 degrees Celsius (yes it can get that cold in the south of France), putting on your nice dry wetsuit, layering up with a fleece over the top, adding a thin waterproof just to be on the safe side in case it rains. Then ten minutes into the work day being soaked in 11 degree water by an overexcited orca doing a mini-breach beside you as you bring the first buckets around the pool.

Weather is a favourite topic to complain about for a trainer. Regardless of what the weather forecast is, if it isn't a mildly breezy sunny day then chances are it doesn't matter where you are in the world you will be uncomfortable. If you work somewhere up north then most likely you will be unable to feel your feet for the entirety of the day and will be wrapped up in so many fleeces you can't bend your elbows.

If you are down south then you will spend the summer season scratching your hundreds of mosquito bites until your skin looks like you have some sort of infectious skin disease.

Or perhaps the age old debate of wetsuit versus swimsuit, sweating away half of your bodyweight in a skin-tight piece of neoprene or slathering on copious amounts of sunscreen trying not to burn.

Another fun game trainers like to play is 'What is this stain on the back of my hand/wetsuit/face?' In case you are wondering the answer can be anything from seagull poop to fish guts to orca snot. It's real glamorous.

These are just some of the highlights of our basic job description but what a lot of people don't understand is the unpredictability of working with animals.

Just because our payroll says we finish work at 18:00 doesn't mean that we always do.

If an animal is pregnant or has just given birth to a calf, then trainers will be on night-watches. Staying overnight and watching the animal to make sure he/she is ok. In theory it sounds easy but staying awake in the dark when all you have to do is watch an animal and count its respirations every 30minutes is much harder than anyone would ever think.

If something happens or goes wrong it is your responsibility and therefore you can't afford not to remain vigilant.

We invest so much of ourselves into our animals that we cannot help but become deeply emotionally attached and involved. This usually means that our own mood reflects how the animals are behaving. For instance whenever I skype my Mum in a bad mood the first thing she will ask me is if the whales were being difficult during the day because she knows that all we want is to make sure the whales have the most positive, fun day possible, all day and every day. Which basically means that when a trainer spends three weeks hand-crafting a new enrichment device and then the whales hate it because one of the ropes on the side looked suspicious and the ball was a weird colour of green, we don't have the best day. Yes, killer whales can be that picky about their toys.

Days can also become incredibly difficult when the whales don't want to focus on anything we want to do because they would rather spend time together.

Let me give you a completely fabricated example of this.

Let's say I have Wikie with me before lunch with a bucket full of fish beside me and the trainer to my left asks Moana to gate through to the front pool for a quick play session before we go to our lunch break.

I glance at Moana to see him leaving the back pool nice and quickly and I glance back at Wikie, my hand automatically going into my bucket, ready to reinforce the separation but instead I see that her eyes are going wide and starting to show red around the edges.

Both of these behavioural signals show me that she is uncomfortable.

As trainers it is our job to set our animals up for success and give them the most positive experiences possible.

I quickly call out to the other trainers that Wikie isn't comfortable with the separation and I try to gain better control with her by asking her to come to a hand target. She hesitates, one eye on my hand and one eye on the gate. She ever so slowly starts to come back to control. She touches my hand with her rostrum and I bridge her with my whistle.

But as soon as the whistling of the air pressure starts to signal that we are closing the gate, she splits from my control like a bat out of hell and rushes the gate.

I sigh in frustration, roll my eyes and call to the other trainers that Wikie is no longer in control.

I hurry to the front to see what is going on with the two whales. Moana has also split from control and is now swimming with his mother. More than likely Wikie told him using a series of whistles and clicks that he was not allowed to leave her side. Perhaps she was anticipating being separated alone for the lunch hour, which often isn't her favourite thing. We allow them to swim together for a few minutes before we call them both over using the recall.

This time we are lucky and they both come to control.

We decide to re-try the separation. This time Wikie is calmer and she decides to let us close the gate. I reinforce her for staying in control. Later on in the day we plan a 'false separation' between Wikie and Moana.

This means asking them to separate and then putting them straight back together again.

This shows the whales that we will always allow them to go back together again after a period of time has passed.

Trust between whale and trainer is imperative. The whales need to know that we will give them everything they need and want, and more.

If the two animals succeed at this false separation then they will be heavily reinforced while alone, probably almost a whole bucket of fish and throwing a toy in the pool for good measure, then they are further reinforced by being put together again.

In this way one of the most important things to reinforce are gatings. We want the animals to know that if we are going to ask them to do a difficult separation then they will be rewarded with everything they like, such as rubdowns, toys and, of course, fish.

Even though this was a completely made up example, in some instances the situations are not so easily resolved. Sometimes, there can be dominance or social issues that come into play within the group.

Within the Marineland pod, Inouk is the most submissive animal. Even though the four of them are a biological family, with Inouk being Wikie's brother and so an uncle to her two sons, he can still bear the brunt of frustrations from the other three from time to time.

Sometimes in situations, like the one I just mentioned, Wikie could have become frustrated by the separation plan and potentially taken her frustrations out on Inouk if he had been in the same pool. Either by aggressing him or by controlling him.

With Wikie being the dominant female, she is always in charge and she definitely doesn't like it if she doesn't get her own way. Oftentimes in situations where you have whales weighing thousands of kilos figuring out their complex social dynamics, you feel more than useless pathetically slapping the water and hoping that a stainless steel bucket of fish is going to get any of them to listen to you.

This is another reason why relationship is so important. When the furthest thing from an animals mind is their appetite, they may still listen to you simply because it is you who is doing the asking. Not because we pretend to have any sort of power over them, but because they have a trust in us.

Killer whales are master manipulators, between themselves and with trainers. We often wonder who is training who, but with regards to situations where the animals are out of control, it becomes glaringly obvious how controlling the dominant female can be.

When Wikie gets annoyed at us for asking her to do something she quite simply doesn't want to do, she will split from control and do her best to stop the rest of the animals doing anything for us either. She will gather the three boys around her and keep them swimming with her until she is ready to negotiate with us. Even if one of the boys (usually sweet little Keijo) will try to come over to one of our recalls, she will start whistling to him under the water. You can see clear as day on his face exactly when it is happening. His eyes will go wide and roll in whatever direction his mother is, he will look at us with his big dark eyes almost apologetically and then dutifully swim away to join his mum.

Wikie reigns supreme at Marineland Antibes.

When situations like this arise we have no choice but to leave the animals on a big time out. When they are repeatedly not coming over to control then we simply have to ignore the unwanted behaviour. Sometimes we will leave for thirty minutes or an hour, and then come back hoping that they have worked it all out between themselves.

Often when we come back they will all be swimming peacefully together and ready to cooperate. Sometimes we come back and Princess Wikie is still throwing a hissy fit. However if we can't get control of the animals for an extended period of time then there is a good chance that we might need to cancel or postpone a show or interaction.

Luckily, the majority of park guests are incredibly understanding that we never punish the animals and that if they prefer to swim together or need time to sort out whatever is going on in the group then we will give them the time that they need, even if that means there will be no show.

However Kohana, the dominant female at Loro Parque, was a different kind of animal altogether.

A striking behavioural signal from a pissed-off killer whale to a trainer, is the head nod and stiff surface swimming. Killer whales make this sharp bobbing motion with their heads as they swim if they are angry and it is very obvious when it happens. Usually if the whale is very annoyed they will follow this up by swimming stiffly at the surface, head nodding intermittently.

Even though killer whales cannot communicate to us through speech, they are very clear with their behavioural signals. It is our job to interpret these behavioural signs to figure out what the whale wants and then try to make that happen for them. Like I said before, we always want the animals to have the most positive day possible.

The best plan of action is to wait until the whale calms down and begins swimming normally again, then call them over. You don't want to call them over while they are exhibiting aggressive precursors because then you could potentially reinforce the aggressive behaviours themselves, which would cause the whales to display them more frequently. In the same way, you wouldn't give a child an ice cream right after they threw a tantrum because they saw the ice cream truck but were told they couldn't have any because would ruin their appetite for dinner.

If you are stuck in a situation where no matter what you try, the animals are giving you the 'middle flipper' as it was so delicately coined by Cat Rust, you see the hours ticking by and you realise that the day is starting to spiral down and down until you have tried everything you can think of.

When the animals still don't want to cooperate even though they haven't come over to control in four hours and there are three buckets full of fish for each animal still chilling in the fridge, we begin to realise that the whales quite simply couldn't care less about what we have to offer them in that moment.

Thankfully these afternoon-long social problems typically only happen once or twice a year, but it is a great way to show that the animals are not working with us for fish. They couldn't care less about the buckets full of herring that we have stashed away for them if they have more important things to do. The fat reserves of killer whales means that they can easily go three weeks without eating.

Killer whales are complicated creatures and when they are in a bad mood, your day will inevitably go from bad to worse.

Luckily though, the reverse is also true. When the whales are having a great time, it becomes impossible not to feel buoyed up by their infectious energy.

When your whale is getting really into a session, maybe they are jumping super high on every behaviour you send them on, or they are just really responsive to your movements, you feel like you can do anything. When they make cute little vocalisations and follow you around the pool simply because they want your attention, it melts your heart.

I love creative and silly sessions with Wikie. It's happened countless times now, but there will be several of us around the pool, not a fish or a bucket in sight, and we will all be in fits of hysterical laughter because she is swimming between all of us inventing her own games to play. One trainer will send her off to splash another but she will come up at a different trainer on the far side of the pool and completely soak them. Or she will decide so swim herself to the middle of the pool and rest on the bottom until someone does something interesting and she will then come over with her tongue hanging out of the side of her mouth like a dog.

It is incredible how deeply the mood of the animals can affect our own. In the same way, there is no denying that this job greatly affects our personal lives.

Our job field is not only very competitive but highly geographically specific, meaning that aspiring trainers have no choice but to be flexible with moving their lives around, oftentimes even across oceans never mind state lines.

If you want to be in with a chance of a job then you need to be willing to relocate.

Especially in the case of working with killer whales, considering there are only two facilities in Europe that house orcas. In Western Europe there are only twenty-five paid positions available working with killer whales.

This means that a lot of trainers end up living very far away from their families, and often because we earn a relatively low salary, are unable to afford frequent visits home.

For some people living far away from home on a Caribbean island might be the ultimate dream, especially if they are lucky enough to have their partner there with them.

For others, they search for a way to bring the job closer to home, to be able to bridge the gap between their dream job and realistic family life. It is a lot to ask friends or family to take an eight hour plane journey with a hefty price tag for a visit once a year.

More often than not, this results in the dissolution of a lot of friendships. It takes a lot of commitment to withstand the distance and so you will find that the majority of trainers have only a couple of very close friends who are professional Facetimers.

It can also be very difficult for trainers who have children, often female trainers leave the field in order to have kids due to a combination of long working hours and generally low wages.

And that's the kicker.

We do this job because of our passion for the animals and companies know that there are hundreds of other applicants nipping at our heels, ready to take our position if we no longer want it. The fact that we are so easily replaceable when we start out, combined with the fact that our employers know we will do anything in our desperation for a job, means that we do a lot of work for very little in return. None of us get into it for the money, but when reality sets in after a few years and suddenly you become overwhelmed with bills and taxes and weddings and babies, it is no wonder that so many of us choose to move on to something more lucrative.

Even if we don't eventually decide to search for a new full-time job, a lot of us have secondary employment. Trainers become yoga teachers, personal trainers, tutors or even writers like myself in order to try and generate a little extra income on the side in order to keep themselves above the red line.

When things get tough, either through homesickness or downright poverty, we are lucky that our work colleagues become our family. People who understand the multiple different ways your personal life can completely suck because of this job and are there to not just pour the wine or scoop the ice cream but volunteer to help you with the hard stuff.

When you are sick, someone will always drive you to the doctors or drive back and forth from the hospital to bring you clothes and food. If your car gets a flat tyre, someone is there to help you change it. When you can't understand the scary looking tax letter literally written in a language you do not understand, they will be there to translate and help you reply.

I am incredibly thankful that I have found this here at Marineland. I am lucky to be surrounded by people who care not only about the animals but also about each other.

Family and friends will always find it difficult to play second fiddle to a job, but the ones who realise how important it is to us, how it means far more to us than just a job, they are the ones who are worth waiting for and making the extra effort to stay in touch with.

Aside from my family I have only two best friends at home in the UK. Dee is more like my sister. We have known each other so long and even though she is two years older than me, I am the put together, organised one. She visited me in the Dominican Republic and flew home as fast as she could towards air conditioning and modern plumbing after her enlightening weekend in non-touristy Punta Cana. We have been kicking ass at long distance friendship for years with her off on a basketball scholarship for four years in Savannah, Georgia and then later at Loughborough while I was interning and moving my life across the world. No matter how long it has been since we have messaged each other, we both know that we can pick up the phone at any time if we need each other and we will both be there.

Louise has a much more conservative life, as a primary school teacher in Scotland it has always been me jetting off and leaving her behind as I went on adventures. Even though I keep pestering her to visit me wherever I am, we always check in with each other's lives and meet up whenever I am home.

It's all about effort. The ones who matter will make the effort to stay in your life and others won't.

Leaving behind friends and family is just one of the massive commitments we make to our jobs and to the animals.

Even trainers who live in the same area as their families struggle with the unpredictability and long hours that the job demands. A lot of relationships with partners or family members disintegrate because they just don't understand the dedication to the job.

They lose patience when you cancel a dinner date for the third time in a row because you had to stay at work to dive a pool, or a long-term partner loses his temper when he has to postpone date-night for the millionth time.

It can be very frustrating for the people on the outside to always have a loved one who has their mind constantly on work.

It is difficult to explain to people that you are unable to leave work, not because your boss is ordering you to stay, but because you care too much about the animals to leave them when they need you.

Finding the balance is a never ending struggle and in the majority of cases, the job will always mean more than anything else.

The animals will usually always come first.

When you make the choice to become a trainer you learn to expect the unexpected, in both your everyday life and your long-term career. Often the hardest realisation is that just because it is what you want to do right now, that doesn't mean that you will always be able to.

In whichever case, it is never a bad idea to have a back-up plan.

CHAPTER 5 – ON MY WAY

For me, my back-up plan was having a degree in something that could easily be applied to any number of job fields if my incredibly specific and insanely difficult career goal fell through in the future. In actual fact psychology turned out to be the perfect choice for me.

Being brought up by a psychiatric nurse meant that I had a very good understanding of mental illness and psychotherapy from a young age. I found studying the way the human brain worked fascinating and would often find myself reading textbooks simply because I was interested in what I was reading, rather than because it was required by my professors.

Despite my interest in the subject matter, I found the transition from high school to university incredibly challenging. I had made the decision to live at home and commute on the train each day in order to be able to save money on rent and keep my part time job. I knew that if I was able to save money during the school year, I would be more likely to be able to afford to intern with marine mammals during the summer months.

I chose to study at Glasgow University almost completely because it looked like Hogwarts. (Google image search it and I dare you to contradict me).

But in actual fact I found myself only ever attending lectures in the ugliest building on campus, a depressing grey tower built in the eighties at the very bottom of the hill. Far, far away from the swooping arches and high bell tower of my Harry Potter dreams. Those first few months were horrendous.

Taking three separate science courses meant that my first-year schedule was brutal. Having to attend three hour labs each day as well as lectures meant that I was required to be on campus from nine in the morning until six in the evening five days a week. Add on an hour-long commute on the subway and over ground train each way and I slowly spiralled into a gloomy fug as we headed into winter and I literally felt like I was living in darkness. Having been brought up in the countryside, I really wasn't coping well with spending all of my time in a dirty, noisy city. To top it all off, I had absolutely no idea how to write a proper university-standard essay and was failing all of my classes.

For the first time in my life I felt like I was losing my grip on everything.

I wasn't enjoying my courses and I couldn't understand why my grades were so bad because I was studying hard and attending all of my lectures. I was required to be at university so often that I was only able to pick up weekend shifts and wasn't saving nearly as much money for future internships as I thought I would have been. And to top it all off, I was so exhausted by the time 6pm came around that when everyone in my classes and labs were heading off to the student union to socialise before going home to their student accommodation, I was trudging back to the train station, huddled under my umbrella, the overflowing puddles soaking into my boots and freezing my feet.

When the Christmas break came around and I was faced with my first set of exams, I had a breakdown in front of my mum. I ended up curled on her lap like a four year old, my face buried in her hair, sobbing that I was letting her down.

I remember expecting her to tell me suck it up and get on with it, that she had raised me better than this. But instead she took a long look at me and asked me seriously if I wanted to pack it all in. She told me that if I was finding it all too difficult and I couldn't cope then she would support my decision if I wanted to quit.

Before that point I hadn't even questioned the fact that university was going to be the path for me. I was a straight- A student and my degree was going to be completely free. Why wouldn't I go to university? But my mum was right, if I was only making myself miserable, and failing everything anyway, what was the point in continuing?

But in that moment I realised that I wasn't going to university simply because it was expected of me, I was going there because I wanted to get a degree. I wanted to have that accolade.

When I told my mum this she nodded once, firmly pushed me off of her lap and told me that I wasn't allowed to breakdown like this again.

From now on I had to find a way to cope.

With that said, I started watching YouTube tutorials and listening to podcasts on how to properly structure essays to university level and I realised that it hadn't been what I was writing that had been causing me to fail, only the way I was writing it.

I formed a good friendship with a group of girls who also lived at home and were commuting to university just like me and we managed to get each other through it. Walking each other to and from the train station, huddled together wrapped up in our hats and scarves or taking shelter in a warm coffee shop next to our subway stop before early morning lectures.

One of the girls in our group, Gail, a tall drink of water with impossibly straight hair and a genius mind, was a dab hand at chemistry labs. And praise be to the Lord, her lab was always three days before mine. With her help each week on my lab reports, a strong friendship group and a steady improvement on my grades, I soon managed to claw my way out of the hole I had found myself in.

By the end of my first year I had managed to get by.

As an added bonus that first summer, my Mum had managed to save up for another trip to Orlando since my swimming career was no longer draining all of her resources.

For my birthday earlier on that year my Mum had gifted me the Marine Mammal Keeper experience at SeaWorld. A full-day program with the opportunity to go backstage in several different departments and meet lots of different animal species.

So at 7am we turned up at the employee entrance with me quite literally shaking in my boots.

I was desperate to make a good impression.

A heavily pregnant trainer quickly came and retrieved me from the security office and introduced herself as Maggie. I was ushered into the bustling fish kitchen, my eyes bright and excited despite the early hour, imagining the day when I would be one of those interns lucky enough to wear the dark navy SeaWorld t-shirt and a tag with my name on it.

Maggie ushered me over to a stainless steel countertop that was overflowing with buckets full of shrimp and capelin.

She asked me if I wanted to help prepare the diets for the otters that morning.

When I eagerly followed her instructions to place the exact number of each fish species onto each little otter bowl and plunged my hand into the piles of crustaceans she looked impressed. After I was done and rinsed my hands under the faucet she told me that most people on the program politely decline that particular task.

"Thanks for letting me do it, I want to become a trainer myself", I eagerly mentioned, drying my hands off on my shorts, which would continue to smell of shrimp for the rest of the day.

She raised her eyebrows and smiled, becoming interested "What species do you most want to work with?"

We were walking to one of the backstage SeaWorld golf carts that was about to take us to our next destination and we had barely hopped onto the back seat before the words were out of my mouth "Killer whales"

This time the expression on her face was slightly different, and I wondered if I had said something wrong. I realise now that she could see the passion and excitement in my eyes when I said it, but she knew this world. She knew that my odds of actually becoming a killer whale trainer, especially being European, were slim to none.

But for the first time in four years, ever since I had come back from my previous trip to Orlando and started telling people what I wanted to do, I was taken seriously. She didn't laugh at me, or tell me it would never happen, she didn't tell me it was a pipe dream. She decided to listen to me and give me advice that would turn out to be invaluable in my career.

She told me to join IMATA (International Marine Animal Trainers Association) so I would be able to see the job postings board to look out for available internships. She told me which internships would look better on my CV, the right questions to ask, the right way to present myself. And I know, without a doubt, that without her advice my career would not be what it is today.

In 2016 I was lucky enough to visit Orlando again during vacation while I was still working at Loro Parque. On a whim, I stopped at the dolphin stadium to ask if a trainer named Maggie still worked there. To my utter amazement not only did she still work there but she actually remembered me.

Apparently I had stood out during the program. It probably had something to do with her being eight months pregnant while she did my tour, that I dropped my burger on the floor mid-bite when I met the head killer whale trainer in the cafeteria (I would like to think that I am more professional nowadays) and that I pretty much bombarded her with questions in a thick Scottish accent for five hours of her work day.

Six years had passed and we were both completely different people.

It was a really wonderful moment, for both of us.

To be able to go back there after six years, find her and tell her that I had succeeded in my impossible dream of becoming a killer whale trainer. That against all the odds I had made it happen and that she had been the one who had made it possible for me to start, was something really special.

One of the reasons we trainers love our jobs so much is that we have the ability to inspire people, and not only did Maggie gave me an incredible day filled with animal interactions that I will never forget, but she also started my career and helped me on my way to my dream.

While I was at University I remember spending hours in the library reading articles about training techniques and researching internships, or looking at the IMATA job board and daydreaming about one day when I could make that my life. Contrary to my high school record, my grades at university were never spectacular, probably because half of my brain was always somewhere else.

I never managed to completely enjoy my four years at university, with the exception perhaps of my final-year project when I somehow managed to convince the psychology department to allow me to study sea lion behaviour instead of human behaviour. I think I basically steamrollered my poor tutor who was supposed to be giving me ideas when I strode into his office on the back of a PowerPoint presentation during our first meeting, outlining what exactly my project was and how I had dates set up with the safari park already.

As a result, while all of my friends were stuck for hours in dark and stuffy labs poring over statistics, I was chucking toys at sea lions and filming them playing for hours at a time while munching KitKats with the trainers and generally having a grand old time. Due to this my final year at university was the most enjoyable as it allowed me to involve my passion to some extent. Pouring over research papers can't possibly be boring when you are reading about baby walrus enrichment.

I had managed to wrangle a research position at Blair Drummond safari park in the sea lion department because I had already been an intern with them for two years previously.

After writing down every piece of advice I could glean from Maggie and my Marine Mammal Keeper Experience tour, I realised that in order for me to get internships I was going to have to do my research. I had to accept the fact that the United States were pretty much off-limits due to visa restrictions and I needed to start looking closer to home.

So I decided to email Blair Drummond Safari Park, located in Stirling, around an hour's drive from my house to see what kind of volunteering opportunities they offered. I was told that I would have to come up for a couple of trial days on the pet's farm department and so I spent a few days dodging llamas, herding alpacas and being chased out of enclosures by a very grumpy penguin.

Despite all of this they seemed to take a liking to me and I was finally sent for a trial day in the sea lion department. At the time it was run by a very hard-headed, strong-minded woman. I quickly realised that I would need to make a good impression on her if I wanted to have a hope in hell of continuing to come back. It took over a month of weekends for me to prove to her that I was the volunteer she needed but in the end it was agreed that I would be allowed to assist the sea lion team every Saturday indefinitely.

I was euphoric at securing my first 'official' internship position. I ended up staying for two years.

I have some incredible memories from my time spent there. Those days were the light at the end of the tunnel for me. Each week day was spent slogging through piles of work for university and never ending train journeys. But at the end of each Saturday spent scrubbing pools, hosing down enclosures and gutting fish, I would feel so buoyed up with happiness that it would carry me through the rest of the week until I could go back and recharge my batteries.

It may not have been heaven to everyone but it felt like it to me. The majority of keepers who work in the UK are very jaded about the industry.

The majority of the facilities were built in the sixties or seventies and are badly in need of a complete re-model and all departments are incredibly short staffed. Regardless, the majority of facilities do incredibly well with the resources that they have.

In spite of poorly designed exhibits and lack of funds, the trainers care fiercely about their animals and work themselves to the bone to give them the very best care. It was not unusual to see trainers turn their hand to carpentry to fashion a personalised training stand for a sea lion with nifty rubber cushioning. Or for trainers to spend their hard-earned wages on a succulent-looking salmon that was spotted down the local market to give to the animals as an evening treat.

For my first year there I spent each day scrubbing sea lion poop off of surfaces and scooping it out of the pools. Cleaning glass windows, chopping and weighing fish, power-washing the kitchen and making tea.

But even though I was doing the most menial tasks every day, I was on my way.

I felt like it was my first step, that I was moving forward, and that was worth the world to me.

Every Saturday evening as I was driving home I would have the music turned up loud in the car and I would be singing at the top of my voice. I would proudly wear my navy blue fleece with *Blair Drummond Safari Park* and the outline of a sea lion embroidered on the left breast as I popped into the shops for a Saturday night treat on my way home, hoping that someone would see it.

Even my Mum complaining that I stank of fish the minute I walked in the door couldn't burst my bubble, as she ordered me to strip and quickly bundled my uniform into the washing machine. Then I got to ease into a roasting hot bath, my toes tingling after freezing all day in my welly boots in the cold Scottish weather and feeling the now-familiar ache in my muscles from doing hard physical work all day.

That is when I knew that without a doubt, this is what I was meant to do.

That I could drive an hour each way, freeze to death in the pouring rain, end up with fish guts in my hair and sea lion poop on my face but finish the day with a smile from ear to ear.

The two sea lion trainers there, Steven and Adam, really taught me my basics in training and started moulding me into the trainer I am today.

When I showed them that I was dedicated enough to drive an hour through snow covered roads to get to work, have to break the ice on the boot dips and gut fish with frozen hands, they took me seriously.

They would let me watch their sessions and then patiently explain them to me afterwards as I jotted it all down in my little notebook. They even took the initiative to invent a proper intern program course for me to follow as they started allowing me to work with the animals.

The biggest thing I have to thank them for, is how much they believed in me.

They would eventually allow me to run my own sessions with individual animals and even progress to handling two sea lions by myself on stage and run show behaviours. They corrected everything from my positioning, my training techniques and my presence in front of the animals.

They even went so far as to try and help my truly awful hand eye coordination.

If there is one fault that I have as a trainer, it is my throwing arm. I had major problems with throwing fish simultaneously to two sea lions who were positioned on two different stands. This meant that one animal was two meters away and the other was four meters away and I continually messed up reinforcement by missing the sea lions' mouths.

To attempt to rectify this, while the group of sea lions were outside trying to catch some non-existent rays of sunshine though the perpetually grey Scottish skies, both Steven and Adam stood valiantly on the wooden stands holding buckets up to their faces as I tried to throw pieces of waste fish to improve my aim.

Needless to say I definitely did not manage to hit my mark every time and I just hope herring guts are good for the complexion.

I have a sinking feeling that their effort was wasted considering I still can't throw an ice ball or a herring more than a distance of three meters no matter how much I have practiced over the years. It really is quite pathetic and a source of amusement for whoever is beside me at the time. Quite probably I am lucky that I work with an animal that has a giant mouth so there is never really any fear that I will miss where I am aiming a fish these days.

*

Even though I was interning steadily once a week and learning a lot, I knew that in order to beat the rest of the competition I needed to make my CV stand out.

By this point I had managed to save up a good bit of money from working late evenings and Sunday mornings as a swimming teacher and lifeguard. So I started hunting google for things I could do towards the end of the summer holidays or in the October break close to home. I thought about volunteering at a seal rescue centre or a bird of prey facility, then an advertisement caught my eye. It was a picture of a blue yacht filled with teenagers wearing the ugliest anoraks you have ever seen all clutching binoculars and cheering.

It was an advertisement by the Hebridean Whale and Dolphin Trust (HWDT) asking for people to volunteer aboard their research vessel for weeks at a time in order to monitor and record marine animals off the coast of Scotland.

It was very late in the evening and I was sat at home on the squeaky leather couch with my laptop open on my knee and an empty box of doughnuts by my side when I picked up the phone to call my mum at work and ask her if she thought I should do it. There was only one place left available for the dates that I could make and so an hour later I had reserved my place aboard *Silurian*. Without giving one thought to the fact that I get incredibly seasick. A month later I found myself on a ferry heading across to the Isle of Mull with my anxiety kicking in full blast as I started to fully realise that I would be living on a very tiny boat with six strangers and no mobile phone reception.

In the open ocean, in a freezing Scottish Autumn.

Despite my reservations, the research week turned out to be one of the best things that has ever happened to me and I recommend it to anyone considering it.

The Highlands and Islands of Scotland are like a completely different world.

Nothing else exists up there and you might as well have stepped into the 1700s because all you will see are mountains, trees and deer. Especially in the remote places we were exploring, the majority of which were only accessible by boat or by foot as there were no roads.

It is quite simply magical.

The jagged and snow-capped mountain peaks rising up out of the lush green hills surrounded by white sand beaches and crystal clear blue waters are so breath-taking that it captures a part of your soul and never gives it back.

At the end of the week I found myself sitting alone on the prow of *Silurian,* my feet dangling down on either side of the bow sprit. I was enjoying the last few hours of the relaxing ebb and flow of the tide that was rocking the boat. We were harboured in the bay of a small island, a mug of honey and ginger tea that helped the nauseating sea sickness was warming my hands as I watched the sun rise over the hill.

I came to realise then that you don't need a lot in life in order to be happy.

In fact I think that may well have been one of the happiest weeks of my life, even though there was no wifi, no phone, no TV and it poured with rain for 80% of the time.

I have never felt more at peace with myself and I have never slept more soundly in my life.

The sheer perfection and magnificently untouched wilderness that is the North of Scotland captured my heart and I fell in love with my country.

My favourite day spent on-board *Silurian* will stay with me forever.

We awoke in a remote Loch in South Uist, surrounded by barren stone and scrubby marshland but surprisingly clear skies. The water was lovely and still so we all gladly grabbed our buttered toast or porridge and headed up to warm our faces in the weak Scottish sun above deck.

Our skipper cheered us up immediately by getting out the chart and telling us that although we were heading out into the Little Minch again (yesterday's crossing had been horrific with large swells and stormy grey skies), I enjoyed revisiting both my breakfast *and* my lunch that day. However for this day, the wind had changed direction so there would be a flat calm.

As we set off from South Uist into the sun, we kept our eyes peeled for minke whales. They had been reported frequently in the same area last year however we were soon well out to sea with no sightings.

We all remained cautious about the weak sun in the morning, keeping our waterproof oilies on, not daring to hope it would be warm enough to begin peeling off our layers. I hadn't been able to locate my sunglasses that morning, so the first real opportunity I had to use them aboard I was left squinting into the glare.

I was first up to the mast to take point on scanning the waves for animal sightings. Due to the complete bliss of a flat calm sea, any surfacing cetaceans would be easy to spot.

We continued further into the Minch until we had left Uist far behind.

There were quite a few other yachts out and about alongside us, clearly taking advantage of the good weather.

After my hour standing at the mast scanning the waves I went on break for fifteen minutes. The hard sail the day before had taken its toll on me, we had been so relentlessly pounded by driving rain and waves that I had grown so cold by the time we anchored that it took three hot water bottles and a cup of hot chocolate to thaw me out. The constant battering of the swell on the boat takes its toll on your body and I was exhausted. I was nodding off on deck, enjoying the blissful heat of the sun, when the first mate Emma nudged me and asked if I would like to go up the crow's nest.

I jerked awake with my heart pounding in excitement and a little bit of fear.

I slung my camera across my back and stuck my foot in the first rung. My oilies made it harder for me to climb as the thick waterproof material didn't allow my legs to stretch properly. My hands cramped up just as I reached the underside of the crow's nest from hanging on so tightly as the boat rocked from side to side. Emma shouted up for me to take my gloves off and I think I managed to shoot her a look that said "Are you mad? You seriously want me to take my hands off the rigging?!"

Gloves remaining on my hands, I managed to hoist myself up onto the spreader and into the basket safely.

The view was incredible, miles and miles of ocean stretched out in all directions, no land in sight.

I took my camera out and got snap happy, careful to keep my footing as every movement the boat made was enhanced by how high up I was. My heart jumped when someone on deck called in a sighting. My eyes scanned the seas for whatever animal was in the area.

A largely curved black dorsal fin was slicing through the water only 50m away from the boat on the starboard side. I could see it was a dolphin (and not a common) but I wasn't sure what species exactly. Another dolphin soon surfaced and we killed the engine, I was lucky enough to be looking in the right direction as one of them stuck its whole head right out of the water to get a good look at us directly in front of the boat as our on-board researcher confirmed that they were white beaked dolphins. Emma grabbed the photo ID camera in an attempt to snap them for research but they soon gave us the slip, with the last glimpse being the three of them 400m away in the distance.

I had picked the best time to spend an hour in the crow's nest and I scampered down again feeling elated. The weather continued to improve throughout the afternoon and our oilies were soon thrown below deck.

As we approached the small island of Barra hours later, we were suddenly surrounded by minke whales. One, two and then three small dorsal fins accompanied by large puffs of breath. Emma rushed up on deck with the ID camera, and we were lucky enough for one minke to surface on the port side, getting a great view of its back, dorsal fin and flukes as it disappeared beneath the bird-strewn waves again. We seal spotted over hot chocolate as we got the first glimpses of the white sandy beaches of Vatersay.

The waters were millpond still as we motored into the mooring, the ocean feeding into a perfect half-moon bay where the waves were met with soft sloping sandy beaches protected by sand dunes. The disturbed seals were spy hopping to check out our boat.

Due to the gorgeous weather and the stunning landscape it was soon decided that we were all going to go for a swim and dinner was postponed until afterwards. We beached the dinghy and marvelled at how clean the waters were and how pure white the beach was. It was so warm and beautiful I would never in a million years have guessed I was still in Scotland.

I quite honestly didn't know it could be so beautiful, it was a far cry from the dreary city centre of Glasgow.

I felt like I had disappeared into the pages of Outlander.

We soon trekked up the beach, making our way over the sand dunes in order to cross over to the other side of the island, the dunes magically cancelling out the sound of the sea on either side and we became engulfed in a meadow full of wildflowers.

The Atlantic side of the island was just as beautiful, with a bigger beach and more powerful waves. Unfortunately it was also colder. With the water at a chilly nine degrees Celsius and me standing only in a swimming costume, I gritted my teeth and gathered my courage to run in. The water left my skin stinging and red it was so painfully cold, my lungs contracted until I could barely gasp a breath but I still dunked my head under. I came up squealing and jumped about in a vain attempt to re-awaken my circulation. When that didn't work I tried swimming. Fast. That had a better effect. I swam out as far as I could and then paddled back in slowly to shallower, and warmer water.

Once I had gotten used to the temperature I lay floating on my back and just tried to remember the moment.

For that one moment in my life, absolutely nothing else mattered.

I was just a girl floating in the ocean in a gloriously untouched environment.

There were no pebbles or stones or seaweed under my feet, nothing but gently sloping white sand for miles, there could be no more perfect place to swim.

Once back on board *Silurian,* we hung our costumes out to dry and watched the sun slowly sink behind the hills, its glowing orange orb reflected by the calm waters.

It was a simple, perfect day.

The waters surrounding the Scottish isles are full of marine life, hence why the HWDT do such important research work there.

Killer whales are not uncommon in the area but unfortunately, even though I signed up for a discounted trip the following May, I was never lucky enough to spot any.

I was still 100% committed to my dream of working with captive cetaceans but I had gained a newfound appreciation for the researchers who were out facing the elements on the ocean every day trying to study and save the wild counterparts of the animals we work with every day.

If people can begin to put aside all of their prejudices against captivity or their hate towards certain groups of people and open their minds to other opinions and points of view, we can all make more of a difference to the lives of killer whales, and other marine animals, both in captivity and in the wild.

My first experiences of working with marine animals in a safari park and in the open ocean had whetted my appetite and I was soon eager for more.

CHAPTER SIX – PUTTING IN THE HOURS, FOR FREE.

The field of marine mammal training is so incredibly competitive that interning quickly becomes a necessity and not an option. In order to even be considered for a job then you must intern and volunteer, oftentimes you are required to have completed more than two separate internships in different facilities to even be considered for a job opening.
Because of this level competition, everyone is vying for the internship with the best hands-on experience, the longest running time or at the most well-known facility to make a CV 'pop'.
In a similar way, the internet trolls who are trying to psych you out about the swim test are also really good at making you feel insecure about your level of experience.
Not only in chat forums but increasingly on social media. It is not unusual to find individuals posting photos in the water with dolphins or holding a target pole to show that even though they are only on their second week of an internship, they have already become so advanced and trusted by the trainers.

This is becoming an increasing problem in a number of facilities. The Social Media Intern (let's call him Jeff) is never far away from his smartphone and is always asking trainers if they can take a photo of him for his latest #dolphintrainer Instagram post. Not a day goes by where Jeff is not uploading stories and perfectly filtered snaps of his awesome summer with the dolphins. While Jeff is busy trying to get a Snapchat of the sunrise over the dolphin lagoon, the other interns are already in the kitchen up to their elbows in capelin.

As trainers, we understand that interns want to collect memories from their time spent with us and the animals, and usually we will make sure that interns go home with photos and videos of themselves with the animals that they love.

But getting a certain amount of likes on Instagram is not why you complete an internship. Neither is it the reason why we get into the field.

You are interning to gain as much experience as possible and squeeze every bit of knowledge that you can out of the people around you.

When I was interning I was desperate to get photos with the dolphins. I wanted to post them on Facebook and show everyone back home that I was chasing my dreams. I wanted them to be jealous and prove to people that I was going to succeed.

There were times when the trainers actively asked interns if they had a phone or a camera with them because the trainers wanted to capture a special moment on film for that intern. But there were other times when a snap-happy intern would ask a trainer to take a photo at an inconvenient or inappropriate moment and I could see from the trainers face that it had been a mistake.

Trainers spend their lives studying behaviour and psychology. We will always recognize interns that are focused and hard-working and reward them either periodically or at the end of the internship by offering to take photos as a memento. So it is a much better idea to leave the phone or camera in your locker and concentrate on building your professional reputation and future career, because you will get a much bigger reward in the end.

Unfortunately it is normal for an aspiring trainer to have completed three or more internships before getting hired. This leads to the majority of us feeling like we are never going to get the level of experience required or that our bank accounts simply cannot support us taking another three months off work.

The reason everyone has so much experience is simply because everyone wants to be a more desirable candidate for a paid position and the more experience a person has, the more likely they are to get hired. The field of marine mammal training is so small that there are only a handful of paid positions available for the hundreds of people fighting tooth and nail to be accepted.

Gaining experience is just the first stepping stone to breaking into the field. Networking is one of the most valuable tools available in any job field. Considering the size of the field of marine mammal training, networking is arguably the best tool you can use when searching for employment. So when interning or visiting facilities the most valuable thing to do is to leave a good impression of yourself, it's not just about logging hours of experience to fill up an empty CV.

While you are on your internship, ask the trainers how they got to where they are now, ask if they have any advice for you going forward, form bonds with them so that they will remember you in the future and potentially recommend you for a paid position later on.

If you are travelling, take the opportunity to visit zoos and aquariums in the area. Politely ask to speak to the trainers or keepers if they have a spare moment in their day, mention that you are a member of IMATA or trying to break into the field.

Be personable and ask intelligent questions.

There is nothing worse than an aspiring trainer asking questions for answers they could have found with one Google search. If you are serious about pursuing training as a career then do your research before speaking to trainers so that when you are in front of the people with all of the answers, you will be able to fully tap into that wealth of knowledge and use it to help you figure out how it can work for you when you go home.

Don't come up to a trainer after a show and say

"How do I get to become a dolphin trainer?" or "Can you mention me to your supervisor?"

Ask questions like

"I have been doing a lot of research on these two separate university degrees, one is a lot more tailored towards animal behaviour and the other has a heavy focus on biology but is more appealing to me as a field of study, do you have any advice about which course would better help me in pursuing marine mammal training as a career?"

Ask. Intelligent. Questions.

"I have recently completed two separate internships (insert details of each facility) and would love to talk to someone in your department about the requirements for prospective trainers that your facility has. If your supervisor or manager (do your research and find out their name and background if you want extra points here) has a spare few minutes throughout the day I would love to have a chat if that is possible."

In this way whatever trainer you are speaking to will have the impression that you are clearly serious about pursing this as your career but have also taken the time and effort to research your visit. In the same way, making a good impression is vital on an internship. When interning you should always do more than what is asked of you. Always find something to do. If you are asked to go and drain buckets before a session, don't just drain the buckets. Ice them, carry them out to the docks and place them where the trainers will need them. If you have been asked to go and set up a session for a trainer to join you, don't just return to the office and report that you have completed the task assigned to you, look around and find something to do in the same area until the trainer arrives.

It doesn't matter if you are only sweeping leaves away from the entrance or organising the life-vests in exact size order, trainers will notice your extra effort and you will create a good reputation for yourself.

Even if trainers are not telling you anything, we are constantly observing and analysing behaviour. We can't help it. This means that even if you don't think that we are noticing something going wrong, trust me we are.

Even though networking is one of the easiest ways to gain employment, that doesn't mean that it is more important to make friends than to do your job. Making friends with the trainers, hanging out with them outside of work, is all completely fine but just because they have a good opinion of you in their spare time does not mean they will automatically have a good professional opinion of you as well.

After all, your ability to chug a beer in 30 seconds has nothing at all to do with how well you can train or care for animals.

When you are just starting out as an intern you are so full of hopes, dreams, passion and (if you are smart) a whole lot of fear. Fear of failing, fear of how long it is going to take to find a job, fear that you aren't good enough or fear that you will never find a job at all. But with enough hard work and dedication you will always find a way to make it happen.

Not a lot of people have the dedication that it takes to put themselves through years of unpaid work before even having a chance at a paid position. Interning and volunteering is tough, there is no doubt about it. There is a high level of expectation on any intern at any given time. Every intern knows that facilities are more likely to hire from the intern group than from the pile of CVs cluttering up a human resources desk. If trainers see potential they will discuss it within the team, so leaving a good impression is crucial.

It is all about balance.

Network successfully and professionally, be yourself, remain focused, concentrate on your work while at work and always go the extra mile.

Generally in most internship positions the day will start in the fish kitchen. A morning prepping in the fish kitchen can last between one to four hours, depending on how many animals' diets you are preparing and how many trainers help out daily.

Now in my personal experience the best way to get through fish kitchen is to turn the music up as loud as it will go, accept the fact that you will end up with capelin in your hair and get into a good rhythm of moving hundreds of kilos of fish from bucket to bucket and just get it done.

Even as a trainer no one comes into work wanting to do a kitchen shift.

We want to be out there with the animals, playing, training, and generally having a great time. However, kitchen is without a doubt one of the most important parts of the job and interns are usually essential in helping it to run smoothly.

Generally, interns will be responsible for sorting through fish and making sure that no fish that is broken, discoloured, missing fins/eyes or smells funny is ever put into a bucket.

Cetaceans are incredibly sensitive to GI tract issues and illnesses, so to keep bacteria at bay, fish is heavily scrutinised for flaws before being put into a bucket. The fish is thawed strictly within a certain number of hours of being fed to animals (usually the night before) and buckets are always heavily iced and stored in refrigerators before being brought out to session.

Kitchen can be incredibly physically demanding. There is the lifting of the 25kg fish boxes, hauling them around to get the fish out of them and then breaking your back bending over deep metal sinks to sort through the tonnes of fish within. Once the fish is sorted, you then need to lift the buckets repeatedly over to the scale to weigh them and then transfer the fish into the animals' individual buckets.

Can I get a "whoop whoop!" for repetitive strain injuries and herniated disks from my fellow trainers reading along please?

Kitchen may be hard physical labour but it teaches new interns that this job is not easy.

Our job is not just about swimming with dolphins, playing with sea lions or cuddling orcas.

If individuals can't handle a 5am wake-up call followed by four hours of lifting 25kg boxes overhead and spending the rest of the day stinking to high heaven of fish and picking scales off your hands past dinner-time, then they are not cut out for the job.

After the buckets are prepared for the day the kitchen must be cleaned.

I can honestly say that the fish kitchens of any facility I have ever spent time in are better cleaned than the majority of restaurants and certainly better than my own kitchen at home. Disclaimer- I do have a very clean kitchen but unfortunately it will still never be as clean as a fish kitchen floor.

Trainers are sometimes so short for time during the day that we have to take our break while washing or collecting buckets and so will have a snack in between sessions in the fish kitchen. We use fish-gutting knives to cut oranges and lay our sandwiches down on the surfaces where three hours before it was covered in fish scales. This is because every single day, often multiple times a day, the fish kitchen is scrubbed within an inch of its life. Interns and trainers alike will be on hands and knees with hoses, brushes and even toothbrushes covered in anything from soap to bleach to strong floor cleaner, even power-washing on special occasions. All to make sure that every inch of every surface is spotless.

The recurring nightmare of any intern is the scale-check.

Every so often a trainer, or most often the intern co-ordinator, will inspect the kitchen and individual buckets. Now bearing in mind that one average herring has hundreds of silvery scales on its body and on an average day at a large facility around 250kg of herring will pass through a fish kitchen, it is very easy to miss one rogue scale that has stubbornly stuck to the side of a bucket or on the corner of the ice machine. It is not unusual to be out at dinner on your weekend off (meaning that multiple showers and hand washings have taken place since you were last at work) when you suddenly notice a herring scale stuck to the side of your middle finger which you then have to try to discreetly peel off in front of whoever is unlucky enough to be in your unrefined company.

The reason facilities are so strict about scale checking and thorough cleaning is because a scale left to dry on the inside of a bucket or any surface can breed bacteria underneath it. Which, because those buckets and surfaces will be used again the next day to prep fresh fish, the bacteria could easily make its way into the stomach of an animal.

That isn't to say that every tiny piece of bacteria would be fatal to an animal, humans invented the five second rule after all, but we always err on the side of caution to make sure we are doing our absolute best to care for our animals. Even if that means scrubbing and re scrubbing every stainless steel bucket a facility owns.

In this way, internships can often be consumed with menial and laborious tasks, not just restricted to the kitchen.

One of the jobs I hate the most is cleaning up algae from pools. No matter how much you scrub or sweep or scoop the green stuff away, it will always come back.

I have spent many hours scrubbing algae off the sides of floating platforms in open water facilities and scooping it off the surface of the water at others. The problem with algae is that the type found in the majority of managed care facilities is not dangerous to the animals.

In fact the animals love it.

They will rip long fronds of it off walls and platforms and joyfully drape themselves in it and swim around with green fuzzy mouths for hours.

It also filters the harsh rays of the sun and so protects the animals' eyes and skin.

But thanks to the common misconception that algae is only produced in dirty water, it needs to be removed from the environment before guests are allowed to see it.

All algae presence actually shows is that the pool water has a healthy ecosystem.

The majority of facilities pump filtered seawater into their tanks, which when combined with a long exposure to sunlight and an excess of naturally occurring nutrients in the water, such as nitrogen and phosphorus, results in a lovely big algae bloom.

Which then leads to trainers spending hours hanging off the side of a dock scrubbing the stubborn green stuff off with a Scotch-Brite and probably ripping most of the skin off their hand in the process.

The animals probably wonder at the stupidity of the humans removing the fuzzy fronds of enrichment that Mother Nature so kindly provided.

Despite the menial tasks and physically demanding workload, what really makes the endless hours of interning worth it, are the learning opportunities.

When the fridge shelves have been meticulously taken out and individually scrubbed, soaked in bleach, rinsed and put back.

When the toy bins have been arranged according to animal preference and ease of trainer access, potentially also colour coded if you are extra organised.

Most facilities will have presentations or lectures given by trainers on the theory of training, explaining not only the foundations of positive reinforcement and operant conditioning but a whole smorgasbord of terms and definitions to explain the techniques trainers put into practice daily.

In the modern marine mammal training world there is only one way we train our animals and that is through positive reinforcement training.

Now the principle of positive reinforcement is rooted in operant conditioning which was originally theorised by the behaviourist BF Skinner in the late 1930s. Operant conditioning details that the probability of any given behaviour increasing or decreasing will depend on the consequences that follow the behaviour. This basically meant that if an animal, say a dog, lifted its paw and was rewarded with a treat for it then it would repeat the behaviour in order to get the treat again. If the opposite were to be applied and the dog was punished with a swat on the nose every time it lifted its paw then it would decrease the amount of times he lifted his paw to avoid the punishment.

Punishment is a tricky term.

Technically there are two ways to punish an animal. Positive punishment involves adding something to the animal's environment so it will decrease behaviour such as a swat on the nose. Negative punishment involves removing something an animal likes from its environment so it will decrease behaviour. Like taking away a bratty teenager's cell phone, or a dog's favourite toy. However, punishment is not something that can be used with orcas because they are far too intelligent to give in to any trainer stupid enough to try it. There is no way you could even try to force a 3000kg animal to do anything it does not want to do. Therefore we work only with positive reinforcement. Reinforcing our animals when they do a behaviour correctly and simply ignoring unwanted behaviour.

This means that whenever an animal does a behaviour that we wish to see more of then we reinforce it with things the animal likes. This can involve throwing favourite toys into the water right after the behaviour is exhibited and allowing a play session, obviously it can mean a handful, or even a whole bucket, of fish being given or a long rubdown.

Anything the animal likes can be used as a reinforcer.

When attempting to train complex behaviours we need something more than just reinforcement to communicate to our animal what exactly we are looking for.

That is why we use a bridge.

A bridge is simply a marker that the animal either sees or hears that lets them know that they have done the behaviour correctly and that they will receive some kind of reinforcement for it. Now for sea lions, a bridge is most often vocal, it will be a trainer saying 'yes' or 'good' at the moment of the desired behaviour.

With killer whales and dolphins we use a whistle bridge. Standard dog whistles are used in most facilities because cetacean hearing is in a much higher register than our own, therefore the high pitched whistle is an easy way to bridge the gap between behaviour and reinforcement. The bridge should be sounded exactly at the apex of the behaviour, precisely when the animal is performing the exact behaviour you want. Unfortunately a lot of error can occur here with 'bad bridging' and can result in animals performing strikingly different behaviours to what trainers desire. For example an animal performing a back breach behaviour falling directly flat on her back should be bridged when she falls directly onto her back. However if certain trainers begin bridging her for the height of the behaviour, therefore bridging too early, and she falls slightly on her side and the trainer reinforces anyway because it was very high, that animal will keep performing high back breaches but falling to the side. Eventually after multiple bad-bridging the behaviour will look completely different. This is why trainers regularly have meetings to talk about the criteria of animals' behaviour.

Now in the special case of Morgan, the hearing impaired killer whale housed at Loro Parque, a light bridge is used. Special lights were installed in all of the pools both under the water and at the surface allowing her to be bridged for any given behaviour at any time. For instance, if she was performing a 'fast-swim' behaviour where her body is submerged then the underwater light bridge will be flashed. If she is performing a bow and is above the water, then the surface light-bridge will be flashed.

The bridge isn't the only important communication tool in training. We also have to be able to communicate to our animals when they have done something undesirable or performed a behaviour incorrectly.

Of course when an animal is incorrect they will not hear or see the bridge, but on top of that we use something called an LRS, which stands for Least Reinforcing Scenario. This basically means that during the period where an animal would usually receive reinforcement, instead they receive a three second period of neutral response from the trainer.

This method was originally created by SeaWorld to be used for training killer whales positively. After they realised that killer whales did not respond well to earlier training methods, where things like food deprivation were still being used, because trainers simply did not know what else to try.

In this way the trainer is able to simply ignore undesired behaviour and move on to something else. The incorrect behaviour can either be repeated, or if the trainer thinks the animal is confused or frustrated then they can move on to something different and try again later. Attentive and calm behaviour by the animal during and following an LRS can also be reinforced, allowing the animal to learn from its incorrect behaviour.

In this way the LRS reduces frustration and allows animals and trainers to set themselves up for successful and positive sessions. After the clear success of modernised positive reinforcement methods and the introduction of the LRS to improve clear communication, these methods were then adopted by the majority of zoos and aquariums around the world.

Killer whales are highly complex intelligent animals and they find a lot of different things reinforcing, which makes our jobs fun because we have a lot of tools at our disposal.

If a whale does a really good training session we can open up a gate with other animals that whale particularly enjoys spending time with, which is more reinforcing than staying in a pool alone even after being given a bucket of fish.

For a lot of individual killer whales fish is the least reinforcing thing in a trainer's arsenal.

Fish is boring, fish is always the same and it is always there.

For instance I have known Wikie, the dominant female at Marineland to come back from doing the most spectacular front-flip I have ever seen her do, see me waiting overjoyed ready with a massive handful of fish, for her to firmly close her mouth and present me with her dorsal fin instead. This is a great example of killer whale personality. She knew that she had done a spectacular behaviour and that I wanted to reward her for it but she made sure that I knew which reinforcement she wanted for her behaviour. A back rub. Not herring.

Who is really training who?

I had one trainer tell me that in order to work Freya, the previous dominant female at Marineland, you needed to learn her handbook. This was an imaginary list of rules that Freya had made up by herself and expected trainers to learn and stick to while training her. Examples included things like feeding her one herring at a time and NEVER tail first, head first only. Or when trainers came into the pool area in the morning she must be greeted first, before any of the other animals, or she would throw a tantrum. Equally she had to be the last one to be told goodnight as trainers were leaving the pool in the evening.

These little idiosyncrasies are things that all whales have, and some whales share, but it is our job to figure them out from the signs that our whales give to us. Kohana shares the herring quirk with Freya in that she will firmly close her mouth and refuse to accept large handfuls of fish, if a trainer persists in trying to feed her like that she will split from control and start head nodding her way around the pool like the diva she is.

The importance of keeping reinforcement variable is to always keep the animals guessing.

If the whales know that every time they do a correct behaviour then they will always be reinforced the same amount of fish then they will soon lose interest, the game is no fun when you always know what is going to happen.

But if they get reinforced sometimes with a big handful of fish, or a rubdown, or a frozen ice block, or jello cubes, or single herring, the game suddenly becomes exciting.

These basics of training are taught both in theory and studied in supervised practice in the majority of internships and they provide the base of experience for interns to build on.

After interns have attended such talks and lectures they will have the opportunity to observe sessions and take notes, connecting the dots between the theory lessons and the practical applications.

When the guest lifejacket closest has been tidied, ransacked by guests, and tidied for the millionth time that season, for a glorious few hours a day interns get incredible opportunities.

Depending on which facility you intern at, those opportunities will differ. At one internship I was allowed to run sessions with animals under supervision. In another I was allowed to act as a B point for a trainer, holding the animal in control and playing with it while the trainer set up guests in the water or needed an extra set of hands for a training session. In another internship I was never allowed to hold an animal by myself at all.

The feeling of being able to take an animal by yourself in a session while you are an intern is exhilarating. The sheer joy and buoyancy that you feel afterwards that leaves you with a grin on your face for the rest of the day.

Allowing interns to practice what they have learned in a classroom is essential to their learning. Yes, as an intern you will always make mistakes, but even trainers are constantly making mistakes. It is how you learn.

This steep learning curve is what sorts out the interns who will persevere with the job even when it gets tough, from the interns who will give up because they don't have the commitment needed to get through the hard work and long hours.

*

My first proper internship was at Dolphin Encounters, Nassau, Bahamas.

I had been trying for months to find an internship program in Europe that would take me. But after being rejected either because of my nationality or because I simply didn't speak the language of the country, I decided I would need to start looking further afield.

After a long Google search and several unanswered enquiry emails, Dolphin Encounters were kind enough to email me back explaining that they did accept international interns visa-free for short term internships and we set up a date for a phone interview a week later.

When I secured my place on the internship, my mum decided that it would be a great opportunity for her to fly out with me for a couple of weeks and have a Caribbean holiday.

I took my position as intern incredibly seriously. This wasn't just goofing around with sea lions in Stirling, this was training dolphins in the Caribbean.

This was The Goal.

I had been emailed a list of clothing items to bring with me. A plain white T shirt, plain navy blue shorts and a plain navy sun cap.

I must have dragged my poor mum around the shopping centre into every sporting goods store I could find until I finally found a plain navy sun cap. Not navy with a white stripe, not navy with a tiny logo above the ear.

Plain. Navy. Only.

I had been given instructions to meet the intern coordinator at the harbour under the bridge to get the ferry across to the island along with the rest of the staff on my first day.

When the morning arrived, I was barely able to eat breakfast, I was so consumed with nerves and excitement as I shrugged on my backpack and flip flopped my way down the hill in my plain navy blue cap and shorts.

I steeled myself as I rounded the corner into the ferry boat terminal and was met with a sea of personnel yawning and drinking coffee. I nervously squinted up at the signs to see where the ferry for Dolphin Encounters was, my contact lens sticking slightly in my left eye, making me worry that I hadn't thought to pack a spare pair since I wouldn't be able to wear my glasses. I quietly made my way through the crowd of people and sat down on a bench.

I was extremely nervous. I was sat there clutching my backpack to my chest and scanning the crowd for who I thought might be the intern coordinator, waiting for her to come and give me some kind of direction.

It is quite an experience, being the only white person in a room. When I think of it now it screams white privilege to never even have thought about it before. In the village where I grew up there were no black people. There wasn't one single person of colour in my high school. And suddenly I was in the minority.

It is something white people don't ever think about, being in the minority, but when you are suddenly crammed onto a boat with two hundred black individuals and you are the only person with different coloured skin, it gives you an incredibly humbling realisation of the extent of white privilege. For the first time I realized how much discrimination people of colour still have to face daily.

The intern coordinator came and found me as I followed the crowd sheep-like onto the ferry, assuming that was the direction I needed to go in. We made our way over to the island through the most picturesque azure blue reef-filled waters and after we arrived, I was given a quick briefing and tour of the facility. I think the whole briefing lasted about ten minutes as a trainer hurriedly ran through the kitchen detail as I struggled to understand his Bahamian accent and kicked myself for not bringing a notepad. Being the only intern for my season at the facility gave me a huge amount of responsibility but so many amazing opportunities.

I attacked that internship.

I wanted to prove to all of the trainers that I was the hardest working intern they had ever had.

Despite my abrupt briefing and lack of notepad I committed it all to memory and the next morning I was blasting out fish kitchen with the rest of the trainers, stacking the buckets in the correct order in the fridge before anyone had to remind me where they went.

One piece of advice I would give to any intern - behave like every single thing you do on your internship is what is going to get you the job.

I would finish my lunch ten minutes early every day and excuse myself to go into the kitchen and take out twenty four dolphin buckets and carry them across the docks to their stations so that they would be ready and set up for the trainers coming back from lunch.

I would prep all of the hydration tubes and organise them according to time of use so they were easier for trainers to reach. I would ask trainers questions about their sessions once they were done and show that I had been paying attention to what they were doing.

And every morning I would volunteer to do the fence check.

Because Dolphin Encounters is an open water facility, meaning that the dolphins are in a natural ocean environment, it was essential to check the fences to make sure they were intact. Not so much to stop the dolphins from getting out, but to stop sharks or other unwanted sea creatures such as jellyfish or stingrays from getting in.

The majority of trainers at Dolphin Encounters hated doing the fence check.

For me fence checking was not a job.

It was thirty minutes every morning where I got to swim in a Caribbean lagoon surrounded by tropical fish and with dolphins swimming alongside me on the other side of the fence. So not only did I get to have an amazing start to my work day but I also got into the trainer's good books by saving them from ruining the hair that had taken hours of painful pulling and twisting the night before.

If there are any Caribbean ladies out there reading this – I have the utmost respect for your pain threshold and dedication to your hair.

For the daily fence check, the animals were always gated away into other lagoons for safety reasons.

The majority of people think that dolphins are majestic sea creatures that save humans from sharks and are never aggressive. I used to dream of swimming like a mermaid alongside a pod of bottlenose dolphins, but unfortunately any time I have ever done that I have never left the lagoon unscathed.

The first time I swum naturally with dolphins like this was on my second internship at Dolphins Plus in Florida. I was having the time of my life with a pair of fins strapped to my feet, cruising along underwater with the dolfs.

Until I made the mistake of becoming a little too dolphin-like by swimming only in butterfly kick on my back, whereupon a randy juvenile male decided he liked the look of me and started nibbling on my fins to start his dolphin courtship.

With a trainer on the platform telling me to swim on my front for a few laps of the lagoon and ignore him completely I made it out of the water without further incident.

As a working trainer in the Dominican Republic we used to try and avoid swimming in the female dolphin lagoon in free time as much as possible because the girls were so pushy.

I remember being forced to go in and retrieve a ball that had gone rogue during one particularly energetic enrichment session and as soon as I stroked out into the deep water I was surrounded by grey dorsal fins. Like an adult being attacked by over-excited children in the middle of a ball pit, I was fighting a losing battle with six female dolphins over a ball they no longer had any interest in, but also did not want to let me have.

Wincing as I finally stepped onto the platform, triumphantly clutching the bright red ball but with my thighs stinging from tail fluke slaps where dolphins had sped past me. My ribs already bruising from where their rostrums had rammed into me as they tried to re-capture the ball. My entry into the water had clearly re-ignited their interest in the game.

The first time I was allowed to do a fence check at Dolphin Encounters, with a trainer in the water supervising me, I had my first 'flipper' moment.

I was checking the seal on one of the gates at the bottom of the lagoon, hooking my toes around the wire below me when I heard a series of sharp clicks above my head, followed by short high whistles. I looked up and saw that Goombay, one of the adult male dolphins, had swum over to investigate what I was doing. His sweet dark eyes were following my hands as they re-tied the rope around the bottom of the gate, small tropical fish flashing their colours as they darted through the fence between us.

It was the first time I had been face to face with a dolphin underwater, albeit with a fence between us, but my mind immediately went to the scene in the movie *Flipper* where Elijah Wood stares into Flippers eyes underwater. It was the moment I had dreamed of having since I had first watched the movie as a child, it was that magic moment I had been lacking during my swim at Discovery Cove. I let go of the fence to take a breath at the surface and he followed, I got my breath back and dived back down to the bottom, he followed me again.

I knew I wasn't allowed to put my hand through the fence and touch him but I put my hand up to the barrier, the sunlight dancing in rainbows across the back of my hand and placed it in front of his rostrum. He floated there staring at me, clicking away.

Even though I wished I could have stayed underwater with him all day, neither my superiors or my lung capacity would have allowed it, so I resumed my duties around the lagoon with Goombay following me along the entire fence perimeter until I exited the water.

One of the dolphins who was actually used in filming scenes for the movie *Flipper* was at Dolphin Encounters when I interned there. Even though he was much older than he had been in the movie, and looked very different due to age, I honestly felt star struck meeting him for the first time.

That movie, along with *Free Willy,* had inspired my love of these animals. Being allowed to interact with the dolphin who played Flipper would almost have been like someone sitting me down in front of Keiko and telling me to scratch his tongue.

Because I was incredibly focused on my work while I was there and was careful to try and make a good impression, I was lucky enough to be rewarded with some really incredible experiences with the animals.

Nassau is a very small island, so everyone hung out in the same places, interns and trainers alike. We spent late nights drinking and getting to know one another. They taught me how to play dominoes properly (Bahamians are very competitive about dominoes), promised me that I would not get sick from eating some dodgy-looking street market barbecue chicken, and tried (and failed) to teach me how to dance.

A combination of hard work, networking and being yourself will always pay off. I wasn't working hard because I expected to get anything in return, I wanted to prove that I could be an asset to the team and I was genuinely enjoying every single minute of the job. But because they knew that I was willing to work hard, they rewarded me for it.

The whole time I was there I was dying to get photos with the animals but I resisted, not wanting to make the wrong impression and never asked for one. My camera was always in my bag in my locker in case I was ever offered the opportunity. Just before my last day, one of my good friends on the staff came into the locker room and grabbed my camera out of my bag and declared that she was going to be my photographer for the day. I ended up with over 400 photos that she and the other trainers took of me prepping buckets, endless selfies of themselves, the dolphins of course, me getting ambushed in the kitchen with buckets of ice water being poured over me and precious moments of me with the animals.

At the end of the day after the guests had left, they put me into the water with two of the dolphins and ran through a number of behaviours with me.

Positive reinforcement works with humans too.

One specific piece of advice I will give any intern who also comes from a cold climate and is unused to wearing flip flops for long periods of time.

Watch where you are putting your feet.

On my last week there I was running to get buckets out of the kitchen, missed a step and fell down a flight of stairs to land in a heap in front of a group of cruise ship guests coming in for their briefing. Thoroughly embarrassed I limped off to the kitchen with my newly broken toe in search of ice.

When the time came for me to leave Dolphin Encounters I was crushed. I sat on the fine white sand of Cabbage Beach, letting the grains run through my fingers and let myself cry. I had made so many friends and had discovered a new side to myself. A slightly wilder and more relaxed Hazel that never appeared in Scotland because I was always too busy working and planning.

It seemed so unfair that I had found somewhere I belonged, but the very next day I was going to have to get on a plane and head back to gloomy Glasgow to complete another semester at university.

Luckily I wasn't alone on the beach for long before my new Bahamian friends came and picked me up, shoved a rum in my hand and said goodbye to me in the best way they knew how, with a massive party.

My second internship was a lot more turbulent than my first.

My plan B had been to intern at dolphin quest Bermuda because as a British colony they accepted British students into their program visa free. However when I learned their internship was almost 4 months long, I realised I couldn't do it in my summer break from University.

Having no patience and being completely convinced that I was leagues behind every other aspiring trainer, there was no way I was waiting over a year to intern again.

I started looking for somewhere I could go the following summer and I applied for an internship in Florida.

At the time of me sending in my application, they had unfortunately not updated their website which stated that their internships ran for eight weeks. I was delighted. An ESTA visa would allow me to enter the United States for exactly 90 days, I wouldn't even need a visa to go for eight weeks.

I completed my phone interview with no problems and had a really great conversation with the intern coordinator on the phone. I hung up the call feeling buoyant and positive about where this would take me. Several weeks later I received the conformation email along with several other girls, that I had been successful in my application.

I was euphoric, but the feeling didn't last long as soon as I scanned the rest of the email and my eyes stuck on one sentence. The dates of the internship had been changed. It was now twelve weeks long. My heart sunk and I felt a sense of overwhelming, multi-faceted panic set in.

I had made a serious mistake.

I immediately emailed back explaining that the dates given on the website did not match the dates on my acceptance email. I explained that I would no longer be able to do the internship visa-free as planned and asked if they had any previous experience with this situation. Unfortunately because they had only recently changed the length of the program, I would be the first to have to search for a visa and I would be doing it completely on my own without guidance if I still wanted a place on the internship program.

I had a nightmare time applying for a visa, I spent months dealing with the stress of filing the right forms and literally hundreds of rejection emails, all while trying to keep my head above water at university.

I finally found a sponsor willing to take me on, and only because I had recently written an essay discussing the effects of dolphin therapy on the symptoms of autism (not exactly the paper my professor had been expecting when he set the class assignment, but I did end up getting an A for it).

After four months of stressing over the visa, all that was left was to hop on the ferry across to the Embassy in Belfast, Ireland and get my papers officially signed and stamped.

I was terrified by the thought of living in Florida for three whole months, in a place I didn't know and with people I had never met. After the nightmare application process and the sheer expense of the visa combined with flights and rent, there was a lot of expectation from this internship.

I have suffered with anxiety for years and I get a lot of questions about how I have been able to move countries so many times and do so many things alone while battling anxiety. The answer is that my Mum is too good for this world and that my passion was what continually drove me forward.

I was so anxious about the thought of flying out there alone and starting it all by myself that my Mum decided to fly out with me and take the first couple of weeks as a holiday and make sure I was settled in. When we drove up to the intern house in the rental car and unloaded all of my stuff, I was met, very enthusiastically, by two girls who would become good friends of mine.

As an introvert by nature and having my anxiety only barely contained (back then I barely understood my anxiety or how to control it) I was scared of making the wrong impression and stupidly decided that I needed to appear cool and relaxed like them and asked my mum to go back to the hotel to let me unpack with the girls.

Unfortunately what I didn't realise was that they were only on their lunch break and had to go back to work. By the time I realised that in fifteen minutes I would be alone in the house with no way of contacting my mum or any way of getting to her hotel, she was already long gone.

So instead of being the new 'cool' and 'relaxed' intern, I was stuck in the middle of a group of excited girls I didn't know in the beginning stages of a full-blown panic attack.

I somehow managed to concoct some stupid story about how I had forgotten anything to eat and how I should really have lunch with my mum. So the girls very kindly drove me to the hotel before they went back to work, probably thinking I was the weirdest person on the planet.

By the time I reached the door of the hotel, with no key of course, I was already almost hyperventilating and crying uncontrollably. When the door wouldn't open and my mum wouldn't answer, my mind went out of control imagining all kinds of situations. That I had told her to leave and she had gotten into a car accident, that she had decided to go somewhere and wouldn't be back for hours, or that she had decided to go back to the intern house to check on me and now she would be worried about where I was. I sat down on the ground and waited for the panic attack to pass.

After ten minutes or so I stood up and looked down at the parking lot to see my Mum walking towards the hotel room.

Her hands were full of groceries and she was looking up at my bright red, tear-streaked face in concern. She rushed up the stairs, genuinely worried that something terrible had happened to me. I felt so ashamed explaining to her that nothing was really wrong, everything just felt wrong.

She sat down on the bed facing me with her arms crossed, no doubt thinking about the amount of money and time she had spent helping me to get to this point and instead of being happy about it I looked miserable.

She gave me a very firm talking to, which at first made me feel worse, but it was what I needed. She needed me to prove to her that I would be okay staying here by myself for the summer. She wouldn't be able to leave me there knowing that I could be having anxiety attacks daily during what was supposed to be the best summer of my life.

She ended up driving me back to the intern house, helped me to unpack and busied herself cooking some meals to freeze so at least I wouldn't starve on my first week.

I'm not going to lie, I was terrified when she left, my last link to home was gone and I was left in a completely new place with a bunch of strangers and a weight of expectation on my shoulders.

I learned a lot about myself during the three months I spent in Key Largo. I made some incredible friends and had some great fun exploring the Florida Keys with them at nights and on the weekends. But I also learned that I am a very introverted person. For years I believed myself to be an extrovert because I was competitive, loved performing and made friends easily. But when I lived in a busy house with four other girls, I often found myself sneaking away down to the canal docks or onto the balcony alone just to get some space.

I also learned that no matter how difficult it was to get myself there, and get over the anxieties I had about being away from home for so long, it was definitely worth it.

Aside from all of the new experiences I was having in my personal life, with regards to the work I was doing, most of my previous experience had all been hands on and I had never had time to learn the proper theory of training. With this internship I was able to attend lectures and take quizzes to test my knowledge. Suddenly, things I had been doing for two years in sessions now had names and definitions and by the end of the internship I felt like everything I was learning about training was fitting together and making complete sense.

An amazing thing about interning is being able to meet so many different people from different walks of life and really embrace other cultures. You may be practically bankrupting yourself to pay for flights, rent and food while working for free, but you are gaining so much more in life experiences.

As an intern you really begin to appreciate what it means to do this job for real. And you quickly realise that it is not a job but a way of life.

Right in the middle of my internship one of the dolphins had an unfortunate accident and swam into a mangrove tree within his sea lagoon resulting in a broken jaw. This meant that immediately the plans of every single person working at that facility changed within ten minutes. Several of the other interns and I had been planning a trip to the cinema that night and we had all really been looking forward to it but the moment we heard what had happened, it was completely forgotten about.

The vet from the equine stables an hour away was immediately called out on an emergency consult with his X-ray machine. Trainers were calling friends and loved ones, cancelling weekend plans and evening dinners because everyone knew they were staying at work until the dolphin was ok.

No manager had to round everyone up and order people to stay, no one was complaining over the schedule or about missed time off or unpaid hours, it was automatic.

There was no other option in anyone's mind.

Even trainers and interns who had not been at work that day when it happened, drove in and stayed to offer extra help.

By five in the evening a secure medical bay pen had been hastily constructed. The large body sling had been brought out and the dolphin was calmly eased into it and slid onto the padded mats for the X-ray to be taken of his jaw.

The X-Ray imaging took less than five minutes as the portable machine was moved around different angles of his head. He was then slowly lowered back into the water, two of his trainers staying in the shallow pool with him to make sure he didn't hurt himself further by swimming into anything else.

Waiting for the X-ray and the results took hours as they had to be sent to the lab for printing. By the time it was all done it was already dark, and yet everyone was still there, talking quietly and waiting by the side of the lagoon.

Eventually the results came in and an operation was scheduled for the next day. In the meantime there was nothing more to be done than give him more pain medication and stay with him.

Trainers volunteered to stay the night in pairs and of course it ended up being the trainers who had the best relationship with the animal. They probably wouldn't have gone home even if the supervisor had tried to force them to their cars.

The next day, I was lucky enough to be able to come in to work and observe the surgery that they performed to re-align his jaw. They set up a camera in the makeshift operating room in the vet's office so staff and interns could observe from the trainers office. It was a gruelling surgery. The inability to use anaesthetic on cetaceans because of their respiratory anatomy means whenever they need surgery it needs to be done while the animal is still awake with the use of numbing agents, sedatives and local anaesthetic.

Cetaceans are conscious breathers which means that they need to think about every breath that they take, so if they were put under a general anaesthetic they would suffocate. One of the main reasons why we form such close relationships with the animals and take so much care with our voluntary husbandry (medical) training. Their lives can sometimes, quite literally, depend on it.

The surgery took less than an hour but involved the drilling of metal screws into his lower jaw in order to re-align the bone. Incredibly the dolphin lay still almost throughout the entire procedure with his trainer beside him the entire time. Honestly I don't know who was having a more stressful experience, the dolphin or the trainer.

We form such close personal attachments to our animals that we would do almost anything to stop them from being hurt. So when one of our animals is sick or in pain and there is nothing we can do about it, we suffer along with them.

The hours that the team put in to make sure that the dolphin was as comfortable as possible in the lead up to, during, and in recovery from the operation was phenomenal. From assessing his physical condition to ensuring he was getting enough to eat and enough fluids, to assessing his attitude, observing him from the dock and diving to clean the mesh of the medical pen twice a day.

Happily, thanks to the commitment and care of the team he made a complete and full recovery. He had a few weeks where he had to wear what we affectionately nicknamed 'braces' as the screws stuck out a little from his jaw and were covered with a shield so he wouldn't snag them on anything as he swum around. Only a few days after the procedure he was back to the same happy-go-lucky dolphin that he had been the week before. After the 'braces' were removed he was only left with a slight curl to his upper lip, a happy coincidence considering his name was Elvis.

This is just one of many examples of awesome animal care I could give from facilities around the world. At the end of the day the most important thing about our job is caring for the animals.

Accidents and illnesses are not the only way that trainers can have their schedules interrupted by their animals. Slightly more heartening is when animals give birth.

An air breathing mammal giving birth in an aquatic environment is always stressful for the trainers and risky for the animals, both in captivity and in the wild. I have been lucky enough in my career to witness two separate dolphin births and they are definitely not experiences you forget in a hurry.

Again during my internship at Dolphins Plus we got a call through on the radio that across the road at our sister facility the heavily pregnant Nika was about to give birth. We had just started our lunch break and looked towards our intern coordinator in a silent plea to be allowed to go.

She grabbed the radio, stuffed her sandwich into her mouth and raced out of the door with us. There was no way any of us were missing out on the opportunity to see any of it.

When we arrived, the facility was shut to guests and only staff were present.

The photo department were eagerly dotted around different points of the lagoon, all desperate to get the best photo of the new-born. The research department had underwater cameras and hydrophones in the water trying to catch something never-before seen that could help in better understanding mother and calf behaviour. The trainers were all focused on Nika and how she was feeling.

She was doing so well, appearing calm and swimming with an experienced mother, Samantha, by her side. She was even swimming over between contractions to get a rubdown or simply lie beside her trainer.

At one point her trainer asked her to lay on her back and she touched the baby dolphin's flukes before he was even out into the world. She delightfully turned around and announced to us that it was a boy!

At that point I remember feeling so lucky to have the privilege of seeing tail flukes being born, never mind a whole baby. I knew that because this facility was closed, all of their guests were being diverted across the road to us for the afternoon so we interns needed to be back in around thirty minutes to make sure everything was prepped and ready for a packed afternoon. There was only a very small chance that the baby would be born before that.

Fifteen minutes later a shout came from the other side of the lagoon that the dorsal fin was out! By the time Nika had swum over to our side, she gave a massive push right in front of us and the tiny little baby dolphin slipped out in a stream of blood as the umbilical cord tore away.

He looked so tiny and floppy it seemed ridiculous that he could ever swim or survive in the water, but Nika was soon right beside him, helping him up to the surface to take his adorably feeble first breath. Everyone had tears in their eyes as we jumped around hugging each other and holding our breath as Nika started to figure out how to be a mum.

To be able to witness a dolphin being born right in front of your eyes is an immense privilege. Dolphins are pregnant for a whole twelve months, killer whales for eighteen, meaning that we spend a very long time in nervous anticipation whenever an animal is pregnant. With any labour, there can always be unforeseen complications and dangers, but when it goes right it is breath-taking. You feel honoured to be able to witness life coming into the world, especially in what is usually the mystery of cetacean birth under the waves. We all stood united in that moment, trainers and interns alike, humbled in the presence of new life come into the world.

We stood there smiling through the happy and relieved tears that fell down our faces with our arms around one another, watching Nika fuss over her new baby as Samantha swam by her side, making sure she was coping.

We might have to work incredibly hard, in the beginning for free and then eventually for a pitiful salary, but when the up side of that hard work is getting to see a baby dolphin be born, it hardly counts as work at all.

There are a lot of people who think our job is easy and only involves playing with dolphins all day long. But most people don't get to see the hard work that goes on behind the scenes. The long hours, the physical labour and the personal sacrifices.

The reason we push interns so hard and ask so much of them is because the job will only get harder.

Trainers do everything interns do and more.

We still do fish kitchen, only we are the ones responsible if any mistakes are made and bad fish makes its way into a bucket. We still scrub docks and net algae out of pools only we do it frantically in between sessions. We still scrub floors and walls and coolers while the animals demand our attention, and we do all of this because we put the animals first. Always.

CHAPTER SEVEN – LEAP OF FAITH

Once internships have been completed and you think that you have enough experience to start applying for jobs, it gets really stressful. Most people will apply to countless facilities and never hear back from them at all.

At this point you have gained as much experience volunteering or interning that you think you need. Perhaps you cannot afford to take another three months off to do unpaid work and interning again is no longer an option. So for whatever reason the only thing you can do is keep applying, cross your fingers and pray.

This is one of the reasons why networking is so important.

I had applied to several different facilities and had received many rejections before I managed to get my foot in the door by having made a good impression on the head trainer of Dolphin Encounters, Bahamas.

Once my internship at Dolphins Plus in Florida had ended, I gathered my courage and fought down my anxiety about travelling alone, navigated the humungous Miami International Airport, and hopped on the shortest flight of my life (a whole thirty-five minutes) to visit my friends in the Bahamas.

But it was much more than a social visit.

My main intention was to speak to the head of the facility and inquire as to the possibilities of getting a job there the following year as I had fallen in love with the people and the island from my previous internship there.

My life outside of work with the friends I had made had been exciting and full of laughter. I loved the laid-back Caribbean island with its white sand beaches and deserted islands only a ten minute boat ride away. The oceans so full of colour and life of all kinds just waiting to be explored. And of course the wonderful dolphin family that lived at Dolphin Encounters.

I clicked with the facility, the way they worked suited me and the location was quite simply paradise.

Considering I only had one final year left of university, I knew it was time to get serious about my chances of finding a job when I graduated and if there is one woman I owe my career to (except my Mum of course) it is Kim Terrell.

Legendary woman.

She was the director of animal training at Dolphin Encounters for a good many years before she retired and she ran that facility with an iron fist. Although she was an incredibly strict boss, I have never seen someone more loved and respected by her staff or seen someone train animals like her.

It was like she could magically communicate to the dolphins, she would have the most hyperactive inattentive eight month old dolphin sitting up in front of her, eyes front, within half a session. Or the grumpiest, stubborn old matriarch acting like a puppy dog who wanted her belly scratched.

I think she already knew what I wanted to talk about from the moment I asked to have a meeting with her, and I was terrified. She might be an incredible person who I have a lot of respect for, but she is also a very intimidating woman. It's a miracle I wasn't hyperventilating by the time I walked into her office, stinking of desperation.

She crushed my hopes and dreams of working in the Bahamas as kindly as possible, basically telling me that due to recent visa restrictions it would be almost impossible for me to live there even if they gave me a job up front.

Through the ringing in my ears, I do remember her saying to me that she was sure I had a bright future in this industry and that I could not give up.

So even though it was definitely not what I wanted to hear, leaving her office with her good opinion of me was like carrying around a little token of good luck in my back pocket that helped me to go back and complete my last year of university.

The months that followed were a continuous stream of sending out CVs and cover letters to numerous facilities across the globe, in the vague hopes that one would eventually reply.

After several months of applying and hearing nothing back, Kim contacted me to say there was a job available in the Dominican Republic and (if I was willing) she would recommend me to the director. I was astounded that she believed in me so much that she would be willing to do that for me. Needless to say I said yes.

She knew how dedicated I was to pursuing marine mammal training as a career as I had made the extra effort to physically fly myself to the island a year later to enquire over a job. This showed commitment and passion, and even though I didn't have a lot of contacts in the field at that time, Kim most definitely did.

The first thing you feel when you secure your first paid position is joy and relief. It has finally happened! You have proved wrong all of those people who told you that you couldn't do it. You are a marine mammal trainer! Congratulations!

Now you get to worry about whether you will actually be good at the job or not.

On entry-level positions, a lot of the time you might be called a trainer but most of the time you will be doing the same level of work as an intern.

If you are really unlucky you will start at a facility you have never worked at before, surrounded by interns about to complete their season who all know how to do your job a lot better than you do. But don't worry, the first year or so of being a trainer is an even steeper learning curve than as an intern. You have so much to prove and so much still to learn, my best advice would be to just enjoy it. Animal training is always changing so that means that you are always learning, whether you have six months experience or thirty years. No two animals are exactly the same, no two facilities are exactly the same and animals are most often completely unpredictable so you will always make mistakes. And that is ok. The only thing you can do is learn from those mistakes and commit them to your 'I will absolutely never do that again' mental folder and vow not to be so stupid in the future.

When you show your bosses that you have successfully made the transition from intern to trainer and can handle being treated seriously, you will be rewarded for it.

The first few years as a trainer are full of exciting milestones.

The first time you run a session with one animal completely alone, the first time you hold two dolphins in control at the same time, the day you get your bridge, your first blood sample, your first hydration. All of these moments, some big and some small, are making you into the trainer you are going to become. And the best investment you can make is in yourself.

So four months after I graduated from university I was sitting on a plane heading to a country I had never been to before, where I knew no one and where they spoke a language I didn't understand. I was terrified.

The night before I left I had a breakdown in front of my Mum and once again she calmly told me that it was my choice, no one was forcing me to leave, I could quite easily stay at home in Scotland forever. That is when I realised that the only thing more terrifying than leaving, was staying and giving up on my dreams.

I have continued to apply that philosophy in my life whenever I have been faced with a new challenge or whenever my anxiety is stopping me from trying something new. If something is risky but I know that it will help me to grow as a person, then 100% I need to make that leap, no matter how scared I am of doing it.

When I was offered the job in the Dominican Republic at Dolphin Explorer I knew there was no way I could ever turn it down. With this field being so competitive, when you are finally offered paid experience, regardless of where it is, you accept.

I soon found myself in a third world country living with someone I had never met before in a cockroach-infested apartment in a very dodgy neighbourhood.

This huge culture shock was a lot for me to cope with and the truth is that my passion for this job helped me to deal with the anxieties that the move brought with it.

Yes I had anxiety attacks about finding somewhere to live, about getting lost, about getting robbed or shot or run off the road (all things that actually happened to various people I knew while I was there) but if I had to go through that to work with dolphins then I would do it.

It sounds crazy but that's the level of dedication that it takes.

Dolphin Explorer was going to be the third natural seawater lagoon interaction facility that I had worked at so I knew roughly how it was going to work.

There were various lagoons holding dolphins in various social groupings, mums with calves, females, juvenile males and sexually mature males.

Separating animals into groupings like this keeps the risk of aggressive incidents between animals minimal. Because dolphins are so sociable they will undoubtedly get into fights with one another daily, both in captivity and in the wild.

Especially when males are trying to have sex with females who are totally not into it. Or when mothers are trying to protect their calves from jealous females, or juvenile males, or even other female playmates simply because they just want to be with their baby.

Animals are not machines and their moods are constantly changing which means, as trainers, it is our job to adapt and adjust depending on the mood of the group.

Usually each dolphin will have a handful of other dolphins that they really like to spend time with. There will be a few others they will tolerate being around but aren't particularly interested in, and the rest of the animals they simply can't stand to be close to.

As trainers it is our job to figure out which dolphins like each other and try to group them accordingly to keep everyone happy.

The best way to picture this is as cliques in a stereotypical American high school. You will try to let the jocks all be together because they like to rough-house and have a lot of energy, however you would keep them away from the nerds who are quieter and prefer to sedately converse with one another. But you would perhaps put the debate team and class valedictorian together with either the nerds or the jocks for short periods of time because they have enough in common to socialise with each other.

When I arrived at Dolphin Explorer, they had a reputation for being a high turnover facility, meaning that trainers never really worked there for a long period of time.

There were various different reasons for this.

Once a trainer has a minimum of one years' paid experience under their belt, they will have a good chance of getting offered jobs at places closer to home or higher on their list of preferred facilities. For a lot of people, the culture of the Dominican Republic was a difficult one to weather and withstand and it usually pushed trainers back to more 'comfortable' countries quite quickly. The company was also very demanding.

We would often be working several hours overtime every day without being paid or seeing any hours given back to us. The company continually tried to squeeze in more and more programs during the day until we were literally finishing one encounter, grabbing the buckets of our next dolphins and starting another one. Therefore, trainers were exhausting themselves trying to take on more work than anyone was capable of doing.

The plus side of this craziness is that when you start there as a trainer, you learn very quickly.

There are so many ridiculous moments and stories from my year in the Dominican.

The time my friend Anne wasn't looking where she was going and accidentally walked off the side of the dock and fell three metres down into the fur seal lagoon in a heap of empty buckets and fish juice. I am forever glad that I witnessed it, wetting myself laughing as she clambered out onto the platform, checking that all of the fur seals were safely in their pens and she hadn't accidentally landed on one.

Once, one of the enrichment balls got blown out of the dolphin lagoon by high winds and one of the trainers valiantly dove out into the ocean to retrieve it. The winds and current were so strong that he ended up being brought back in by a local fisherman, but he did have the ball tucked under his arm.

I once got bitten right through my left foot by an eel that was lurking undetected under the platform during my last session of the day. This ended with me attempting to gauze and bandage my own foot while bleeding profusely on the dock because I was adamant I was not going to a Dominican hospital.

In the end I had no choice, the company piled me into a van and off I trundled to the dodgiest hospital I've ever been to where the tetanus injection needle got stuck halfway into my arm and I was halfway through cleaning my own foot with betadine and rubbing alcohol before the nurses realised they had forgotten to do it.

I made a best friend for life in the form of Anne, an incredibly talented trainer from England and fellow only child. We would enjoy frequent movie nights featuring various Disney classics or Game of Thrones marathons and often eat chocolate bars for dinner.

I had some really incredible moments with the dolphins, when we had a quiet day and we were allowed to have 'free sessions' with the animals, meaning that we got to free dive and swim with the dolphins in the lagoon. There is no better feeling than grabbing a mask, snorkel and free swimming in the middle of a tropical lagoon with a pair of bottlenose dolphins.

Well, some trainers would disagree if those dolphins were Dali and Vicente.

Dali and Vicente were a special pair. And that's putting it nicely. Very few trainers wanted to work with them because of their aggressive history. They loved to play games with guests in the water, usually games that involved herding people out of their depth or biting toes. They had never done any serious damage but it was enough to put trainers off working with them.

For aggressive animals you always have to be on your toes and two steps ahead of them, watching for any precursors and anticipating the animals' behaviours. You have to be ready to accept any consequences of your own mistakes, meaning you could end up getting bitten or rammed by a rostrum yourself.

But I loved figuring them out.

Some of the best dolphin programs I have ran and sessions I have had have been with those two dolphins. When they know that you will give them everything they want if they do what you ask, those dolphins are electric. And building a relationship with a difficult animal like that, makes it ten times more rewarding when you have it.

Of course I made a lot of mistakes with them in the beginning.

The first time I went swimming with Vicente by himself he bit me twice on the calf.

One of the managers had told me how well they both responded to trainers who got into the water with them instead of just standing on the platform, so I decided to get off the platform and into their world.

For the first ten minutes Vicente loved it.

Swimming with me was different for him. I had a good breath hold, I took toys out with me and I swam quickly. I got wrapped up in how much fun I was having swimming in a Caribbean lagoon in crystal clear waters with my dolphin, having another 'flipper' moment, that I forgot to pay attention to his body language. Turns out that he had been getting bored of me swimming around beside him for a while and because I hadn't been reading the signs he was giving me, he decided to be a little less subtle about it and bit down on my leg.

Now, he didn't even break the skin or leave a mark, but it was a clear enough signal for me to return to the platform and re-evaluate my swimming sessions with him from then on. He also decided I wasn't swimming back fast enough for his liking and so bit me on my big toe just to make sure I got the message.

Needless to say I became much more attuned to his precursors after that.

One incident with Dali that stands out for me was when I had him alone for a program late one afternoon and the guests were walking down the metal stairs to the side of us, coming into the water. It was low tide, so there were a lot of stairs for them to walk down and they were often slippery. One large man lost his footing and thudded down the last couple of steps, landing with a splash on top of the platform directly behind me.

Even I jumped and Dali immediately split from control.

I called out to the other trainers to warn them that Dali was not with me and made sure the gentleman behind me was no worse for wear after his tumble. He assured me he was fine and assumed his position in the line.

I waited for Dali to come back.

It was completely understandable that he swam away, he got a fright. A very large stranger landed very suddenly and unexpectedly into his home. After a few anxious minutes, I finally saw the shadow of his body as he swam back to me.

Because he had split from control, even though he came back to me, I needed to give him an LRS before moving on with the session.

Remember an LRS stands for least reinforcing scenario, I needed to ignore the unwanted behaviour of splitting from control.

So Dali accepted his LRS calmly which I then decided to reinforce due to his frustration-related aggressive history. He ate his capelin and I turned to the guests to explain the session, whereupon he took his opportunity to give my hand a sharp bite.

He didn't even break the skin and it wasn't even painful enough to make me gasp aloud, I honestly don't even think the guests noticed anything, but he was communicating to me in the only way he knew how. He trusted me every time I stationed him at the stairs to keep him safe and in that instance I had failed, so he was telling me that he wasn't happy with me.

You will find that in most cases of aggression like this, the animals are frustrated and trying to get their point across to us dumb humans.

Once again I ignored his biting behaviour and continued to have a positive and enjoyable program with both Dali and the guests. At the end of the program I asked the same man who had fallen into the water to, *very carefully,* walk back down the steps towards me and Dali.

This time Dali stayed with me, was well reinforced, and learned that the next time he was stationed at the stairs nothing bad would happen.

In a similar way one of the last sessions I ever had with Dali and Vicente involved an 'Explorer' program with a large Russian family.

It was the session from hell.

The tide was very high meaning that the four children were unable to stand on the platform and instead were clinging onto the fence behind them or being swept away with the waves into the middle of the lagoon, toes floating ripe for the picking for my nibble-happy animals.

The adults spoke little-to-no English as they bobbed around in their life vests and were clearly only interested in what they could do with the animals.

I managed to get through the behaviours with the children with relatively little issues but when I asked the father to come to the front in order to do his handshake with Dali, the problems started.

Before every session we would explain to guests not to reach out and touch the face of the dolphins, because they don't have hands that they can use to protect their eyes or blowhole, and fingers poking into those areas could be potentially harmful to the animals.

But instead of reaching gently for Dali's pec flippers like I had instructed, he proceeded to lunge out with both hands in some sort of attempt to wrangle Dali into his embrace.

Immediately Dali was having none of it, his eyes rolled white and he jerked away from the man.

I gave the man a warning and then explained again exactly what I wanted him to do, asking him to stretch out his hands and demonstrate to me that he understood what I was saying. Once I was comfortable that he understood, I sent Dali again. This time the man moved his hands to either side of Dali's face, fingers grabbing right where his eyeballs were.

I was worried Dali was going to simply lash out to the side and gnaw on the man's meaty forearm but instead he sank low under the water in front of him as if making up his mind.

Then he came back to me and bit my hand. Hard.

This time the Russian man realised he had done something seriously wrong as I gritted my teeth and ignored the stinging of the cuts on my hand in the salt water. As I bit my tongue in an effort not to lose my temper, my hand throbbing under the water and my eyes filling up with tears, not from pain but from rage, he visibly recoiled against the fence.

I took a deep breath and asked Dali for a calm behaviour in front of me to re direct him.

I don't blame Dali one bit.

If it had been me I would have taken a chunk out of that guests arm, but after months of me working on his aggression he knew that he absolutely should not bite the guest.

So instead, to make sure I understood his frustration, he came over and bit me.

Painful, but effective.

In this way, among other reasons, I found the facility incredibly difficult.

The sheer volume of guests we were experiencing daily was exhausting not only for us but also for the animals. The lagoon platforms were poorly structured and didn't rise and fall with the tides meaning that some days you would be treading water battling a strong current, unable to even find your dolphins as they floated two feet in front of you in the turbulent waters, and other days your feet would be killing you as you crouched on the metal grate in two feet of water.

This is one of the main problems with poorly-constructed sea pen facilities, regardless of how large and spacious they are. The ocean is an unforgiving environment, and as such, if the facility is not properly constructed, it will give both you and the dolphins a hundred more problems than you would have in an enclosed, easily controllable pool.

A highly unexpected and completely bizarre problem that occurred while I was working at Dolphin Explorer that took us weeks to figure out, was that the back lagoon dolphin pod (the juvenile males) kept popping up to station with black marks on their sides. We tried to figure out if it was bruising or some kind of fungus or even a virus when suddenly the black spots opened up into full blown sores. Samples were taken and swabs done, cultures were examined, but no sign of bacteria or virus or other cause was found.

It was perplexing.

It was only when we sent a diver in to examine what was happening with the dolphins that we found out there was a large species of carnivorous fish living under the floating platforms. These fish had swam in through the fences while they were still small, found a nice cosy habitat under the docks, grown too large to leave again and started feasting on the dolphins flesh.

It was like something out of a horror movie.

As soon as we found out, we gated the male dolphins into a different lagoon and called in local fishermen to catch and remove every single one of the fish that had made their home under the docks. For three days straight these men would leave the facility with the biggest smiles on their faces, clutching buckets filled to the brim with fish that were, apparently, very tasty once barbecued. Even though it is more natural for the animals to reside in a natural seawater environment, it definitely is not problem-free.

Nowadays the popular thing to suggest is that we 'retire' our killer whales to a seaside 'sanctuary'.

Let's discuss this for a minute because it is at the core of the majority of debates about captivity these days. Not a day goes by where I am not told by an activist on social media, that 'at the very least' I should allow these animals to live the rest of their lives in a sea pen. Those are the messages I don't mind receiving, I can understand that these people simply want what they think is best for the whales.

The death threats are a little more difficult for me to read.

The majority of people who suggest putting the orcas into sea pens usually don't have a great idea of the sheer amount of work that would go in to making them halfway successful.

Let's imagine that we were going to put all of the whales born in captivity into a sanctuary build out on the ocean somewhere.

How is this sea-pen going to be built?

In order to have a clean and healthy aquatic environment, water needs to be filtered.

In pools that is done by using filtration systems and in the majority of lagoons the nets have enough space to allow the flow of water through the enclosure.

Will this material be resistant to the elements and to the whales themselves?

From working with killer whales you will find out that they like to destroy everything. Give them a plastic toy, it is broken in a few days. Give them a stronger plastic toy, they will puncture a hole in it so it fills with water and sinks to the bottom. Give them a rope toy and they undo all of the weaving so it unravels and you can't give it to them anymore for safety reasons. Re-paint a pool and they will entertain themselves for hours opening holes in the paint and slowing picking away at it until there is just a wall of grey concrete again.

Is it going to be strong enough to withstand ocean currents in all weather conditions as well as the pesky curiosity of a destruction-happy killer whale?

There are currently eleven individual killer whales residing between Loro Parque and Marineland.

Is the plan for all of them to go into this sanctuary together? Is it just one big open pool for them to swim around in or is it possible to separate the animals? As we have already discussed, cetacean society is highly complex and they simply cannot spend every single minute of every day with each other because they will get into arguments and get bored with one another's company.

Inbreeding will start to happen from unrestrained natural reproduction and aggression will occur at a higher frequency as the animals grow sick of spending time together.

If we are able to build multiple pens, how do the gates work? How many pools will there be?

Most importantly, where will the sanctuary be built?

Presumably somewhere with very deep water and lots of space for the animals to roam, while still being in a contained environment. This probably means it will have to be somewhere relatively far out into the ocean and potentially somewhere with very harsh weather conditions. The difficulties with the sea pen constructed in Iceland for Keiko's failed release is detailed at length in Mark Simmons' book *Killing Keiko; The True Story of Free Willy's Release to the Wild* and really makes you realise that sea pens are not a miracle solution for any animal.

If a sanctuary was to be constructed in the middle of a harsh environment, which the majority of areas deemed appropriate for such large mammals are, how are we supposed to protect the whales? What is to stop anyone who has a boat just from driving right up to the edge and having a little look or touch? If these pens are difficult to reach and difficult to access, how are veterinary staff supposed to check them over regularly to ensure good health? None of the animals currently residing at Marineland or Loro Parque, with the exception of Morgan who was rescued in her early years, have ever been in the ocean and so the move would put them under so much stress it would be incredibly risky even to attempt it. We would be dumping them into a completely foreign environment with too many different elements for them to understand and comprehend.

This amount of stress could quite literally kill them.

Trainers once tried to introduce live fish into the tanks with the whales as creative enrichment, hoping that the whales would hunt together and have fun as a pod. Instead they all completely freaked out, swam as far away from the fish as possible and refused to come to control for the rest of the day, even once the fish had been successfully retrieved and removed by trainers. They may not be domesticated animals but they are not completely wild either. During Keiko's three year re-training effort he was eventually able to successfully retrieve partially stunned fish that had been thrown into his sea pen, but he was never observed hunting and catching live fish on his own either in his sea pen or while in the open ocean. Wild instincts can often be buried very deep down within an animal, and in some cases impossible to find.

We haven't even begun to talk about pollution yet. The ocean is so incredibly toxic these days that we would actively be putting these whales in worse condition by introducing them to the ocean. Their immune systems would not be able to cope with an unknown pathogen. They would be at high risk from developing pneumonia and other respiratory infections as well as gastro intestinal problems.

If those weren't enough problems already, who is going to take care of the animals once they are there? Are we trainers, who unarguably know them best, going to be allowed to take care of the whales we have devoted our lives to, or are the animal-rights activists going to assume that role?

Are we supposed to just hand over our animals to people who don't know the first thing about them? These people don't know how Kohana likes to eat her fish, how Skyla likes her jello cut up. They don't know Moana's little idiosyncrasies (hell even I don't!) as well as his trainers. They don't know or understand these whales as well as their trainers do. They might be trying to fight for what they believe is better for them, but just because it is what they think is better for the whales, does not mean it is what the whales themselves would want.

We should not decide what is best for an animal simply based on our own preferences and desires.

And ultimately where is the money going to come from?

The price tag for Keiko's failed release was over ten million dollars for three years of keeping one animal in a sea pen and we are speaking about eleven killer whales only in Europe.

If we are never going to release them into the wild then they will live in this sanctuary for potentially up to fifty years. So for fifty years these animals need to be fed and taken care of, and that is only if they don't breed. If breeding is not controlled by drugs, accidents can still happen while on birth control, or separations then more orcas will be born and so the project continues indefinitely.

Trainers need to be paid to look after them, and fish needs to be purchased to feed them. Toys and other enrichment devices will undoubtedly need to be purchased to stimulate them mentally, as leaving the whales to simply swim around with no mental or physical stimulation would be barbaric. So how is the money going to be generated?

The logical answer is to charge admission for people to come and see the whales. A logical way to make sure the animals are getting enough exercise and mental stimulation is to train them. This keeps them thinking and stops them from getting bored, in the same way a wild killer whale figures out how to efficiently hunt their pray, a captive killer whale enjoys figuring out the puzzles we trainers give them.

Leaving the animals all together in one sea pen continually without any stimulation at all, simply arriving to feed them their fish and leave again, would be criminal. The animals would quickly become bored and take out that boredom and frustration on each other which would lead to escalating aggressive incidents. If these aggressive incidents turned nasty and a whale got seriously injured and any wounds became infected due to the high bacterial content of unfiltered saltwater, who pays for the vet treatment and medication? And more simply, how is that whale supposed to be separated from the rest of the group for treatment or for their own safety? Is husbandry training still going to be allowed in order to monitor the health of the animals and detect any infections? And if so, how to we trainers get close enough to the whales in order to do this?

So what this leaves us with is a very expensive, very risky idea that results in the exact same situation for the animals, after putting them through an extreme amount of stress.

They would effectively be going from a stable, protected environment in a marine park to a dangerously uncontrolled project in the open ocean.

But people find the word 'sanctuary' more acceptable because it sounds better, it is softer on the ears than 'captivity'. It gives a nudge to 'rescue' and lets people think that they saved the animals from their concrete prisons and put them in a glorified net in the ocean.

I am not saying all of this because I don't want what is best for the animals.

I would love for the animals to have deeper tanks and more space to swim even though that is not the most pressing need for any of the whales. The whales born in captivity are inherently lazy, they simply don't need to swim miles to find fish, their fish comes to them.

In a similar way I would much rather sit on my sofa and order a takeaway pizza than head out to the forest and attempt to catch a rabbit to roast.

I want them to be given better enrichment devices and more mental stimulation through play and interaction at all hours of the day. With the potential of adding in underwater elements that are safe for the whales to play with such as underwater currents or kelp. We trainers need to get more creative and spend more time with the animals to give them the variable changes that they need. People often wonder why trainers collapse onto their couches and beds, exhausted after a day's work, barely able to tear open the bag of chips that will most likely become dinner before passing out before 9pm. It is because we exhaust ourselves running around with the whales, playing with them, inventing stupid games that they find new and exciting. Trying to keep up with a killer whale is a massive challenge, trying to always surprise a killer whale is almost impossible. But we do it.

More research projects need to be conducted so we can figure out how to save their wild counterparts. More conservation projects with schools and other facilities need to be undertaken to spread the word about the importance of working to save wild animals. In 2015 SeaWorld Parks and Entertainment proposed a revolutionary idea, to not only expand the orca pools by an extra five meters in depth, but also to implement more enriching exhibits, proposing the addition of underwater currents and naturalistic plant elements and foliage. This was the Blue World Project.

When trainers heard about this we were ecstatic.

Not only was the company proposing to put their profits directly back into the care and wellbeing of the animals but they were listening to public outcry that the current pool size was simply not enough. SeaWorld was moving with the times and modernising. They wanted to give the orcas more space, more enrichment and make a move towards more educational shows while still entertaining the public. This was innovative and revolutionary. However, less than a year later the company pulled the plug on the whole operation.

Stocks and profits were so low because the keeping of killer whales in human care were going out of favour in the public eye. It was decided that they simply could not afford to spend millions to improve the quality of life of the animals if no one was going to pay to come and see them anymore.

Instead CEO Joel Manby announced a company-wide ban on the breeding of all captive killer whales.

This is an excellent example of how activists campaigning not only directly affects the lives of the animals, but is detrimental to their well-being. People are so eager to jump on the bandwagon that they don't stop to think about the consequences of their actions. Because anti-captivity activists were gaining so much momentum with the Empty the Tanks movement, among others, SeaWorld and other companies began to listen and predicted future profit margins based on their decline in visitors. Therefore, to preserve profit and to be able to keep the orcas in the good standard of care they are accustomed to in the present day, they were unable to spend the money needed to further improve their quality of life.

For me the Blue World Project will always be a lost dream and I will always hope that they will revisit the idea in the future.

Because it was the future of orca care in zoological settings.

More space, more education, more enriching, more conservation. That is exactly what the orcas, trainers and guests need but are unable to attain because of anti-captivity campaigning and boycotting.

It is time that activists and trainers all came to an agreement.

It is clear that we all care about the animals and people who are suggesting that we send them to sea sanctuaries are coming from a good place. But they are misinformed. Sea sanctuaries are not the miracle solution that people want them to be.

If we all worked together to bring more profits into marine parks and zoos around the world, then our organisations could not only provide outstanding care for our own animals by building them better habitats and exhibits, but we could then also redouble our donations and efforts to conservation projects around the world. Together we could do so much more good for killer whales (and all animals) everywhere.

*

Aside from the unpredictability of sea pens, another difficulty of Dolphin Explorer came from the sheer number of dolphins we had at the facility. There were thirty one when I worked there, and because our main aim was running programs, there was relatively little time in which to do any training.

Husbandry behaviours such as blood draws are essential to train voluntarily in order to reduce the stress on the animal that would occur from putting them under anaesthetic, as would usually happen with terrestrial mammals. Secondly, cetaceans respiratory systems do not function like ours do, being conscious breathers if they were put under anaesthetic then they would stop breathing and suffocate.

This is the main reason why trainers focus so much time and attention on training essential medical behaviours in a voluntary and stress-free way.

At Dolphin Explorer, even though all of the animals were trained on voluntary blood-draws from their tail flukes, they were not routinely trained on injections for things like antibiotics, should they ever be necessary.

If an animal is eating well then it is easy to administer antibiotics or any additional medicine they may need within their fish, however if the animal stops eating then an injection will be needed. A couple of months before I left the facility, Vicente became very sick. He had been off his food for two days before we decided we needed to step in and get him out of the water for emergency fluids and medicine.

I remember standing on the warm sand at the edge of the beach holding one of the massive sponge pads that stank of damp. The sun was just leaving the beach and settling behind the palm trees, casting a rosy glow on everything surrounding me. The salt was cracking on my face every time I yawned and my hair was a birds' nest on my head from eight hours spent running dolphin interaction programs in the ocean. Despite my deep tan, the top layer of skin on my arms was a dull red colour and throbbing with enough heat to tell me that I had burned right through my cheap sunscreen bought from the local supermarket. I tried to stifle another yawn but failed miserably, eight months of no vacation time and only one day off a week was starting to take its toll. Every part of my body was starting to hurt.

I was waiting for my friend and roommate Anne to appear through the gap in the palm trees from our maintenance/storage area with the stretcher. I looked above me at the seagulls coasting along, shadows falling off of their wings as they flew into the sun. The sea lions were grunting and snorting to the other side of me, lolling lazily in their enclosures, peering at us out of one cracked eyelid like a grandpa trying not to wake up from his nap.

Anne finally crashed through the trees, much to the annoyance of the sea lions who immediately started barking their frustration, a heavy stretcher unravelling around her.

A petite English rose with pale skin, a smattering of freckles and long brown hair, bleached blonde at the ends from the salt water and sun.

"Can you help me with this, I don't know why it's so tangled"

I glanced behind me towards the dolphin lagoons, at the Dominican trainers already halfway up the docks with the other sponge and stretcher poles and knew we were already behind.

I dumped my sponge onto the sand

"Well two heads are better than one"

I started un-ravelling the mass of material and we eventually got it folded correctly and tucked under Anne's arm. I hoisted the massive sponge under my own arm and we set off running towards the dock. The pearly white sand rushed between my toes as I ran and as I hit the wooden dock with a thump, my feet, calloused from months of working barefoot, didn't even flinch as I ran towards the sound of our Director shouting commands.

We finally reached the dock and set our materials down at the side of the lagoon under the heavily judgemental gaze of our vet. A terrifyingly brilliant English woman who scares the living crap out of most grown men. We hurriedly jumped up to the high dock and grabbed the last masks and snorkels out of the bin, meaning that we got the duds. My snorkel had a hole in it so for every breath I took I got half a mouthful of saltwater too, Anne's mask was missing a clip and so was held together with a cable-tie instead.

I floated at the surface of the water, mask starting to steam up and the snorkel biting into the soft flesh of my gums. There were twelve of us trainers in the water as we waited for the incompetent photographers to lower the 250kg net down from the high platform. Our Director was screaming at them to stop twisting the net because the weights would end up on the wrong side and could potentially ruin the whole catch.

Trying to figure out what everyone was saying with my still-limited Spanish and my ears half under the water was a challenge. I was trying to keep my eyes on what the Photographers and maintenance staff were doing with the net but also on my dolphin floating in the middle of the lagoon just beneath the surface.

I watched Dali swim protectively around Vicente as he floated, lethargic, staring at us.

He hadn't eaten anything in two days and if we didn't get fluids and antibiotics into him soon then his condition could rapidly become fatal. The previous two days had involved me and other trainers attempting to entice him to eat some fish, swimming out from the waist-deep platform to get to him and offering him touches and rubdowns whenever he swam over to us. A couple of days previously, when he had been showing signs of illness but had still been eating, we had managed to get a blood sample from him voluntarily which had shown us that his white blood cell count was up, he had some sort of infection and needed antibiotics. Unfortunately by the time we diagnosed him he had stopped eating and didn't want to come to control.

Which is why I was floating in a saltwater lagoon at 6pm about to catch a dolphin.

Thankfully Dali and Vicente had already been gated into the far right holding lagoon while the large aquarium at the back was under maintenance. Meaning that there were six less dolphins to worry about and the lagoon was much smaller.

Even though I was a girl and foreign I had begged to be allowed on Vicente's catch team. In extreme cases like this one, when it is necessary to get in and physically catch an animal, the strongest and largest trainers are chosen in case the animal begins to fight against its restraints. Given the fact that Vicente was already incredibly weak and I had a good relationship with him, they let me be on his catch team.

As the photographers lowered the net slowly from the high platform down to the side of the lagoon where we were waiting in the water, the two dolphins started swimming, they knew what was coming.

Dali was especially annoyed. He wasn't the sick one after all.

As we grabbed onto the net, making sure the weights were on the right side, all twelve of us got ready to dive. I looked at Anne who was on my right side and she nodded at me in encouragement. She knew how worried I was about Vicente. I looked to my right and found Britney and I nodded at her in encouragement, she was on Dali's catch team, she needed all the luck in the world.

Collectively we all took a breath and dived, straight down the fence to get the net to the bottom. Trainers in the middle pulled it flush to the sandy bottom, making sure it didn't snag on any rocks and trainers at the sides pulled it tight to the corners to stop any holes forming. Those of us with better breath holds stayed down and started to pull the net forwards, the two dolphins circling a few meters above us.

Once my air was gone, I shot eight meters back up to the surface and gasped in a breath, quickly looked around to get a visual on the animals and make sure that they were clear of the net and dove back down again. Once the net was across the bottom of the whole lagoon we synchronised and pulled it up on all sides at once.

I handed my piece of net off to one of the newer photographers who looked like he had no idea what he was doing or why we were catching a dolphin.

"Tiralo con fuerza cuando nos decimos" or "Pull hard when we tell you to"

I stared at him through my mask until he nodded that he had understood. At least I hoped he understood, if the net wasn't pulled tight enough we could either drown or be crushed by a 170kg dolphin.

I looked around me in the lagoon and saw Dali floating on the other side and Vicente close to my left shoulder. The other trainers were spread out across the surface, looking like whack-a-moles with their heads out of the holes.

Spotting that I was the trainer closest to Vicente, our director instructed me to try and calmly get my arms around him.

I nodded and slowly approached Vicente.

I swam carefully, trying not to make any sudden movements. He was floating at the surface, breathing frequently but making no noise which wasn't a good sign. Dali was squealing like a toddler having a tantrum and we hadn't even done anything yet. Vicente was clearly very weak. I stretched out my left hand towards him and stroked the palm of my hand along his side, just above his pec fin. The last of the sun's rays were dancing over his skin under the water, illuminating his old shark bite scar.

He didn't move when I touched him.

Taking a deep breath, aware that he could move suddenly at any time, I switched arms, placing my right palm at his side and slipping my left arm over his back, in front of his dorsal fin.

He still didn't move.

I floated there for a few seconds, treating water carefully, trying not to put my weight onto Vicente any more than I had to in order to stay afloat.

"Alright everyone, slowly take your positions on Vicente"

At our Directors urging the other four members of the Vicente catch team joined me on him. One beside me on the head, one on the tail and two on the dorsal.

He didn't move.

"Ok Dali team when you're ready"

I couldn't see the Dali team because they were behind me and on the other side of Vicente but I could hear a lot of grunting and splashing. Thirty seconds later I heard the command to pull the net up, seconds later I felt the cords under my feet and I could stand on the net instead of floating at the surface thanks to thirty pairs of hands taking our weight from the high docks.

I sneaked a glance over at Dali and I saw him thrashing around madly trying to break the hold of the six trainers on him. I grimaced, poor Britney, she was getting rag-dolled.

But I wished that Vicente had been reacting the same way, he was far too calm and docile. There was something seriously wrong with him.

We walked him slowly and carefully over to the side of the lagoon where the photographers let go of the net so we could step off onto the platform. Other trainers stepped in with the stretcher and we eased him into it carefully, tucking his pec fins to make sure we didn't damage anything. Finally he was in the stretcher and on the count of three we tucked the poles over our shoulders, the cold metal biting through our wetsuits, and lifted him clear of the water. Even with eight of us on the stretcher he was incredibly heavy. Once we got to the side of the lagoon we lowered him onto the large sponges, folded the stretcher away from his sides and re-assumed our restraining positions, we needed to apply only the gentlest of pressure considering he didn't have much fight in him, poor soul.

Dali was another story.

As I poured water over Vicente's back, being careful to avoid his blowhole, I watched Dali thrashing from side to side, effectively dragging the trainers around the lagoon despite their supportive net floor.

Britney was nothing but a small head of light brown hair among a crowd of dark-skinned Dominicans surrounding her. I hoped she would get out of the way when they released Dali.

"Okay net down!"

The shout came from our director and three of the four lines of workers dropped the net into the water and scrambled up to the top deck to help pull the water-logged net out of the lagoon on one side.

As the support went from underneath them, the trainer team on Dali started to struggle. He started to pump his tail up and down, giving Miguel the ride of his life trying to keep his hold on the flukes. Luckily they managed to stay at the surface. Finally the net was out and clear of the water and the team could release Dali.

I heard the tinny vibration come from the head of the Dali catch team as he counted down through his snorkel and everyone braced themselves for the release. As one, the trainers on Dali pushed away from him as far as they could get and he took off in a swirl of white water, his tail flukes pumping.

Then the water went still

"Everyone ok?"

I was trying to help prepare the endoscopy tube and ties needed for Vicente while scanning the surface of the water to see if anyone had been injured. I saw Britney raise her hand up and form the 'ok' sign, along with the majority of the others.

"Hazel, I need you to move back to the dorsal now"

George, our director, was asking me to give him, the vet and another trainer space to work around Vicente's mouth.

In order to get the tube into his mouth and down into his first stomach they would need to hold his mouth open with gags. For the hundredth time I wished it was possible to anaesthetise cetaceans for procedures like this, if only their respiratory anatomy allowed it. It was so much easier for terrestrial mammals, who as unconscious breathers like us can continue breathing reflexively under anaesthetic. A simple tranquillizer is all that is needed. Cetaceans do not possess that reflex, needing to actively think about every single breath they take.

Anaesthetic is suffocation to a dolphin.

I stroked Vicente's back gently, trying to give him what little comfort I could, eventually bringing my lips down to kiss his soft back.

I looked up at our director.

"I want to be on the Gag"

George sighed and began shaking his head but before he could reply I butted in again

"This is Vicente, if he is going to cut his teeth on anyone then it's going to be me"

He looked at my determined face for a couple of seconds before he took the soft terry-cloth towel gag from Angelo and instructed him to trade places with me.

I took a deep breath and steeled myself as I got into position, this was not going to be pretty.

I clambered over George's back and knelt in front of Vicente's rostrum, squeezing over as far as I could on the narrow dock to allow the vet, Michelle and her assistant to manoeuvre the tube and hydration fluid. The dock was soaked at this point, wet wood leaving imprints in my shins as my toes began to prickle with pins and needles.

With all of the trainers out of the water and already rolling up the net, Dali was floating calmly in the middle of the lagoon like butter wouldn't melt in his mouth, watching us curiously. Little stinker.

"Are you ready?"

I looked up in front of me and nodded at George, now standing over Vicente's body, one leg either side.

I nodded and asked Vicente to open his mouth and as carefully and slowly as I could wrapped the soft gag around his lower jaw. He stayed calm, making only the smallest vocalisations, so I bridged him with my whistle to let him know that he had done a good job.

I took a deep breath and prayed that he wasn't going to hate me forever for what we were about to put him through. Without this gastric tubing he would almost certainly die, but there was no way for me to tell him that. As far as he knew everything hurt and we were only making it worse.

I asked him to breathe for me and he did, however feebly, and I saw one of the trainers observing the procedure automatically start counting his respirations.

I took a deep breath myself and asked him to open his mouth again.

This time when George wrapped his gag around Vicente's upper jaw, he twigged what was going on and he started to fight us. He started making high-pitched vocalisations and thrashing his head back and forth so George and I were forced to allow ourselves to be thrown about to avoid damaging his jaw. I had to bite my lip to stop myself from crying and I wanted to scream at him to stop fighting us because we were trying to save his life.

I so badly wanted to stroke and hold him to communicate that it would all be ok, but I couldn't move my hands from the gag.

He didn't have much strength left so after a couple more feeble swings he exhaled in a great puff and inhaled wheezing slightly.

Michelle gently nudged me out of the way as she approached with the gastric tube and George and I held his mouth open for her. It was a delicate task, careful not to pull too far or we could break his jaw, and careful not to hold him too loosely or he could snap his mouth shut on the top of Michelle's (or our own) hands.

I could see his blowhole creating various different shapes in a never ending pattern as he vocalised in a high register that human hearing could barely detect. His eyes were bugging wide as she slid the lubricated tube down his throat.

I watched the white tube disappear down his slimy pink gullet.

Luckily cetaceans have no gag reflex and she managed to get the small flexible tube down without incident. With the tube in place, we all took a breather and waited while Michelle fitted the funnel to the end and mixed the antibiotic solution with the bottled water.
"It's ok baby, you're going to be Ok"
I kept uselessly whispering to him even though I knew he couldn't hear me "It's just another hydration, we do them every day"
Even though Vicente was trained on voluntary hydrations and I did them daily myself with him, he was not an easy dolphin to hydrate. Venus was a dream, she would float completely still and rest her pectoral flippers on your feet with her mouth wide open while the tube would glide effortlessly down her throat. She would eagerly gulp down a litre of bottled water and follow you with her mouth open if she saw you carrying the hydration tubes. For her, hydrations were a positive experience and reinforcing in themselves.
Because captive dolphins' fish is delivered frozen and is subsequently thawed, it loses some of its water content. In order to replace that and ensure the animals are well hydrated we perform hydrations and also occasionally feed unflavoured jello and ice cubes.
The majority of dolphins don't really seem to care about hydrations, they are all trained with successive approximations so the procedure doesn't stress them out and they are a lot more interested in getting their favourite toy to play around with afterwards. Any animal that can swallow a herring the size of my forearm in one gulp can swallow a tube the size of my index finger no problem.
When I was first learning to hydrate Vicente I remember not understanding why the water in the tube wasn't going down properly.
The tube was into his stomach but the water was not exiting the funnel. I had to wait until he breathed before putting the tube down past the epiglottis, feeling the blockage on the end of the tube before I applied the tiniest amount of pressure, twisted my wrist ever so slightly and the tube glided freely downwards again.
That was usually the most difficult part, once the tube goes into the stomach the water goes down, the tube comes out, job done.

But I was left staring in bewilderment with Vicente floating in front of me, his freckled pink belly soft against the sides of my feet and his eyes blinking innocently up at me.

I called my mentor over and he started laughing, apparently dolphins have such good control over their internal muscles that sometimes they can squeeze the tube from the inside, effectively blocking it off and stopping the water from entering his stomach. Vicente liked to play games with his trainers but this day he wasn't playing.

As Michelle got ready to pour the antibiotic solution down the funnel I sent up another silent prayer that he would let himself swallow it.

The first half of the funnel went down smoothly, but he soon began to buck his body on the soaked sponge and then tried to gnash his jaws together to get the tube out of his sensitive stomach.

George and I had to fight him a little to stop him from closing his mouth on either of us but we never wanted to be too forceful with him, meaning we both ended up with some superficial cuts on our hands.

"Just a little more."

Michelle was eyeing the solution in the funnel like it was liquid gold, praying that he would take it all.

Finally the antibiotic solution and water was into his stomach, the poor dolphin was exhausted by fighting us in his weakened state and lay on the yellow sponge, each breath coming heavily.

But it wasn't over yet, Michelle prepared a smaller electrolyte solution to reverse some of the effects of his dehydration from the previous days of not eating. Even though this solution was smaller than the last, after only a few seconds, he started regurgitating and water came pouring out of his mouth either side of the tube, accompanied by a disgusting rumbling burping noise and an unearthly smell.

"Wait, wait, wait!"

George frantically signalled to Michelle to kink the tube to stop any more water coming out of the funnel as we waited for Vicente to calm down again. We were both looking in his mouth and around the sides of his head to see how much water had come back up in an attempt to judge how much antibiotic he had lost. Once he was calm again we tried to give him some more electrolytes but as soon as he started bucking we removed the tube from his throat.

He was done.

His stomach was clearly so sore from whatever infection he had that even just a couple of litres of water was too much for him to handle.

We unwrapped the gags from around his rostrum and he closed his mouth, defeated. I handed off the towel to someone behind me, it was now in tatters, cut by his sharp teeth.

I knelt by his soft grey head, looking into his sombre black eyes and stroked him, murmuring words of comfort that he could not hear.

Michelle quickly and efficiently injected him below his dorsal fin with a second antibiotic, and then took a further blood sample to be analysed.

As soon as the last vial was filled with his dark red blood we pulled the stretcher tight around his body again. I could see his skin starting to slough more than usual because of his contact with all of the materials, grey skin was sticking to the sponge and the stretcher.

At least we had given him a good exfoliation treatment.

We lifted him to the very edge of the dock and on the count of three released one side of the stretcher, allowing him to fall the three feet drop back into the lagoon with a neat little splash.

I dropped the stretcher and ran around the corner of the dock to grab Vicente's bucket, just a formality at this point. Prepared in the morning along with all of the other animals diets but thrown away again every night, uneaten.

Miguel and I called both dolphins over to the side and to my delight and surprise Vicente came over beside Dali. He had no interest in eating, even though I tried to entice him with a delicious-looking herring. I myself hadn't eaten in more than eight hours and even raw fish was starting to look appealing.

I wasn't surprised that he didn't eat but I was incredibly happy that he didn't appear to be too traumatised by the catch and forced hydration. I gave him some cuddles and gave him a stern talking-to about taking care of himself and staying alive until morning.

I caught up with my supervisor on the way to the showers and asked him if he needed people to stay the night to watch Vicente but he told me there was no point since we had already done everything we could. As he walked away across the beach towards the trainers hut, I looked behind me at the dolphin lagoon. Dorsal fins cut across the surface and dolphins splashed out of the water playfully in the main lagoon. But I stayed waiting on that dock until I saw Vicente's dorsal fin finally poke out of the water as he surfaced to breathe, Dali by his side.

Later that night as I peeled off my wetsuit in a freezing cold shower, my skin feeling raw and abused by the sun, all I could think about was Vicente and if he was going to be alive in the morning or not.

Thankfully, going into work the next day Vicente seemed to be doing better and even came over to me and accepted a handful of capelin. He seemed to be on the mend.

Given the stress his body had just been under, he should have been given time to rest and fully recover from what we learned was a stomach infection, possibly caused by eating something nasty that had drifted into his sea pen.

The day after we had hauled him out of the water our supervisor handed Anne Vicente and Dali's buckets and told her to go and do an explorer program with them.

My mouth fell open in shock and my chest grew tight.

I felt so protective over Vicente in that moment that I could easily have said something to my supervisor that would have lost me my job, but I managed to bite my tongue.

At least it was Anne doing the program. I knew that she would do whatever she could to conserve Vicente's energy and not ask too much of him. She mouthed 'sorry' at me as she walked away with my boys' buckets. The sick thing to me was that the only reason Vicente was forced to do that program was because the company was over-selling programs to guests. If there was a demand for a dolphin swim, we would sell it.

Even if the dolphins had already done four programs that day, save fish! They need to do a fifth!

I was mad that our supervisor didn't find a way to move a Funtastic program into the Dali and Vicente lagoon because that way all that Vicente would have to do were maybe a couple of kisses and a handshake with Dali covering the rest of the more high-energy behaviours.

But he had given Anne an Explorer. The Explorer program required dolphins to do fast-swim rides like dorsal tows and belly rides as well as jumps. Usually it was Dali and Vicente's favourite program, it was high energy and fast paced and they responded really well to it. But in Vicente's fragile condition I just couldn't believe he was being forced to do it out of sheer company greed. As far as I am aware the company has since changed management and the dolphins are doing less programs, there are more trainers, the lagoons have been reconstructed and the training is better. At least I sincerely hope so.

*

The year I spent in the Dominican was undoubtedly the toughest of my life so far.

Working in the open ocean meant constantly battling the elements, whether that was scorching sun and dehydration or battling our way through a dolphin program with tropical storm force waves hitting us in the chest for six hours.

Not only was the work more challenging than I could ever have expected but I began to really struggle in my personal life.

Soon after I arrived on the island I got into a relationship with a Dominican man which lasted almost the entirety of the year I lived there. The relationship is still difficult for me to talk about because I feel deeply ashamed of the choices I made to stay with a man who manipulated and emotionally abused me for months.

Toxic relationships like my own were often commonplace on the island, several good friends also found themselves soon being controlled and manipulated by their Dominican boyfriends and were often swindled out of large amounts of money.

People who live there often talk about the 'Dominican bubble', when you are on the island, the rest of the world simply doesn't exist. The Wi-Fi simply wasn't good enough to do anything other than attempt a heavily pixelated Skype call. Streaming movies online or binging on Netflix was often out of the question with frequent power cuts. Once, we had a record eight days without running water in our apartment building and it was only after we all started washing our hair in the pool that the building manager finally paid the bill to the water company. The only music ever played on the radio is bachata, a specific style of Latino music, the preferred artist being Romeo Santos. I'm sure other people find the music soothing and exotic but every time I hear it my blood runs cold and I feel like my ex is standing right behind me. You would think that years later I would have recovered from the psychological after-effects of the relationship, but all it takes is a few guitar chords and the crooning Spanish voice and I am transported right back to the girl I became on that island.

But I loved him.

I was young and wore my heart on my sleeve and he took full advantage of everything I offered him. He wasn't the most attractive man in the world, many would say he was quite the opposite in fact, but he was charming. That same charm he used to make me fall in love with him was soon used to manipulate and twist everything that was my reality.

At more than fifteen years my senior and my superior at work, he used my naivety and relative inexperience against me.

Even after I found out he had a wife, all it took was for him to deny my accusations before I was once again completely blinded by love for him. Any time I challenged him about her, he would manage to twist everything around so that he was completely innocent and I was the one creating trouble by making ridiculous accusations.

And I bought the lies.

I was so blinded by my love for him that I wanted to believe everything he was saying. Even though I knew the relationship was toxic and slowly destroying every piece of who I was, I couldn't let him go. His emotional manipulation soon became my daily reality, to the point where I could no longer distinguish truth from reality.

I tried as hard as I could to get out.

But every single time that I worked up the confidence and strength I needed to finally end things, he would twist everything around so that it was my fault. He would verbally beat me down until I felt like a pathetic, quivering wreck of a person, who needed to seek comfort in the only person who was there to give me it at that moment. Him.

Our relationship slowly spiralled out of control.

Even what little good memories I have with my friends there are all tainted by his manipulation and jealousy. He would call me right before I was about to go out dancing with the girls and tell me that I was a slut and that he knew I was going to cheat on him. That I should watch my back because the security guards working the club were his cousin's friends, he had eyes everywhere watching me.

In this way he took everything from me.

I am incredibly lucky with the infinite amount of patience and support that my friends on that island, and my family through Skype calls, gave me. Even though my disintegration into a sobbing terrified wreck happened almost every other night, they were always there to help me pick up the pieces and help to tape myself back together.

They may not have known it at the time but I owe whatever pieces of my sanity that I retained within that period to them. They never once judged me, even though they knew as well as I did how stupid I was being. They were simply there to hold my hand and offer their help for whenever I was finally strong enough to get out.

After eight months of being trapped inside the Dominican bubble, I suffered a neck injury on another dolphin catch at work and again found myself in the hospital.

When the doctor who examined me told me that she would not be giving me any time off work to heal, even though I could barely move my neck to the side, I had a panic attack.

Feeling like I was quite literally going to die, my vision blurring as I clutched the sides of the examination table like I wouldn't ever be able to let go. The poor doctor quickly realised that she had made a terrible error and attempted to calm me down. After the attack passed she took my blood pressure, which had quite obviously sky rocketed, and she sent me to have a conversation with another doctor.

In my fuzzy state of mind I didn't even realise that he was a psychiatrist.

After a brief conversation in what little Spanish I was able to use at the time, he signed me off work for one week in order to 'recover'. I felt like a woman in the Victorian age being told to take bed rest in order to get over a bout of hysteria.

As I left the hospital and walked up the road under the baking heat of the sun towards what passed for a bus stop, I had to fight back stinging tears.

I had moved to this island to follow my dream. The dolphins and this job were all I had ever wanted from life, but I had somehow gotten myself stuck in a pit of misery and anxiety and I couldn't see how to climb out again.

When the psychiatrist at the hospital asked me if I had been experiencing extreme stress or anxiety, it was the first time I was forced to admit that there was something seriously wrong.

I had been having regular panic attacks, sometimes even on the dock at work right before a guest program. My obsession with him was putting my career, the very reason I had moved halfway across the world, in jeopardy.

I clutched that little slip of paper that offered me freedom and swallowed the tears as I left the hospital. A week wasn't much, but it was the break I desperately needed.

As I trundled home on the hollowed out van that passed for a public bus service, squeezed between an elderly ladies shopping bags and a man clutching a live chicken, I saw that I had no messages from my boyfriend on my phone, even though he saw me get hit hard by Orion's flukes during the catch four hours earlier.

After waiting by my phone for him to call until late in the evening with no luck, my Skype lit up with a video call from a good friend who lived in Monterey Bay, California.

After explaining my situation to him, he started trying to convince me to fly out to him for five days and get away from the island for a bit.

As ridiculous and last-minute as it sounded, I began to see my way out, I decided to take a leap of faith.

In possibly the most risky and spontaneous decision of my life, I booked a flight to San Francisco for the following morning.

The days that followed were like coming out of smog into fresh clean air. Gone was the dust and constant rabble of the Dominican, replaced instead by the cheeping of birds and sharp scent of pine needles. I took long walks by the sea front, enjoying the silence filled only by the sound of the waves and splash of sea otters searching for clams in the shallows. I walked miles by myself, lost in my own thoughts with my phone switched off while my friend was at work. When he was off of work he showed me around the area and was there to feed me some harsh truths about myself.

He patiently sat on his couch and listened to me as I tried to sort through my complicated feelings while I ugly cried and snotted my way through his only box of Kleenex.

Once I was finished he brushed my tangled hair away from my tear stained face, grasped the side of my face with both hands, looked me right in the eyes and told me exactly why I was worth more than this. He was harsh with me, and some of the things he said made me very angry (mostly at myself), but every word he spoke was the truth. His words resonated with me and I started to believe that I could make my way back from this.

The next day I took the time to visit the Monterey Bay Aquarium and deliberately struck up conversations with trainers and aquarists and reminded myself of why I loved my job. I marvelled at their success in training stingrays and was reminded that my passion in life was my work, not my toxic relationship.

I was finally out of the bubble, I could see that the real world was still there and that I could find my way back to myself within it.

While I was in California, I was chatting on WhatsApp with a trainer I vaguely knew who was working at Loro Parque on the orca team and he happened to mention that they were looking for a new trainer. He promised to pass my details and CV on to the head trainer.

I returned to the Dominican with hope.

I now had not only the promise of escape from the island but also potentially my dream job.

As hard as it was for me those next few weeks, I clutched the possibility of becoming a killer whale trainer close to my chest like a beacon, warding off any unpleasantness.

A month after I returned from California and two telephone interviews later, the job at Loro Parque was mine.

Even though I was well on my way to recovering from the crippling anxiety I suffered for the better part of the year, it was still incredibly difficult landing in Punta Cana at the end of my week in California. I had no idea what I was going to be met with at my house or at work, if he would be waiting for me or if he would be ignoring me as I had ignored him for the past seven days. In the end he chose to make it as hard as possible for me to let go of him and became the most docile, gentle and loving man he could be right up until I stepped onto a plane again.

Every day was a test for me not to go back to him and sometimes I failed.

But I knew that I would choose killer whales over anything else in the world. Even him.

My last day at work with the dolphins was bittersweet. Handing in my notice was relatively easy, as I was now desperate to get out of that place and find my way back to who I had been a year before. The evening before my last day was when the emotion hit me.

I had just finished my last session of the day with my boys, Dali and Vicente, and had escorted the guests out of the water. I floated there with their two grey faces staring expectantly at me. Dali all big dark puppy-dog eyes and Vicente with his adorable freckles. I put my arms around both of them, cradling one head on each shoulder and let myself cry. And it was not a pretty cry.

I was full-on sobbing, clutching on to their backs as if for dear life. I don't know if they somehow sensed that I needed it, those two boys would never normally have allowed me to hold them like that for so long, but they didn't move a muscle. Even when I finally let them go and just sat there in the water, shivering in my wetsuit, they stayed beside me.

I have never wished to have the ability to talk to animals more than I did in that moment. The hardest thing for me was that I had no way to explain to them that I was leaving and wouldn't be coming back. I had spent a year forming a relationship with the two of them, working on developing trust and I was about to walk away from them and never go back.

I desperately wanted to find a way in which to explain to them why I wouldn't be coming back. It took me a good fifteen minutes but I finally got a hold of myself and went to join the others cleaning buckets in the kitchen.

I left the Dominican Republic in August 2015, took a week at home in Scotland to be with my family and try to get a real hold of my mental faculties, then took another flight to Tenerife to start my life over again.

I was sure that everything would be perfect, I had landed my dream job as a killer whale trainer at the age of twenty-two.

Surely   everything   would   now   fall   into   place.

CHAPTER EIGHT – A WHOLE DIFFERENT BALL GAME

Killer whales.

Not exactly a name that endears you to them is it? So why then do people feel such a strong connection to them?

In fact, the name is actually a mistranslation from the original 'whale killers', given to them because they regularly hunt and kill other species of whale in the wild. Over time, and maybe because it sounded better, the name evolved into killer whales.

They are found in oceans all over the world, therefore regardless of where you live there will more than likely be a group of killer whales off the coast of your country.

The two main sub-types of orcas are typically split into two categories- either residents or transients. Resident whales tend to live in shallow coastal waters, do not migrate large distances and eat mainly fish. Transient orcas however, travel large distances to find food, mainly of a mammal variety and rarely stay near the coast. Within these two types there are other more specific sub-species of orcas- Biggs, Offshore, North Atlantic, Southern Resident, Icelandic and Antarctic to name but a few. All of these sub groups feed on specific prey, have their own specific dialect and roam in different areas of the world. They have even evolved to have physiological differences, such as varying saddle patch colour and shape, head and body morphology and even skin coloration.

Now depending on environmental differences and variations in prey and hunting techniques all sub-species of killer whales have varying morphology.

One of the most striking examples being the yellow or almost brown hue of the Antarctic killer whales' skin, where the majority of other species are a bright white. This is thought to be because of specific diatoms living in the frigid Antarctic waters that affects their skin colouration.

Additionally, several member of sea lion eating killer whales in South America have collapsed or slightly bent dorsal fins because they stay in relatively shallow water for their whole lives.

In 100% of male killer whales residing in zoological settings, the dorsal fin will inevitably bend over.

This bending over of the dorsal fin occurs because of gravity. The dorsal fin is made from collagen and there are no bones or muscle within it. Therefore, because captive whales spend a lot more time at the surface of the water, they do not have the water pressure needed to hold a boneless fin of around two meters in height straight. It will most often bend in the direction the whale spends most of its time swimming in, for instance the dorsal fin of Keto in Loro Parque bends to the left of his body whereas at Marineland, Inouk's fin bends to the right of his body.

It is an urban myth that it is a sign of ill health or depression in males. It has however been suggested that genetics play a part in dorsal fin collapse, with some individuals appearing more susceptible to dorsal fin collapse than others. This could potentially be likened to how some humans are more susceptible to wrinkles over time than others, due to the varying amounts of collagen in their skin.

It is however important that trainers continually rub down the inside of the bent fin with our hands to remove any excess dead skin that may build up as a result of them being unable to scratch themselves there. Perhaps in the captive population a collapsed dorsal fin becomes a desirable physical trait as it results in extra massages.

Orcas weight and length can differ depending on their genetics, similarly to humans, some whales are just smaller than others. Captivity and pool size does not limit their growth, using Tilikum as the perfect example, weighing close to 6 tonnes and measuring almost eight meters in length. Unfortunately due to Tilikum's enormous size it was often difficult to allow him the space that he needed to swim, even in the largest pools at SeaWorld Orlando. However, the space an animal has in captivity is not directly an indicator of its quality of life.

There are many animals in smaller exhibits or enclosures that have much more enriched lives because of the dedication of trainers and creativeness of design. On average the pools at SeaWorld are around ten meters deep, given Tilikum's large size that was not a lot of room to manoeuvre.

The largest female orca in captivity is Corky at SeaWorld San Diego, who measures just under six meters and weighs almost four tonnes, making her larger than Inouk! It's no wonder the trainers over there affectionately nickname her 'The Beast'. As previously stated, orca weight and length is a direct result of genetics and it is obvious, even within the limited captive population, how much variance there is.

Corky is also estimated to be the oldest orca currently held in captivity at fifty five years of age.

Despite the large debate surrounding the life expectancy statistics of captive versus wild whales, the average life expectancy of a killer whale is around 50 for a female and 35 for a male. There will, of course, always be outliers who live much longer, and conversely, who live much shorter lives than that.

The famous case of the wild killer whale 'Granny' who was a member of the Southern Resident population of orcas, was said to have died at one hundred years of age.

However, any age given to a wild animal will only ever be an estimate.

Granny was first photographed in 1971 with another adult male who was *assumed* to be her son. Scientists then estimated that male orcas age to be around twenty. Furthermore, they estimated him to be her last calf, and put her estimated age at around sixty years. This is an awful lot of guesswork.

In fact, in later years, researchers changed their minds to say that they were sure that particular adult male was not her son but her estimated age was never revised.

The only certain fact we have about her age is that she was at least ten years old when photographed in 1971 as an adult female with an assumed calf. She died in 2017, so she was at least fifty six years old, potentially older. Still a good long life for an orca, but certainly not over one hundred years old.

Unfortunately mortality rates are extremely high in the wild for orcas in their first year of life. Take the endangered Southern Resident population of killer whales as an example, since 1998 forty four calves were born and survived, but seventy seven individuals died. Looking at the statistics, the majority of individuals who died within that time frame were under four years of age. Recently, the Southern Resident population of orcas received a lot of media attention because of the individual J35 who carried around her stillborn calf for more than two weeks in a heart-wrenching show of what appeared to be extreme grief. Although thousands of people sympathised with her and championed the orcas ability to feel emotion, people completely missed the bigger picture, which is that the Southern Resident population is declining rapidly.

The entire population comprises of only seventy five remaining individuals, which has been steadily declining over the last twenty years due to toxic pollution, heavy boat traffic and over-fishing. The Southern Residents feed primarily on salmon, more specifically Chinook salmon which is at record low level due to excessive fishing for human consumption.

J35 was not the only individual in the Southern Resident population to make headlines in 2018. Three year old J50 was spotted ailing and emaciated trailing behind her pod, clearly sick from starvation. Researchers were frantically trying to supply her with antibiotics even though it was already too late to bring her back from the brink.

Scientists and activists trying to help her even went so far as to throw live Chinook salmon into her path stuffed full of antibiotics. This is a heart-wrenching example of the hardships wild killer whales are facing at this moment in time, directly as a cause of human activity in the oceans. And yet people are still clamouring for the release of perfectly healthy, content captive orcas into this environment.

Regardless of years of advancement in understanding orca reproduction, mortality rates in captivity have unfortunately been very high.

In the early years of captivity, orcas would reproduce naturally with each other but because of inadequate pool size, orcas were unable to effectively nurse or take care of their young. In 1985 a calf, named Kalina, was born to matriarch Katina in SeaWorld Orlando who became the first orca calf to be born and thrive in the care of man. This marked a new age for killer whale reproduction and breeding in captivity. Animal caretakers learned and studied how orcas reproduced, gave birth and interacted with their young, contributing endless hours of observations and biological testing to aid research into orca reproduction.

Eventually resulting in a marked improvement in calf survival rate. Unfortunately not every calf survives and not every orca survives to its average life expectancy, no matter if they are wild or under human care. But that is simply a fact of life. Not every human survives to be one hundred years old despite having access to high standards of medical care, and not every orca in the wild will survive to its average life expectancy either.

Unfortunately in Russia and China, killer whales are still being captured from the wild for display in marine parks.

In late 2018, a brand-new state of the art marine park was opened in Shanghai housing four wild-caught killer whales. The problem to an untrained eye? The park looks exactly like SeaWorld. The shape of the stadium, the wetsuits and the colours are all modelled from what is arguably the best marine park in the world. However, to an 'outsider' it is hard to tell the difference between parks that continue to take animals from the wild for display, and parks who stopped that practice over four decades ago. Therefore, everything gets generalised and people lump every single marine park into one category, screaming for us to release our animals 'back to their home' without realising that they have nowhere to 'go back' to.

The activists are still campaigning to boycott SeaWorld even though they have rescued and released more than 33,000 animals to date and haven't taken an animal from the wild in decades.
It would be incredibly refreshing if everyone could set aside their prejudices and have a mature conversation about what can be done to help marine parks improve the lives of captive animals exponentially. How can we become more involved in conservation projects, how can we give more of our profits to organisations really making a difference to our animals' wild counterparts?
The truth is that we are learning so much about these animals from studying them in captivity.
Killer whale births have rarely been captured on film or seen with human eyes in the wild, it is not truly known how high or low the mortality rate is for new-born calves but it has long been estimated that the number is higher than anyone knows. From statistics gained from captive cetacean births a pattern has been shown, primarily in dolphins, that a first calf will have a high chance of being stillborn or die within the first few months. However, every calf born to that mother afterwards will usually be healthy.
Invaluable information on killer whale nursing behaviour was gained by expert veterinarians and researchers in captive facilities. Milk samples were taken to examine the components, and as recently as 2015, SeaWorld was involved in a ground-breaking research study with the NOAA (National Oceanic and Atmospheric Administration) that explored the percentage offload of contaminants though lactation from mother to calf. This is being applied in the real-world to help the endangered Southern Resident orcas, to see how this is contributing to the high calf mortality rate.
Loro Parque was also part of a study in which researchers are attempting to create a cure or vaccine for wild killer whales that have intolerable levels of PCB toxicity in their bodies. Having access to animals in captivity where the reproductive history is known and having access to fish analysis readily available is invaluable to researchers.
If orcas had never been brought into captivity and subsequently studied and observed then we would never know as much about them as we do now.

It started with research on dolphins, where scientists were continually surprised and pleased by their level of intelligence. This became even more apparent in orcas and research soon began to branch into topics such as teamwork, social interaction, communication and imitation.

In zoological settings, researchers are better able to control the environment and observe animals for hours at a time both above and below the waters' surface. This means that they are able to collect a much more reliable and diverse set of data within a much smaller time period. Research in the wild is much more difficult considering one first has to find the animals and attempt to identify them and they are usually only ever observed from the surface, meaning that the biggest majority of their behaviour is left unobserved. Being able to collect samples from the animals voluntarily and without stress has been a big help in aiding researchers. Especially for those researchers looking to identify environmental stress factors when attempting to help suffering wild killer whales.

One study in particular that had been carried out at Marineland for over ten years came to a head in early 2018 when Wikie suddenly became famous overnight for being able to 'speak'. The media took the most sensational angle they could, as per usual, and portrayed it like we were trying to teach her how to speak. Activists called it a cruel joke, or a circus trick.

Even one of my favourite TV show hosts Graham Norton made a cruel joke on his show saying that if she had the ability to speak she would tell us to put her back in the ocean. Needless to say she has nowhere to go 'back' to, considering she was born at Marineland.

Everyone completely missed the point about what the research was about.

It was never about teaching her to speak. It was about imitation. In order to delve deeper into the world of killer whale communication, researchers wanted to find out how well they could imitate one another.

Wikie and several other whales at Marineland were taught a signal for 'copy', essentially asking them to imitate what they saw or heard another whale or trainer do.

Usually in training, one hand signal is paired with one specific behaviour, but the copy hand signal could be applied to any number of behaviours. So the animals had to be taught that the copy hand signal did not mean anything specific, but instead represented the concept of 'copy what you see or hear'.

In this way they learned to copy behaviours, human voices and other killer whale vocal sounds. Wikie was even able to imitate vocalisations from killer whales she had never met before which were played into the water over a hydrophone.

This incredible research study won two awards at the 2018 IMATA conference with my colleague Gwen Margez presenting on behalf of all of the trainers at Marineland involved in the study since its inception. We learned that not only are the whales capable of complex communication, but that they understand how to imitate one another as well as imitate novel sounds. Researchers found that killer whales also learn the concept of copy significantly faster than dolphins or sea lions.

But the media took this revelation and turned it once again into a reason why they should be released.

But the answer to saving wild killer whales lies in the captive population.

Research has truly never been more important. We allow researchers and behaviourists access to the pools to observe our animals and come to conclusions about their intelligence and social behaviour, to name but a few.

If people start boycotting marine parks so that their profits plummet then all of this research will go down the drain and fifty years from now when the majority of animals are on the brink of extinction people will be wondering why we never did anything to try and help them.

*

My first day at work as a killer whale trainer was surreal.

I had imagined it so many times before and I was worried I would be overwhelmed being introduced to the team and seeing the whales for the first time.

The image I had in my head of a killer whale trainer was not the same image that I had of myself at that moment. I had always looked up to orca trainers as being elite, both physically and mentally, in order to be able to work with the biggest predator in the ocean.

I had always imagined that when I was finally allowed into this exclusive world I would have been the very best version of myself. In fact, I was completely the opposite.

Battling my anxiety daily was leaving me fatigued and mentally drained. From barely eating during my last few months in the Dominican I was malnourished and lacking in so many vitamins and iron that my skin and hair was incredibly dry and my muscles ridiculously weak.

After spending some time at home in a gluttonous wave of steak pies, fish and chips, and a cheeky Nando's or three I had developed a nice food baby that was glaringly obvious in my new wetsuit.

I couldn't have been further from that image I held in my head. But somehow, regardless of how I was looking or feeling, putting on that wetsuit and stepping into the world of orca training felt like it was meant to be.

I didn't feel like an impostor or a girl playing dress up. It felt like destiny.

I remember being alone in the locker room downstairs, situated underneath the whale pools inside an echoing tunnel and pulling on the long wetsuit. I had always avoided wearing long wetsuits before because I always found them uncomfortably tight. That morning was no different, the brand new neoprene had absolutely no give in it and it took me a good ten minutes to get it on.

With the wetsuit finally on and with the blood circulation to my hands and neck cut off, the garish yellow Loro Parque logo proudly displayed on my chest, I splashed some water on my face trying to make it seem less red and took a deep breath.

I scooped up my unruly curly hair and twisted it into a tight bun on the back of my head, smoothing away the flyaways with gel.

It was official. I was now an orca trainer.

I climbed up the steps in the middle of the tunnel and arrived backstage to join the rest of the trainers before the first show of the day, careful not to step outside of the 'red zone' clearly marked on the floor. I was brand-new and so definitely not allowed outside of the indicated safety zone.

The first orca I saw up close backstage was Keto.

Of course I had seen orcas in marine parks before but never in such close proximity. There is a huge difference between seeing them from a stadium and seeing them appear from under the water two feet in front of you.

Everything was the same but different.

The long wetsuit being only the first of many changes. The buckets were so much heavier than I was used to and for the first few weeks my shoulders and biceps were killing me from all of the extra weight I was lifting.

Continually having to be aware of where the animals were, not turning your back on a pool and making sure you were within the safety lines at all times were new habits I had to pick up quickly.

Learning to feed the animals massive handfuls of fish at a time instead of just one or two capelin like the dolphins.

After my first morning, walking into the office in my wetsuit and reading the animal boards and notices, I saw my name on the schedule and couldn't help but smile.

Somehow I had made it happen.

And by some miracle I had made it happen by the time I was 22.

I had never expected to achieve my goal so early in life.

I knew from the minute I had made up my mind about my chosen career that it was going to be an uphill battle. I had almost prepared myself for the fact that it might never happen and I would have to content myself with working dolphins for the rest of my life.

Reading my CV it seems like I simply jumped from one logical stepping stone to another but there was so much hard work and dedication that took place for me to be able to do that.

To this day I can be standing on stage in between sessions just watching the whales swim together or pause in the middle of a rubdown with a whale and I take a minute to appreciate where I am.

I remember the never ending stress of visa applications and the sleepless nights thinking that I was so far behind everyone else. Worrying about the swim test being too difficult and constantly refreshing the job postings board on the IMATA website.

Now when I am face to face with a killer whale, I smile to myself when I think I am one of the ones who managed to make it happen.

I was hired at Loro Parque on a two year contract and during the two years I spent there I formed an incredible relationship with my first whale, Skyla.

A young female killer whale, born at SeaWorld Orlando in February 2004 to mother Kalina. She is incredibly playful and almost hyperactive at times. She loves sliding up on beachings but she will constantly wiggle out of rubdowns in the water. She loves almost all toys and will play with them alone for hours until you take them out.

Sometimes she won't let you take them out, and instead will try to hide them at the bottom of the pool or shove them under a gate and pretend that she can't find them. She can make almost noticeable eye rolls when a session is boring her, but when a session is fun and variable I swear that whale can fly.

She taught me so much in my two years there. She was patient with me and let me learn how to train her in a way that she found enjoyable. I learned so much about who I was as a trainer through working with her, and I discovered the sheer complexity of working with killer whales.

Figuring them out became my new obsession. I loved training orcas more than any other animal I had ever worked with.

Even if you have a lot of previous experience, when you first start working with killer whales, it's like you've gone from being a general in the regular army to a private in the SAS.

It's a whole different ball game.

It takes a certain type of person to be a killer whale trainer.

You need to have confidence in yourself to believe that you can be equal to a killer whale. The ability to keep calm in stressful situations is key, even just running a high-speed show with several animals is incredibly stressful. If one trainer messes up a behaviour and sends something at the wrong time, it can potentially create dangerous circumstances for trainers or animals. If a whale is sent on a stage slide behaviour at the wrong time, or misinterprets a hand signal and that trainer does not communicate to the other trainers on stage that their whale is incorrect, we will basically be a line of human bowling pins with the killer whale as the bowling ball.

This is actually something that I have seen happen twice at Loro Parque. Both times it happened with Keto, both times he had misread a hand signal while being sent from the back pool. This made it even more dangerous because there was no trainer able to communicate or watch his underwater 'run' from the stage. Luckily on both occasions the trainer at the side of the stage spotted his shadow approaching quickly and shouted to everyone else to get out of the way. Both times, Keto terminated the behaviour early, as he exited the water and saw trainers on the stage in his way, he knew that he had misunderstood and pushed himself back into the water early.

Being an orca trainer means learning how to think on your feet, being prepared for any potential situation, very good use of peripheral vision and excellent communication to your fellow trainers and to the whales.

We orca trainers almost have our own language of hand signals that we use. I have often been so used to using it at work that I have automatically raised both hands in a fist to let someone know that I am agreeing with them instead of replying verbally and watched as they looked at me like I was mentally challenged. Raising both hands in a fist indicates that the whale is correct or that you are agreeing with another trainer. Raising one hand in a fist to communicate that the whale is incorrect or you don't agree. Turning two fingers over each other to indicate that you either want to continue the session or you will do something later. With the sheer size and acoustic challenges of the orca stadiums it makes sense to use signals to communicate to each other instead of screaming yourself hoarse trying to make yourself heard only to get a confused 'what?' from the other side of the pool in reply.

I know a lot of incredibly talented sea lion and dolphin trainers who wanted to get into the world of orca training who just had something missing. Usually in this case it is the trainer themselves who decides to leave because they realise that it just isn't working out for them, that every day is too much of a struggle.

The day I handed in my resignation at Dolphin Explorer, my boss at the time was actually an ex killer whale trainer who had spent many years working with the whales at Marineland, Antibes. When I told him I had accepted a position as an orca trainer at Loro Parque, the first thing he said to me was 'there's a good chance you will be back working with dolphins in a year'.

This wasn't because he didn't believe in me, he was just very aware of the reality of working with killer whales. He went on to explain to me the sheer number of people who hated the complexity of killer whales and preferred to stick to what they knew. Obviously as he told me this I had absolutely no idea what I was getting into and could never have dreamed of how different the world of killer whale training would be. But he was right.

I think every trainer has their favourite animal to work with. Whether that is a binturong, an elephant, a sea lion or birds of prey, trainers will usually gravitate towards one species because they match their personality.

Working with killer whales is a partnership.

In the pioneering age of killer whale training back in the 1970s and 80s when dolphin and sea lion trainers were trying to figure them out, they realised quickly that the old training methods used with other species simply weren't working. Old training methods were simple, if a dolphin didn't do the behaviours you asked of it then you didn't feed it until it behaved. Similar to when elderly relatives tell you that if your child isn't behaving they should be sent to bed without their dinner and they will soon learn the consequences. However parenting, just like training, has thankfully changed with the times.

Realising that these methods were not producing results with killer whales, SeaWorld started exploring psychology and modern behavioural conditioning techniques in order to literally write the book on orca training. They invented the LRS and adapted positive reinforcement to allow for more variability and complexity and soon the whales really started responding.

Leaving such a highly intelligent animal to sit alone in a pool for an entire day in a sterile environment would be cruel. That is why we use training to create 'puzzles' for the animals to allow them to use their full intellectual abilities to really challenge themselves mentally and physically. Like the majority of our boyfriends ignoring us in order to play the latest game on their PlayStation, they want to be challenged by the game, and often for absolutely no physical reward.

Orcas will often figure out our puzzles just for the satisfaction of having completed the task, just like a group of guys celebrating winning Fortnite Battle Royale, they don't have anything to show for it except the knowledge that they won.

Even if you are still an advocate for placing these animals into sea pens, it would be a crime to simply place them in the ocean and leave them to swim around in boredom until they died. Killer whales need stimulation.

They may be in a concrete pool, or hypothetically suspended in the ocean within a large net but the environment is exactly the same. A large expanse of water with nothing inside it except other orcas. In the wild, killer whales spend the majority of their time hunting and whatever minimal time that is left over in socialisation or play. Our killer whales are lucky that they get to spend the majority of their time engaging in socialising and play behaviour.

But it is our job to make sure that they are getting the most out of their environment.

Trainers are most definitely not in charge of the whales, the whales are always calling the shots.

When first stepping in front of a killer whale, ready to develop your relationship and learn what it takes to work with an animal like this, you cannot act nervous. If a killer whale senses that you are hesitating or unsure in any way, they will walk all over the top of you. Not in an aggressive way, but they will definitely make sure they are in control.

If you hesitate while asking a whale to do a behaviour, that whale will float three feet away from the platform and eyeball you, as if asking

'Well, what are you going to do now?'

Orcas like to test you, almost as if they want to see if you are worthy to be around them and unfortunately some trainers just don't have the confidence it takes to step in front of the biggest predator of the ocean and say 'listen up, we are going to be a team now'.

Even though you are always asking them and never ordering them to do anything, you have to ask them confidently.

If a stranger came up to you with a product you had an interest in and said 'this lotion is going to change your life, here's some free samples and my contact details in case you want some more at a discounted price' you are going to be a lot more convinced and likely to reach out to them again. But if someone came up to you and said 'I like this lotion and, um, I think maybe you will like it too? But I don't have a lot of money and so I was wondering if you could pay five euros for it?' you probably wouldn't give them the time of day.

Even if you do bring a confident attitude (but always keeping your ego in check of course, killer whales will never hesitate to knock you down a peg or two if it gets too big) there is still more to it. When you first start on an orca team it's like you have gone completely back to square one of the training basics and because of all the safety rules involved in working around the animals, it can be weeks before you are even allowed into the same areas as the rest of the trainers.

After years of research and prototype testing, as an additional safety measure, SeaWorld brought in their mini scuba tanks for trainers to wear in a belt around their waists and implemented them at Loro Parque six months later. Once each member of the team had completed a week long course in how to properly assemble, use and clean the belts they became a permanent fixture of the uniform.

They were made to be as small and comfortable as would still allow them to be functional, but they were still cumbersome and very heavy. For us female trainers, bottles would always slide up and bounce around our waists when we ran because no matter how tightly we secured them around our hips, they would slide up the slick neoprene wetsuit. Carrying an extra 5kg of weight around your hips for ten hours a day definitely took its toll on your back. Learning how to swim underwater while breathing into the small regulator with no mask to stop water going up your nose was actually something that the majority of the trainers, including myself, really struggled with, especially while diving vertically to the bottom of the pool.

With most trainers being strong swimmers and certified scuba divers, we are all comfortable in deep water. In a 'normal' scuba set up, the mask will cover both your eyes and nose, leaving you to comfortably breathe in and out of the regulator.

The hardest part about breathing into these type of small 'spare air' tanks in emergency procedure training is that you need to breathe through your mouth and block off your nose without the help of a mask. A lot of trainers find it claustrophobic and panic-inducing, having the regulator in their mouth and trying to breathe calmly while the stinging salt water is filling your nose at the same time. It is hard enough getting used to this practice while swimming at the surface where you can angle your nose so the water doesn't rush in, however when diving to the bottom there is no way to stop it. The first time I completed my spare air tank course and was completely submerged in the freezing water I was scared.

For me drowning is somewhat an irrational fear but the human instinct when water is filling your airways is to panic. It took months to get to a place where I was able to swim competently with the bottle underwater but I am still never comfortable doing it. Most of the time I always came up to the surface choking on salt water.

In the early days on a killer whale team, most of your work day is spent observing, but as with any job this is a great way to learn, especially for killer whales.

One of the best things about our job is that no day is ever exactly the same because the whales are always unpredictable. This also means that our job is more difficult since we can never rely 100% on previous knowledge. The best thing about observing for months at a time when you start out, is that you will have a bunch of hypothetical scenarios stored away in a filing cabinet in your brain, so that if something similar happens again, you go back to that file and see if there is anything you can use to help the current situation.

When you build this one filing cabinet up into a whole library of archives, you can learn to spot behavioural patterns and begin to anticipate and predict what is going to happen just because one whale swam off in a certain way.

Aside from observation, the majority of your time will be spent opening and closing gates for the other trainers in sessions and in shows, and it is important that gates get opened as quickly and smoothly as possible to aid in the running of a show or session. Even though it may feel like nothing important because you are literally only flicking a switch and securing a latch, gatings are one of the most essential behaviours around the whale pool.

Because killer whales are such social animals, a lot of problems can arise when separating individuals even for a short time.

If one animal wants to remain with the group instead of gating to another pool during one segment of a show or a session then it is likely to 'split' on the gate. This means that the animal will leave its trainer and try to swim back through the gate before it is closed in order to stay with the animals on the other side.

Now if the trainer working the gate is too slow at understanding communication from the trainer in control with the whale and close the gate too early (or too late) that whale may take advantage of your haste or hesitation to split from its trainer.

Killer whales are infuriating.

So many times I have been stood in front of Skyla or Wikie (Keijo hardly ever splits from control the little sweetheart, he'll just keep gazing up at you with his gorgeous eyes looking like butter wouldn't melt in his mouth) and find myself heaving a massive sigh of frustration because they have just given me the orca version of 'F you' and swum off for something more interesting.

To try and avoid this you have to read the situation and rely on your instincts to tell you what the whale is going to do. Interpreting body language is a key part of the job.

If a whale is floating away from you with wide eyes and is leaning towards the gate, then that is a clear sign they are uncomfortable with whatever separation you are attempting. In this situation it is usually the best idea to try and get control of your animal, either by asking them to come over to you with a hand target, or trusting that your relationship and reinforcement history is strong enough for them to choose to stay with you.

Choosing to close the gate in this situation runs the risk of making that individual animal (and usually the rest of the animals in the other pool) incorrect.

When we talk about an animal being correct or incorrect it refers to whether the animal does what the trainer wants or not. For instance an animal can be incorrect on a bow behaviour because they jumped in the wrong position or they can be correct if they jumped on the right position.

The main reason you want to avoid whales splitting on gates, especially during shows, is because it can make things potentially dangerous for trainers working with other animals.

We work in very close proximity to killer whales and so if there is an animal 'out of control' and basically doing its own thing then it is more likely that the other animals are going to become unfocused which can make it potentially dangerous to get close to them.

So, even when you are just starting out, you are collecting memories of each individual, their body language, their precursors and all of their likes and dislikes so that you can adapt your decision making in the future.

As trainers, it is always our job to try and figure out what the whales want and how to make them happy.

If Wikie has spent all night with Moana and Keijo she will usually be tired in the morning, having been swum around by her boys all night, so we will gate her into a pool alone or with Inouk so she can rest by herself for a while. All Mum's deserve a break after all! We might separate an animal who doesn't like being alone in a pool by themselves for a very brief period of time, in order to reinforce that behaviour, before opening a gate with other whales. This shows the animal that we will not leave them alone in a pool for a period of time they are uncomfortable with.

On the other hand sometimes we come around the pool in the morning and all of the animals are floating behind gates looking at one another. Then we can open all of the gates and let all of the animals socialise together, even throwing toys into the water to add to the fun.

We always want to give the animals what they want. It is our job to keep them safe, healthy and happy and by reading their body language like this, we can ensure we do that.

As orca teams rarely get interns assigned to our departments, we take responsibility for all of our own cleaning duties. This includes diving the pools to brush the fine carpet of whale poo that has sunk to the bottom having evaded the filters on its first circulation or scrubbing the scum line of fish oil off the windows until it coats your hands in a white film that stinks like cod liver oil.

And even trainers can't escape kitchen.

New trainers usually end up with a lot of kitchen shifts because older and more experienced trainers are able to do more with the animals with regards to husbandry and training. Therefore, it is more beneficial to have them around the pool instead of buried beneath mounds of herring for four hours.

In this way the first few months of working as a killer whale trainer will rarely deviate from duties expected of experienced interns.

However if you keep your nose down and show that you are really trying to absorb every scrap of knowledge that is thrown your way, you will be rewarded for it.

The first time I ever touched a killer whale, my supervisor at the time pulled me into the office for a quick review of my first month on the job. Yes, I was in a wetsuit working around the pool for a full month before I was allowed to touch an animal. That first month was spent pulling nets and getting checked off on multiple safety procedures such as throwing emergency ropes and buoys and CPR. I had gotten cleared to do kitchen alone after spending four extra shifts in the kitchen with a more senior trainer talking me through it. I was genuinely given a 'running safely on slippery surfaces' test before I was allowed to cross slide-overs and be around the whale pool inside of the yellow safety line.

Enormous binders full of protocols, animal histories and trainer conduct guidelines were read and signed and of course the swim test was passed.

So my supervisor ran through my quick evaluation of how I was progressing and ended the meeting by saying that she was very happy with how hard I had been working. As a reward for that hard work I was going to be allowed to join in with a rubdown session on Keto.

I looked out of the office window and could see the rest of the team raising Keto up on the false bottom of the medical pool. I rushed out of the door and ran over to the other side of the pool, my supervisor close behind me.

I double-checked with the trainer in charge of the relate session that I was allowed to step onto the platform and crossed over the wall, the ice cold water flooding into my boots as I splashed over towards Keto's enormous bulk.

Lying happily on the false bottom while eight trainers massaged him all over his body, I slowly stretched out my hand to his side. Weighing over four tonnes, the top of his back was level with my ribcage, so all I had to do was reach out in front of me and lay my hand on his saddle patch, that light grey area behind the dorsal fin.

It was still slick with water and as I rubbed my hands over him I thought how different his skin felt to what I had been expecting. I had been used to the impossibly smooth marble surface of dolphins, softer than a baby's bottom and almost squishy when you applied pressure.

Keto was solid as a rock.

As I moved my hands over his ebony skin towards his back, I felt the very slight ridges on the surface which stopped it from running completely smooth. I also noticed that even though I was running the flat palms of my hands over his skin impossibly gently, like I would have for a dolphin, the other trainers were all applying pressure with their fingertips or even scratching him with their nails.

It was my supervisor who reminded me that their thick layer of blubber meant that in order to feel our massage we needed to apply a decent level of pressure.

Additionally, we owed him a good exfoliation treatment to aid in the sloughing of his skin, hence the nails. One of the dolphins I had worked with in the Dominican named Ariel had needed us to help her with her skin sloughing. Either she was just incredibly lazy and didn't swim fast enough for her skin to shed off on its own, or she generated more dead skin than the other animals, but I would spend a large portion of our sessions rubbing dead skin off her dorsal fin and back.

It sounds disgusting but it was actually extremely satisfying. Dolphins and killer whales shed their skin in a similar way to humans, only around six times more often, so the process of exfoliation is more or less the same.

In fact, researchers document Antarctic killer whales swimming over five thousand kilometres at high speeds in order to slough their skin in warmer waters. Luckily the whales in our care don't have to exhaust themselves with epic swimathons, but they do enjoy lying back and letting us do all of the hard work. They get a relaxing full body massage and we are left trying to get their skin out from under our fingernails for the rest of the day.

It felt so nice to be presented with a rough dorsal fin surface, spend a few minutes vigorously rubbing away the dead skin cells to be left with an impossibly smooth marble exterior again.

Obviously this feels as good for the animals as a deep exfoliation treatment does for humans. I one heard one of the SeaWorld executives refer to the medical pool as the 'Shamu Spa'.

My fingers were tired after that first rubdown session as I exited the pool, Keto snoozing with his eyes closed as we lowered him back down into the water.

My hands looked like they had been painted black from the amount of dead skin that I had rubbed off and my mum would have shuddered to see the underside of my nails.

Keto may have been the first killer whale I ever laid my hands on, but he was not my first whale…

CHAPTER NINE – FIRST LOVE

Once I was told that my first whale was going to be Skyla, every session was planned out so I could have a chance to start building my relationship with her.

My first few months working with her, I was always by the side of a trainer who already knew and had a good relationship with her. In this way Skyla learned through somebody she already trusted that she could also trust me.

The aim was always to conduct sessions that Skyla would find interesting and exciting and were filled with things that she loved. The base of our relationship was formed on hundreds of rubdown sessions, play sessions, enormous amounts of primary reinforcement (fish) and all of her favourite secondary reinforcement thrown in as an added bonus (Ice, jello and toys). The hope was that her sessions with me would be the most exciting, variable and fun, so she would start to associate seeing me with a positive experience.

Eventually just simply interacting with me would become fun, regardless of what we were doing.

I was desperate for her to like me.

I had waited so long for the opportunity to come face to face with an orca, my childhood dream was now coming true and I did not want it to turn into a nightmare. I wanted to prove that I was going to be good at my job. It was like I was the nerdy kid at school begging for the approval of the head cheerleader- and totally not getting it.

I would give her everything I thought she wanted, her favourite toys, her favourite treats, I would painstakingly plan sessions to make sure they were the most positive and reinforcing as possible. I wouldn't just throw fish at her and hope the relationship would come. I would sit in the office and study her profile (every captive animal has a profile detailing their history from birth) to see how I could plan the best sessions for her. I would drag the incredibly heavy plastic toys all around the pool because I knew she loved to play. I would prepare extra jello and ice blocks as secondary reinforcement. I would rope in other trainers to help me and place them all around the pool because I knew she loved changes within a session so she never knew what was coming next.

I was so eager for her to love me as much as I already loved her so I was thrilled when she would do a perfect session with me and happily accept the painstakingly prepared reinforcement.

But no matter how creative or fun I made her sessions, she would simply take everything I gave her without giving me so much as an inch in return. There were numerous times I left a session with Skyla in the early days fighting back tears because it seemed like she simply didn't want anything to do with me. I would watch her shows and sessions with trainers she had known for a few years already and I was insanely jealous at how obvious their bond was. I wanted to have that.

But I was too impatient. And one thing I have learned now, in any partnership between human and killer whale, it is the killer whales who call all the shots.

And that whale made me work for it.

It was almost like she wanted to see how far she could push me to see how hard I would try to worm my way into her life and her heart. She was like a sorority girl with trust issues, she was friends with everyone but there were only a small few allowed into her inner circle.

But once you were in, you were in.

I'm not exactly sure when the change happened, all I know is that it felt like it took forever. But I was never going to give up.

I kept preparing sessions, I even wrote notes down in my little journal that I kept in the office. After each session I would sit down and take notes on how it went, along with any criticism I had received from senior trainers for how I could improve for the next time. My studiousness was much to the amusement of the other trainers but I wasn't bothered about looking 'too enthusiastic'. I 'Hermione Grangered' my way through that first year with her.

I knew I wanted to do everything I could to be the best trainer possible, and I knew that in order to do that then I needed to establish a great relationship with my whale.

It started with small things.

When I arrived around the pool in the mornings or before sessions she would swim up to me vocalising, looking for attention, where before she would have studiously ignored me. After I had finished a session with her she would do silly little beachings and offer me her tail to rub even though she knew I had already fed her all of her fish for the session- she just wanted me to scratch her tail. Within the sessions themselves she started to offer me more, she would give me better criteria because she knew I would give her the reinforcement she deserved. When other animals decided that they didn't want to do a show she would stay with me instead of swimming off to join the rest of the group.

And in that moment, even if all she would offer me was the most feeble pec wave I had ever seen, I felt ecstatic. Because she was choosing me over leaving to be with the other animals.

Not because I had a bucket of fish behind me, not because I had a toy hidden on the other side of the pool and certainly not because I had cut up her jello into long slivers the way she liked.

She was staying with me because we finally had a good relationship.

Having so many young individuals together in the absence of an older dominant female has made for a very difficult social structure at Loro Parque.

The orca team there has done an incredibly good job of building those original whales into the adult pod they are nowadays.

Currently residing at Loro Parque are four females and three males comprising three adult females, two adult males, one juvenile male and a female calf.

Four captive born whales, Koahana, Skyla, Keto and Tekoa, were all transferred from various SeaWorld parks to Tenerife in February, 2006.

Adan was born to parents Kohana and Keto in October, 2010 with Morgan joining the pod that same year after being rescued in the Netherlands. Morgan gave birth to her female calf in September 2018.

In the early days, Kohana showed the most promise at assuming the role of a dominant female. Genetically at least, she comes from a line of some of the most dominant matriarchs at SeaWorld- her grandmother Kasatka and her mother Takara. In orca society, females are always in charge, with a pod being led by a dominant female. Because Kohana was transferred to Loro Parque at such a young age, she had no female role-models to show her how to be a leader within the pod. Once she had been moved to Tenerife, it was up to the trainers to push her into that dominant role. They would reinforce her when she made decisions and took charge, rewarding her for taking a leading role in the group.

Kohana is still not the most dominant whale I have ever seen. She will try her best to keep the other whales in line but she will only step in when their behaviour gets seriously out of line. Usually, a dominant female really helps us trainers out by keeping the rest of the group under control. Most of the time the other whales are allowed to do whatever they want as long as they avoid stepping on Kohana's toes (or flippers).

Dominance is not indicative of size, Kohana in fact being the smallest adult whale at Loro Parque. One of the most dominant female orcas in captive killer whale history was Kasatka, one of the smallest orcas in the SeaWorld family at only five meters length and two tonnes in weight.

Trainers speak the names of the infamous dominant females with a sense of reverence.

Kasatka, Katina, Takara, Freya…

All killer whales are special for their own reasons but these females are all something extra special. Stories are passed down through generations of orca trainers about these individuals. About how one time they tried to gate Katina alone into the back pool during a show in Orlando and she smacked the gate with her tail flukes. When the whales in the front pool heard the noise they all immediately stopped what they were doing and not one whale would listen to their trainer until she was let out of the back pool. This is how a dominant female should control the group. She is the reigning queen of the pool who with one look or noise can silence everyone else (including trainers) and have them once again completely under her command.

When you work at Marineland you cannot help but hear endless stories about the majesty of Freya's reign as dominant female. Even my director at Dolphin Explorer in the Dominican Republic had framed photographs of himself in his office doing waterwork with her. Every trainer who had worked with her or around her would say how much of a character she was, whether that meant in a good way or a bad way depended on the trainer's perception of her.

Freya usually didn't need to resort to aggression to sort out the rest of the whales in the pool. When the rest of the whales were arguing between themselves, possibly refusing to participate in the show, if the gate was opened and Freya was let out into the pool all of the animals would stop their petty arguing and pay attention to what she wanted.

Her reign was absolute.

If in that moment Freya decided she wanted everyone to do the show, every single whale would have their heads up in front of their trainers to perfect attention in minutes. However that is not to say that Freya always worked in favour of the trainers, sometimes she would perfectly control the group but instead take them all away to swim together with her.

Freya also liked to intimidate new trainers. Potentially seeing us wetsuit clad, gangly limbed, over-eager souls as an extension of her pod, she liked to remind us that she was always in charge. She used to play games with inexperienced trainers, blocking them from crossing over slide-overs, hovering at the bottom of the pool and waiting until they tried to get across before shooting up out of the water two feet in front of them. Like a troll lurking under a bridge waiting for her toll.

Despite this intimidating and controlling aspect of her personality, as was required of her as the leader of the pod, Freya trainers' eyes will always mist over as they talk about how much love she shared with them. Even though it took a long time to get to know her and to win her affections, once they had a relationship with her, she stole their hearts. And in the majority of cases, took them with her when she left this world.

When the four whales at Loro Parque were first moved together, there was a period of adjustment where Tekoa was aggressed a lot more frequently as all four of them settled into their hierarchy. Thankfully, serious aggressive incidents between the whales are now few and far between.

The whales at Loro Parque are maturing, they have moved past establishing themselves in the hierarchy and things have settled down significantly. Five years ago Kohana might have aggressed Tekoa for three hours straight and his whole body would be covered in fresh rake marks left from her sharp teeth. These days she may just give him one small scratch, or even just a jerk of her head is enough to remind him to stay in his place.

It does look serious and fresh rake marks are bloody and sore, but you should never forget that these are killer whales. They are not little fluffy bunny rabbits who love cuddles and would never dream of nibbling on your finger.

These are the top predators of the ocean.

Intelligent, highly social beings who have the ability to experience emotion and form bonds with each other and their trainers, but they are also perfectly capable of messing up another orca who has been pissing them off.

Killer whales establish dominance in a number of ways. They of course use their whistles and clicks as communication to the other animals but they also use their physical force.

Orcas use their teeth for almost everything, play, mating behaviour, to explore their environment and when displaying aggression.

Raking is a term used for when whales scratch other whales with their teeth, sometimes going deep enough to cause significant bleeding in times of serious aggression.

Once when I was at Loro Parque and Skyla was doing a show with another trainer, I was backstage on the microphone speaking the show lines. Skyla was supposed to be participating in a show segment with Kohana but in the previous segment Keto had been out in the show pool.

To change segments meant removing Keto from the show pool, closing the gate and leaving Skyla and Kohana in the front pool together. Now on any given day Kohana and Skyla are best friends. They are the mean popular girls that don't let anyone else into their clique. But for some reason that day Skyla decided she didn't want to stay with Kohana and split to the back pool to be with Keto.

Unfortunately that then meant that we had Skyla and Keto out of control during a show and we were unable to close the gate between the show pool and the back pool. The trainer working Kohana decided to break with her instead of waiting until she split from control, which is more positive for Kohana.

At this moment I came out on stage to nervously speak my half-remembered lines in Spanish to explain to the crowd that we had a problem with the whales and so the show would be postponed. Thank you for your patience and understanding.

When I came backstage and took off the microphone I saw Kohana swimming around with Keto very closely by her side and Skyla lying on the bottom of the pool floor.

Looking at the behaviour within the pool it was clear that Kohana had aggressed Skyla for breaking the show and resulting in her own session being terminated early. She had then proceeded to keep Keto under her control close to her and away from Skyla as further punishment to both of them.

Kohana knew that Skyla wanted to be with Keto, and she also knew that Keto wouldn't dare go to Skyla and disobey Kohana even though he wanted to be with Skyla.

Scarily intelligent.

But regardless of the intricate social dynamics that were currently taking place in the pool I was worried about my animal. I had worked at Loro Parque for about a year at that point and had seen whales rake each other superficially before but I had never seen Skyla be aggressed. Because she was the dominant females' best friend she was awarded a certain level of protection, but that rule didn't apply when she pissed off her own best friend.

We knew at that point that there was no saving the show.

With Kohana as angry as she was we knew she would never come to control by herself, never mind let Keto or Skyla move an inch away from where she wanted them to be.

Luckily the public are usually very understanding when we need to cancel shows, given the fact that we can never force the animals to do something they don't want to do and that sometimes they need time to sort their own personal problems out between themselves. Eventually we managed to separate Kohana and Keto together into the front pool, leaving

Skyla alone in the back.

I remember hanging anxiously over the edge trying to see where she was raked and how bad it was. Usually when whales rake each other, even if it is quite deep it won't bleed for very long. The line can be red and look ugly but the salt water limits the circulation and promotes healing so quickly that the bleeding usually stops within a couple of minutes.

But this time Kohana had raked her deep on her peduncle and once Skyla started swimming we could see the thin stream of blood behind her for about half an hour before it began to clot. It was the only mark on Skyla's whole body. Three deep lines about the length of the back of my hand on her right peduncle on the white part of her skin where the contrast with the red made it look so much worse than it really was.

I had seen worse aggressions and so had all of the other trainers on the team before me, so no one was particularly worried about any damage to her health. The wound was deep but relatively small, and the vet had already prescribed a one-time dose of painkillers but it was the first time that *my* animal had been hurt.

I felt so useless because there was nothing I could do to help her, she just needed time to be by herself and metaphorically lick her wounds.

Something that can look like a very serious wound to a human can be healed within a few days on a killer whale. The bleeding stopped itself within a half hour and shortly after that she came over to us trainers and accepted her fish as per usual.

Later on that day she was swimming beside Kohana like nothing had happened.

Although I am sure she was on her best behaviour.

Raking happens both in the wild and in captivity. It is an essential way of maintaining orca social structure. If an animal steps out of line or disobeys a more dominant animal they will get raked. A mother disciplines her calf by raking them to ensure they will not step out of line in the future. A mother will also rake her calf if she decides he is now too old to be reliant on her so she makes sure he knows he will no longer be babied. Young juveniles rake each other frequently in play behaviour, although these rakes are mostly superficial. Females will rake males severely if any sexual behaviour is not tolerated by the female.

In captivity, rakes are not uncommon around the genital slits of males who had been getting just a little too comfortable with a female.

There is a lot of speculation among animal activists that raking does not occur in the wild or if it does it is only amongst juveniles. The second argument is that in the wild they have more space to 'escape' being raked by a dominant animal.

However, killer whale social dynamics are far more complicated to simply allow one individual to swim away from his or her pod to avoid a few rake marks. In the situations I have just described, it is obvious how much control the dominant female wields over the members of her pod.

Even though Keto wanted to swim away from Kohana to be with Skyla, he stayed with Kohana because she told him to. I have seen Wikie, the dominant female at Marineland, force her brother Inouk to swim by her side instead of responding to trainer slaps so that she can continue aggressing him until she is finished her telling off. Even though Inouk knows it is likely he will get raked by staying beside her, he cannot disobey her.

The same is even more likely in wild populations where pods rely heavily on the guidance and leadership of their matriarch for survival. Submissive animals will accept their punishment for disobedience in order to remain under her protection in the same way that calves will endure raking by their parents.

Rake marks are visible in almost any close-up photo of wild killer whales, often the scars are overlapping all over the surface of their bodies.

These scars are particularly apparent in Risso's dolphins as their skin pigmentation changes throughout their lifetime, permanently setting the scar into their skin.

Perhaps the misconception that is occurs more frequently or more severely in captivity is merely due to the close proximity to the animals as it happens.

Aggressive incidents between wild killer whales will usually occur under the surface of the water where people cannot see them and when people photograph rake marks in the wild it is usually several days after the incident occurred and the wound has had time to partially or completely heal.

In marine parks, you can view almost all of it from the surface and visitors snap photos of the fresh wounds only minutes after the aggression happened, making it look much worse than it actually is. I am sure we have all seen over-dramatized photos and videos of captive killer whales bleeding from fresh wounds. A rake mark that can appear severe immediately after the aggression can look weeks old the very next morning.

Killer whales are expert healers given their rapid rate of skin regeneration. Adding in the healing properties of the salt water and their wounds close very quickly.

Clearly we trainers do not enjoy situations like this, we love and care for our animals and never want to see them hurting each other. Therefore, more often than not, when two individuals or sometimes the whole group is involved in an aggressive or potentially aggressive situation, we will always do our best to separate the animals.

Tekoa is the most frequently aggressed whale at Loro Parque but there are also days when Tekoa decides he has had enough and aggresses another whale, although admittedly never Kohana.

Similarly, there are times when Keto is sick of Adan snapping at his tail flukes and so he bats his son over the head with them to put him in his place. Then there are times when Kohana remembers that Adan is her son even though she rejected him at birth and swims along calmly in mother-baby position with him for about ten minutes, before remembering how much he annoys her and she swims away again.

Killer whales, just like humans, are incredibly complex creatures whose personalities are constantly evolving.

I have seen whales get angry at each other through a gate, like dogs barking at one another through a fence, even going so far as to ram the gate with their heads so it makes an unearthly banging sound, but when the gate is opened they will be swimming around peacefully together.

Killer whales are a bunch of over-dramatic divas.

I have had worried guests ask me if the baby is crying through a gate to his mother because he can't get to her and I have pointed out that the gate on the other side is open so he could easily swim around to her but for some reason he is floating static on the other side of the gate, acting like we have torn him away from his mother's side.

Maybe mum has put him on a time out.

With Kohana enjoying her reign as queen of the Loro Parque pod, shadowed by her lady-in-waiting Skyla who is always at her right hand. Keto enjoys a relatively indulgent life as the dominant male of the pod, being both the largest and the oldest, however his son Adan frequently terrorises him. There is however one whale who occasionally challenges Kohana for dominance and is also able to keep the other whales under her influence and that is Morgan.

All of the killer whales residing at Loro Parque were born in captivity, with the exception of Morgan. She was found in shallow waters off the coast of Holland in 2010, emaciated and alone. Estimated to be around one or two years of age at the time of her rescue she was taken to the Harderwijk Dolfinarium for rehabilitation.

She spent over a year recovering there and during the course of the year a large debate ensued over whether she should be released back into the wild, or kept under human care due to her young age and severity of her condition at the time of her rescue.

Eventually the Dutch government ruled in favour of keeping her in human care and she was moved to Loro Parque in 2011 to be with other animals of her species.

Morgan is very well assimilated into the group in Tenerife, despite the popular rumours that she is picked on and bullied by the others in the group.

A rumour, no doubt, spread by the people who are still clamouring for her release.

A few years ago there was a video posted online that quickly went viral and was picked up by several international newspapers claiming that Morgan was attempting to 'commit suicide' and that there was a 'depressed whale locked up in tank'.

Sensationalised video clips and images combined with emotive and persuasive language can seriously misinterpret animal behaviour in any situation.

Nobody wants to read a story about a whale beaching on a slide out simply because they enjoy it. So they take some generic footage of a killer whale sliding out onto a beaching and they interpret it however they want to in order to sell newspapers or get more hits on a blog post.

The specific incident I am talking about occurred at Loro Parque one afternoon after a show. Morgan and Kohana were in the front show pool together after having just finished a really positive show together. Throughout the entirety of that day Morgan had been trying to assert her dominance over Kohana and in fact had been pushing her luck several days prior to the incident.

So when Morgan once again started trying to push Kohana around after the show, she decided that enough was enough. Due to Morgan's relatively dominant personality, Kohana did not go so far as to rake her, potentially for fear of being raked back herself. Instead she displaced Morgan onto the stage, not through force, but through body language and kept Morgan up there by floating close by in the water.

As guests were leaving the stadium, their attention was drawn to Morgan on the slide out. I was standing near the exit and had a lot of people ask me what was going on, I was more than happy to explain to them that the two whales were simply figuring out some dominance issues.

I reassured them that Morgan was perfectly able to remain out of the water for a period of up to fifteen minutes and in the unlikely event that Kohana would not let her back into the water after that amount of time, we would step in to make sure both Morgan and Kohana sorted things out between themselves.

However someone who sold the video to the papers clearly hadn't been within earshot and we trainers were criticised for 'ignoring our whale's desperate plea for help' when in fact we were ignoring them because we did not want to reinforce Kohana for displacing Morgan.

If we had called the whales over at that moment not only would Kohana then be more likely to do it again in the future but we probably wouldn't have been able to separate the two whales immediately because they were still mad at each other.

In actual fact Morgan only remained on the slide out for around five minutes before Kohana let her back into the water. Once Morgan got up the courage to take the plunge back into the show pool, while the guests were still filing out of the stadium, the two females avoided each other for around ten minutes before they started swimming together again. Once we saw they had calmed down we called them over and separated them. No aggression, no problems.

But the media had a field day, once again twisting something so insignificant into something sensational.

After Morgan was moved to Loro Parque and they began training her like the other whales, they discovered that she wasn't responding to the trainers' whistles or water slaps the same way. Experts were called in from the United States Navy to run hearing tests on Morgan. They discovered that she is profoundly deaf in both ears, meaning she cannot reproduce novel sounds, attempt imitation, or produce any type of recognised orca vocalisation. This discovery, combined with her early age at the time of her rescue, and now being a mother to a calf born in captivity, it would be unethical to release her into the wild.

The Free Morgan Foundation, led by Ingrid Visser, are still collecting donations from the general public in their efforts to free Morgan.

Over the past ten years the generous donations made by the general public have been used to fund plane tickets, publicity stunts and camera equipment for the foundation to fly to Tenerife and sit in the stadium of Loro Parque. Where they wait for their opportunity to take photos of Morgan exhibiting behaviour that they can interpret as being distressed or frustrated. The fact that a company can take such an incredible amount of money in charitable donations from people who genuinely believe they are helping an animal in need and use it to fund their own agenda makes me sick. I can understand why the Free Morgan Foundation were founded way back in 2010 when Morgan was first rescued as there genuinely was a possibility that she was going to be released. It would have taken a lot of money, time and effort from both animal activists and trainers alike and there was a slim chance of success. Therefore, gathering funds to help with a potential release effort was the sensible thing to do and I applaud them for trying to be ready for that.

But once the government ruled that release was considered more dangerous to her health and survival than a happy healthy life in captivity the debate was over.

Despite the donations they are still receiving, not one animal is seeing the benefit of this charity. The Free Morgan Foundation seem to be too stubborn to realise that they are not only fighting a losing battle, but they are championing a cause that would do Morgan more harm than good.

The money gained from donations like this from people who have a desire to help animals would be better off going towards conservation projects dedicated to saving wild orcas faced with the threat of infertility, starvation and eventual extinction.

In a similar way I will never understand why anyone would donate money to PETA if they took the time to look into what they do as a company. Yes their marketing team do a great job of making it look like they are the martyrs who stand up for the well-being of animals everywhere, but if you take a closer look you will see a darker reality.

Just do a Google search on their shelter statistics.

However as a company they still receive thousands of dollars in donations a year from people who believe they are doing the most good for mistreated animals, simply because they have the loudest voice.

And why do they have the loudest voice?
Because they spend the majority of their money on marketing.
They shoot shocking ad campaigns, put up billboards and pay
celebrities to endorse their latest agenda. The rest of the money
they spend on suing companies like SeaWorld and taking them to
court over ridiculous things like 'violating the orcas constitutional
rights'.
None of these well-meaning donations are making their way to
animals in need anywhere.
We could all do so much more good in the world if we listened to
one another instead of arguing with each other. I seriously wish
that more people would realise that release would be the worst
option for Morgan, and all of the whales in a similar position, and
focus their efforts and charity on wild animals who really need it.
There were several independent research studies carried out to
explore the vocalisations Morgan could make in comparison to
both her captive companions and wild killer whales. It was found
that Morgan's vocalisations shared absolutely no similarities with
either the captive or wild populations of orcas and therefore it
could be concluded that she has a severe communication
impairment.
One of my funniest memories with Skyla was when researchers
from the Navy Marine Mammal Program in the United States,
came to Loro Parque to re-assess Morgan's hearing and test the
other whales too, several years after the original study.
I had to bring Skyla up on the rising floor of the medical pool,
something she was completely comfortable with, and ask her to
stay still while the researchers placed electrode stickers onto the
skin around her ears for them to play sounds to her.
As I sat in front of her stroking her rostrum and casually chatting
to her, I giggled watching her eyeball these men she didn't know
as they stuck small pieces of white plastic to the sides of her head.
Killer whales and other cetaceans have no facial muscles and as a
result it can be quite difficult to determine or interpret their
feelings from their faces. However their eyes are incredibly
expressive.

When the researchers began playing sounds to Skyla, some of which were recordings from wild killer whales, her eyes were all over the place. In response to one sound they went wide, in response to others they flicked to and fro, and in other cases she narrowed them down in a glare.

I was in hysterics laughing at her adorable reaction. For eight minutes they recorded Skyla's vocal reaction to the sounds and the soundwaves while she adorably turned her head to and fro, like a dog doing a head-tilt.

When research and enrichment become the same thing, it is a good day for all animals.

Luckily orcas use more than just their vocalisations to communicate, their body language plays a large role too, and thankfully Morgan has been able to rely on this form of communication to integrate herself into the pod.

Despite her deafness, Morgan is one of the most vocal animals at Loro Parque, frequently emitting a low 'humming' or 'purring' sound. She is the only orca in captivity known to make continual vocalisations like this, even when she is completely alone.

Skyla actually made a habit of copying Morgan's more ridiculous vocalisations and repeating them later for us, much to our amusement.

*

Once you have begun to develop a relationship with your first whale, you can start practicing show segments in addition to the numerous playtime sessions you will participate in during the day. This means that your manager has built up enough trust in you to think that you will be able to handle the pressure of working with a killer whale in front of a full stadium, representing everything we stand for.

I couldn't wait for that moment.

Sharing all of this with the public is an incredibly important aspect of our job, especially nowadays and shows are one of the main ways in which we do that.

Shows are used as a way to educate the public by showing the physical and mental capabilities of killer whales, as well as the relationships they can develop with us trainers. Although each show has the same basic structure, every show is different, again we always keep the day variable and unpredictable for the animals. In this way, each show will have different whales participating in different segments, sometimes having one whale participate in one segment and sometimes having the whole group participate. In the same way, the behaviours continually change, as does the reinforcement.

Really good trainers know how to create changes the animals will enjoy and not expect. Such as sending or receiving the animal from different areas of the pool or having more than one trainer do a show with one animal.

In this way shows are often one of the most stimulating and enjoyable parts of the day for the animals.

At Loro Parque, new trainers would always start with the 'Quiet' segment of the show.

This was the segment used to showcase the relationship between trainer and whale, it involved lots of rubdowns and slow behaviours, so it allowed new trainers a lot of time to think on their feet if they ever got nervous during one of their first shows.

Loro Parque were very careful about how quickly they went with new trainers.

I had been working there eight months before I was allowed to do a Quiet segment by myself.

Even though the main reason for the slow progression is because of security, unfortunately something that the orca team there is known for is discrimination against international trainers.

Almost every day I had to fight to be allowed to progress in any way.

The majority of the team is made up of a group of local men who fell into the job rather than pursuing it as their passion. Don't get me wrong, there are several truly talented and passionate individuals on the team there who have excellent relationships with the animals.

The problem among the team is that regardless of how hard an international trainer works to learn an animal or be the best trainer they can be, they will always push their fellow Canarian friends up the ladder faster. In this way I found myself falling behind men who had been hired over a year after myself even though there was absolutely no difference in our ability to work with killer whales.

I also made things more difficult for myself because, unable to quietly accept open discrimination, I would call my peers out on it. For every time that I begged to have a session with Skyla, running down to the kitchen to prepare ice blocks and jello cubes and sprint back up the stairs only to see that my session had been given to another trainer, I would question it.

I would ask if they thought I was doing poorly with Skyla and if that was why they would never let me work her but they would never give me a straight answer.

The other women on the team who were in the same boat as me were too scared to raise their voices, either because they needed the job to support a family, or because they were afraid of the repercussions they would face.

I felt incredibly alone.

But after my experience at Dolphin Explorer I was determined not to let anything ruin my dream job of working with a killer whale and so I took full advantage of what little opportunities came my way.

Without a doubt my best memories of working at Loro Parque were with Skyla.

She was an animal who really enjoyed doing shows as she was an insufferable show off. Morgan, arguably the most athletic member of the pod, would occasionally make you wonder if she was going to leap so high out of the water as to touch the roof. Second to Morgan in energy levels was Skyla.

Skyla wouldn't just jump during sessions or shows, if she was in a good mood she would fly. She was a bundle of energy that never seemed to get tired. In fact she would often get angry at you if you stopped her to reinforce because it took too much time for her to stop herself, open her mouth for fish and then go off again on the next behaviour. She would much prefer you to send her on a big chain of behaviours and then just feed her when she was done.

It was such an exhilarating feeling to know your animal that well. Picture it.

You are standing on a stage facing thousands of impressionable tourists. Some are there to learn about killer whales, some are only there because they want to see a whale jump, and some don't even know if they should be there because they aren't sure if they agree with captivity. But they are all watching you. And it is up to you what kind of impression you leave them with.

Standing backstage I could hear the applause from three thousand people in the stands as the intro music began its crescendo. Skyla was floating in front of me, head popping out of the water listening to the music.

I was keeping my eye on David as the music reached the timing we needed to send the whales out on their first behaviour. He sent Kohana on a spin bow behaviour and she took off under the water. I watched her progress, nothing more than a dynamic black shadow under the surface. She reached the gate and I turned my attention back to Skyla. She stared back at me, angling her body towards the gate, ready to go. I slapped my thigh and then pulled my hand straight out from my body, the signal for a back breach behaviour. Skyla exhaled in a rush and dived under the water.

I grinned. She was motivated.

I ran around to the side of the stage, hopping down onto the plastic grille, dodging buckets that had been left on the floor and rushed out to greet the crowd, every nerve I possessed tingling with the rush of performing.

I presented Skyla to the crowd as she launched herself out of the water and landed on her back with an almighty splash. I put my whistle to my lips and got ready to bridge the second bow, her criteria was great, she was enjoying herself.

From the corner of my eye I saw David send Kohana directly on a vertical spin behaviour in the middle of the pool, I bridged Skyla as she arched over the water and waited for her to come back to me. She returned to me at stage at the same time as Kohana finished her vertical spin.

"Send Skyla, quick!"

Came the orders from the trainer on the spotter tone but I gritted by teeth and plunged my hands into Skyla's bucket anyway.

I had admired and even looked up to this trainer when I first started working on the orca team because he had a lot of experience and had one of the best relationships with a killer whale I had ever seen.

However, after months of my hard work going completely unnoticed, several nasty comments from him on my Spanish speaking ability and my mental faculties, coupled with not one single positive remark about my work, my respect for him had evaporated.

I looked up at his face as I walked across stage to reinforce Skyla and I could see that there would be hell to pay after the show for my decision.

Not only had I interrupted the flow of the show by taking time to reinforce Skyla instead of sending her directly on another behaviour but I had disobeyed an order from a senior trainer. It didn't matter that David had sent Kohana too early on a behaviour that was too fast to allow me the time I needed to reinforce, and it didn't matter that Skyla's criteria had been through the roof.

In their eyes I had made the wrong decision. Again.

I sent Skyla on an 'alien' behaviour as quickly as I could because I knew that her underwater run was short and the spotter trainer was already pissed about my timing, but I could almost feel him shaking his head behind me before I turned around to confirm it.

He was now going to bollock me for sending another one-element behaviour covering only one side of the pool.

I could never win.

I shrugged my shoulders back and reminded myself not to worry about what he was going to say until the show was finished. I looked expectantly at the left side of the show pool, the sun hitting the thick glass through the palm trees, casting rainbows exactly where she was about to surface. She leapt out of the water in a great rush of salt spray, straight up in the air, pushing her head forward at the apex of the jump to make the 'alien' shape.

With several behaviours completed it was time to finish the intro to the show.

David and I stretched our arms out in front of us, both hands in fists, and tapped them together, the signal for a slide-out behaviour. Kohana and Skyla dived under the water and beached themselves on top of the slide-out right in front of the crowd to gasps and applause from the audience.

They certainly hadn't noticed anything wrong with the intro.

We gated the two girls back to pool C to allow Keto out to the front with his trainer to perform the 'quiet' segment.

The two whales swam calmly through the gate together and stopped in front of us at backstage. I finally located the small stainless steel bucket with an 'S' scrawled over the lip in sharpie and we reinforced both of them together, a mixture of fish and jello.

As we broke with the animals and allowed them to swim together I remained backstage and tried not to dwell on the fact that, only a few minutes into the show, I had already made a mistake.

It didn't matter how hard I tried, or how variable I was, or how much I adapted my behaviour to follow their criticism, I could never get it right.

A few months before, when I first started performing in the final segment of the show I had been criticised for sending Skyla on too many behaviours, that I should reinforce maximally only a few behaviours, until I was comfortable with the pace.

I had been trying to demonstrate that I was ready for the responsibility and was able to watch the other trainers and send Skyla at the right time to keep the flow of the show going. So the next time I was allowed to perform in the final segment of the show, I gathered as much primary and secondary reinforcement I could get my hands on- jello, ice cubes, hoses, brushes and pool noodles. I only sent her on three relatively easy behaviours that she had a 100% success rate with.

It was an incredibly positive session for Skyla, and for me.

Until the debrief.

I was berated for not watching the other trainers and covering for them when they needed time to reinforce their own animals, I was told that I was too focused on myself and my own animal and would not be allowed to participate in the final segment again until I understood that.

By that point I had learned that answering back and trying to justify my actions resulted in me getting nothing but less time with Skyla and more time in the kitchen.

So I loitered backstage, watching the show from between the slats in the wood. The emotional music when timed perfectly with behaviours can beautifully communicate the depth of a relationship between trainer and whale.

I loved performing in a quiet segment alone with Skyla, unfortunately I rarely got the opportunity.

Ten minutes later it was time for me to take Skyla out again.

David came back from the other side of the stage and slapped the water, calling the girls over to us.

"Quieres mandar un 'Fling' juntos?" Or "Do you want to send a 'Fling' together?"

I nodded in agreement and we waited for the right timing of the music as Paulo opened our gate. We gave the whales the signal for fling, a behaviour where they vertically splash water from the pool with their tail flukes, to both of them.

Kohana and Skyla were great at synchronisation, if you sent one of them too late, the other would wait at the bottom of the pool until she caught up.

David and I came around from backstage and started amping up the crowd, getting them clapping in time with the music and excited for what was to come. The energy within the stadium increased tenfold with expectation and we started pointing to where the whales were headed.

We could see them now, gliding effortlessly across the pool, smooth white bellies contrasting brilliantly with the dark blue water. The surface of the pool was barely rippling until they threw their tails out of the water in perfect harmony, launching a titanic wave of freezing cold salt water over the members of the audience. David signalled to the spotter on the tone box to bridge the girls underwater and they turned around and came back to stage.

I sent Skyla directly on a bow behaviour around the pool, she took off quickly and dove deeply. I smiled to myself seeing how motivated she was, I knew this was going to be one of those shows. She leapt from the water as the music burst into a deafening crescendo and goosebumps prickled my flesh underneath my wetsuit. As she arched perfectly from the water a second time I bridged her, her criteria was so high I needed to reinforce it.

Skyla was an animal that never liked to stop.

She wanted to play until she was tired of it, so she always responded better to trainers who kept her moving and then reinforced her when everything was done. If you stopped her flow she would appear to roll her eyes at you and more often than not, refuse to take off on the next behaviour you asked her to do.

Her energy was so good I didn't want to risk losing it so I threw first one, then two, and finally a third herring into the pool in front of her. They landed with a wet smack, and timed perfectly, she scooped them neatly up into her mouth as she swam back to me.

When she reached the stage in front of me she slowed but didn't stop, peeking her bright eye out of the water as if to ask me 'what next?'

I gave her the signal for a centre belly, knowing that when she was in this kind of mood, she could fly.

She exited the water faster than I predicted and I was too late to get my whistle to my mouth, in a powerful rush of salt spray she was airborne and I had to quickly scream at David not to send Kohana until I had asked for the underwater bridge to be sounded for Skyla.

Thankfully he heard me and after the tone he sent Kohana off on a flip-flop bow. Skyla was already almost back to me so I judged the timing quickly in my head and sent her on a front-flip. I was a little early but if I was lucky, Kohana would be quick and it wouldn't be too noticeable.

I could almost see Skyla's body buzzing with energy and after her acceleration with her tail flukes, her peduncle pumping furiously up and down, I held my breath for the siding bow. I smiled and shook my head in wonder at this amazing animal and her boundless energy.

She was so high on the siding bow that I knew it was going to be an almighty front-flip.

Once more she exited the water to spectacular applause from the crowd, her head coming up out of the water in a rush and tucking her whole body around herself so she re-entered the water on her back, this time with my whistle ready in my mouth, I bridged her. Before she stopped in front of me at stage I asked her to slide out beside me in a beaching behaviour so I could give her a quick rubdown.

She emerged from the water, glittering deep ebony and startling white and stopped solidly beside me.

Her blowhole, the size of the palm of my hand, was moving inquisitively as I scratched her back, her sloughing skin coming off under my nails, making it look as if I had been digging in dirt all day. I massaged her back in long deep strokes, watching the strong muscles give way under my hands, her broad black back glistening under the lights.

I looked over Skyla's back at David to see if he was on the same page as I was.

Thankfully as a trainer who was also on Skyla's team, he was thinking exactly the same thing.

As Kohana returned from a belly spin, he sent her on the last behaviour that had been pre-planned before the show, a bow to the front of the pool.

With Skyla still up beside me on the beaching I made sure to walk into her line of vision, her only being able to see me with her right eye at that moment. I crossed my right arm over my chest and then pointed towards the middle of the pool with both hands, the signal for a front-facing bow.

She exhaled in a rush and hunched her back, sliding herself backwards into the pool and disappeared beneath the surface.

Seconds later the two girls jumped beautifully together in the middle of the pool in perfect synchronisation just as the music came to its climax.

David and I kneeled down on stage in our final present as the audience clapped and cheered. I could see so many children in the front rows, completely soaked to their skin, squealing and grinning with excitement about the orcas. A little further back, adults were left sitting open-mouthed in wonder and amazement. As I always did when we finished a show and watched people gather up their things to leave, I wondered how many we had managed to inspire.

With our whales quickly returning to us for reinforcement for what had been a spectacular session, we turned to our buckets.

I grabbed the biggest handful of fish I could manage and delivered it directly into her gaping mouth.

Almost five kilos of fish in one handful, straight down the throat.

I followed up with more handfuls until I had completely emptied my bucket and then asked her to line up beside the stage to give her a rubdown, god knows she had earned it.

I was still on a comedown from the high of the show.

Working a motivated orca is electric.

Being so at one with your animal, sometimes you feel like you have the ability to read each other's minds. Nothing else exists in the world except you and your whale and what you are achieving together.

It is the closest feeling I have found to racing since I quit swimming.

That surge of adrenaline, followed by a temporary exit from reality into a world that is entirely your own, until it finally ends with applause from the audience and a new personal achievement.
Despite how perfect the final sequence had been, I knew I was not escaping a telling-off for the intro.
As the audience filed out of the stands and the animals were settled, we all gathered beside the spotter, whose job was to take mental notes on every aspect of the show.
As I had predicted he was unhappy about my decision-making in the intro and criticised me heavily for it.
I stood silent and endured the criticism that came my way and made mental notes to try and figure out what they were looking for so I could improve for next time.
Despite the difficulties I sometimes had by not being understood by my colleagues, working with Skyla was one of the biggest joys of my life.
The only other explanation I can offer to feeling at one with a killer whale, is that it feels similar to when you are galloping or jumping a horse. Feeling the animals' energy underneath you, how their muscles bunch when they get ready to match the excited butterflies in your stomach. How, when you let your animal launch themselves into the gallop or over the jump, you are both swept up into this bubble where only the two of you exist, and you don't know where one of you ends and the other one begins.
Sometimes words are just not necessary to make a connection.
Aside from the electric buzz of a speed show or session, I love to showcase the relationship that exists between orca and trainer. I have had tears prick the back of my eyes during a show (mostly thanks to very emotive music) with Skyla because the audience has been so enraptured by watching us together.
Not only between myself and Skyla, whenever I watch trainers who have worked with whales for over twenty years, the relationship between them is so solid and obvious that it takes my breath away. If I can experience what I think is a strong relationship with Skyla in only two years I can only imagine the depth of a relationship after twenty.

One of the things that unfortunately makes it harder to develop a relationship with the whales at Loro Parque are the security limitations. The rules are there for a very good reason, to keep the trainers safe, but it definitely makes it harder to get close to your animal. For example if your animal comes up to you asking for a rubdown by presenting you with their back or fins, you are not allowed to touch that animal unless there is another trainer with you 'spotting' you. If there are other animals in the pool and you are not in a controlled session then you are not allowed to touch your animal even if you have a spotter.

These rules make it a very safe work environment but I feel it also makes it harder on the animals. Don't get me wrong there are plenty of 'relationship' sessions actively planned into the day to make sure all animals and trainers get the time they need or want to rubdown and play with their animals but it does make the job a little more 'hands-off' than before.

A slightly stricter example is that no trainer, even supervisors, are allowed to put their hands into the mouth of any whale. This one sounds like a no-brainer, but many orcas love to have their tongues scratched and rubbed and for years it was almost like a secondary reinforcer to some individuals. At Loro Parque that is now completely banned and none of the animals offer their tongue anymore.

Do they no longer offer it because they don't really want it to be rubbed? Or do they not offer it because they know that even if they do, they will be ignored? It is in these kind of situations where I wish I could ask the animals what they were thinking or feeling.

One of the hardest mornings of my life so far and one of the most upsetting things I ever heard as a trainer was the announcement of the SeaWorld orca breeding ban. As a trainer working for a facility that was housing five of SeaWorld's killer whales, we thought that we trainers would be informed before the general public to whatever decision SeaWorld would make with regards to the animals.

In actual fact, I found out on social media.

On March 17, 2016 the CEO of SeaWorld parks and entertainment announced a company- wide ban on the breeding of all of its captive killer whales. This news was released to the world's media, and by extension the general public, before the trainers knew anything about it.

Needless to say there was an uproar when I finally got to work. Trainers from the team half-in their wetsuits arguing with our supervisor at seven thirty in the morning trying to find out if anyone had known anything about it beforehand or what it would mean for the future of our animals.

Trainers get into the field because of their passion for the animals, so when the well-being of said animals comes into question, tempers can run a little high.

We later found out that even the higher-ups in SeaWorld knew nothing about the decision before the day of the announcement. So along with the personal devastation I felt at such a decision because of my love for the whales, I also felt a massive sense of betrayal from the company. We were always there repeatedly at every hour of every day telling visitors to the park that the animals in our parks are well cared for and content with their lives.

It is genuinely what we all believe and because of that I have never had a problem explaining that to guests. But this decision by the highest ranking individual in the SeaWorld Corporation made it seem as if what we are doing is wrong. That keeping orcas in captivity is wrong.

Why should there be a need to stop breeding orcas in captivity if there is nothing wrong with it?

An hour after I heard the news I was at work. I went into the changing room, pulled on my wetsuit and walked up the stairs to greet the whales and start the safety check-in just like every other morning. But that morning as I walked to the med pool to check the operation of the rising floor I stopped and looked at the whales.

I looked at the whales and I felt sorry for them. I felt no hope. I looked at the six of them and wondered which of them would be the last lonely orca left lingering here in Tenerife waiting to die. I looked at Skyla, my playful happy-go-lucky little girl who was at that moment making excited little whistles at me in greeting as she swam over to my side of the pool, and I felt like crying when I knew that she would never even have the choice to be able to reproduce.

Because it is a choice, they do have a choice.

Only a very small minority of orcas in captivity have been born using artificial insemination.

The first calf to be successfully bred using AI was Nakai, born at SeaWorld San Diego in 2001. SeaWorld originally began implementing its artificial insemination program in order to preserve genetic diversity within its captive population. This eliminated the need to transport adult killer whales between their parks, which is both costly to the company and stressful for the animal.

In order to transport an adult killer whale, weighing between two and three tonnes, you need to commandeer a large empty cargo aircraft, fill the space with a transport tank filled with salt water just large enough for the orca to lie in, without the ability to move and hurt itself. Orcas are unable to be tranquillized for transport, once again due to their respiratory anatomy, unlike the majority of terrestrial mammals which can make transports incredibly stressful for them.

Artificial insemination is a very touchy subject for animal activists and indeed even some trainers. There is large debate about the moral implications of artificially inseminating a highly intelligent animal. If you read articles written about the subject written by activists they use language such as 'held down by trainers and raped'. Although the situation is not quite as graphic or aggressive as painted by that sentence, it is essentially manipulating the course of natural reproduction.

Yet those same activists who admonish the use of positive reinforcement to achieve AI in orcas, applaud the birth of a rare giant panda who was conceived through artificial insemination. There are several differences between orca and panda artificial insemination. In order to inseminate an orca the males are behaviourally conditioned to present their penis and through successive approximations are taught to ejaculate.

This process can take months or even years to teach, with animals often not understanding what exactly the trainer is looking for, some animals presenting urination instead of ejaculation. Eventually the animal learns what is asked of him and with the orcas incredible capacity for cognitive thinking is able to ejaculate with minimal manipulation from the trainer. Personally, I am sure this is anything but a negative experience for the animal, considering if he does the behaviour correctly he ejaculates and if he doesn't then there is no punishment, the trainers will simply try again in the next session.

Whereas with a male panda an electrode is inserted inside the anus while the animal is tranquillized and an electric shock is passed through it in order to stimulate an ejaculation. This means putting the male panda through a stressful tranquilization and a lot of physical manipulation by keepers with a potentially damaging internal electric shock.

In the opposite sex, female orcas are trained to calmly lay out on their back, holding their breath for ten minutes, also trained through successive approximations. In the very first session the orca will only be asked to lay out for one minute, and then the next session it will go up to one minute and a half, and then two minutes and so on until she is able to hold her breath comfortably for ten minutes. Orcas in the wild can hold their breath for around twelve to fifteen minutes, however individuals in captivity typically breathe a couple of times a minute and so require training for longer breath holds.

Once the breath hold training is completed the animal is trained to accept the relatively small tube into their vagina where the semen is simply pushed inside. I was lucky enough to be part of Skyla's AI training team during my time at Loro Parque and saw how slowly and carefully these procedures are trained to ensure the animal is completely desensitized and comfortable. Even though we trained her for AI for over two years, she is still to be inseminated with no official plans as yet to do so.

In comparison, female pandas are tranquilised in order to place the semen sample into the reproductive organs. This eliminates the need for slow and careful training and allows the panda to sleep through the procedure but does involve the drugging of the animal.

The breeding of giant pandas as an endangered species in captivity is, of course, incredibly important.

My point is that there should not be a double standard on artificial insemination just because it is involving an orca.

The Southern Resident population of orcas is endangered and several other orca populations are at risk. In my opinion, with the continual pollution and over fishing of the oceans, all marine animals will be endangered within the next fifty years. Therefore it is essential to continue the breeding of cetaceans in captivity with as much genetic diversity as possible, and artificial insemination gives us that option.

In all other cases of conception in captive populations? 100% natural.

Orcas love to have sex.

We have already established the intelligence level of an orca. Trainers who know the animals better than some of their own blood relatives will attest to it. Even activists hail their 'unimaginable' intellectual capabilities, they even use it as the basis of the argument that they shouldn't be kept in captivity. So what is there to say that they don't know that sex causes babies? Most captive orcas have seen enough sex and killer whale births to know the mechanics of it all. Therefore there is the possibility that orcas are aware of the consequences of their actions and so perhaps choose to have sex because they actively want to have a baby.

Watching female orcas in captivity, it is incredibly interesting to observe changes in female sexual behaviour.

There are some periods where females will be so 'not in the mood' for weeks on end that they will actively aggress any male orca who attempts to mate with her. Batting males with their tail flukes and making sharp turns in the gate channel because the female knows that the adult male is too big and bulky to turn as quickly to follow her.

Then there will be days where it seems like the female has miraculously turned into Jessica Rabbit overnight, batting her eyelashes and posing, so of course all of the males play Bugs Bunny, making cartoon-heart eyes at her. Then the female turns into a master manipulator, often turning two or more males against each other while she plays coy in a corner watching them compete for her. This is usually a nightmare for trainers considering in this moment we have absolutely nothing that the whales want. So we just stand around the pool uselessly holding buckets, staring at what is rapidly becoming an aquatic version of the Playboy Mansion except the female is Hugh Hefner.

To trainers, behavioural changes like this may seem as obvious as a comedy cartoon whereas a member of the public may not be able to pick up on such subtle shifts in behaviour. But it shows us that orcas definitely choose when they want to have sex. And if they can choose to have sex based on hormone changes within their body which are putting them 'in the mood' then surely there is the possibility that they may have hormones that make them want to reproduce in the same way human women are known to get 'broody'.

After all a calf is great for a pod, they provide closer inter-pod relationships, you see the adults engage in more play behaviour and they appear to have a generally positive effect on all animals in the group. So why is it our right to take that decision away from them?

When I looked at Skyla that day I felt like I had failed at my job. Who did she have to protect her? Who did she have that really knew her?

The people who are campaigning to end the captive killer whale industry genuinely believe that what they are doing is for the good of the animals.

It is coming from a good place, a place of love.

However, it is misplaced.

The truth is that they don't know enough about the animals within facilities such as Marineland or Loro Parque or what it takes to care for them properly.

That morning I felt so powerless, I was only one trainer, and a brand-new one at that. My voice was never going to be loud enough to have thousands of activists or CEOs listen to me and my arms were never going to be big enough to wrap around Skyla to keep her safe.

I was overjoyed when in November 2017, a year and a half after the breeding ban was announced, Loro Parque made a statement that SeaWorld had transferred ownership of the whales to them and that they would be continuing to breed the animals in their care. I was delighted that breeding was going to be allowed to continue, at least in Europe, not only for the good of the species but for the good of the animals.

Regardless of how much we care for them or how well we know them or even what company policies are put in place, the trainers never have the final say about what happens to their animals. And even though I had a great relationship with Skyla, I was powerless to determine her future.

Because she isn't and never was mine.

Technically she was owned by SeaWorld, now she is owned by Loro Parque and I was only an employee of that park.

But it doesn't feel like that to a trainer.

Yes, you know it is a job and you get your pay check at the end of every month but no one knows those individual animals or loves them more than the trainers. Imagine the relationship you have with your family dog, a dog you have had since he was a puppy and you know his favourite toys, his favourite tickle spot, and his favourite treats. He always comes to you for his hugs and you are confident in telling everyone that he knows who you are and he loves you, despite the fact that he cannot talk. You judge that information from his body language and his behaviour, the same way trainers do with the whales.

Now imagine that dog is a highly intelligent predatory mammal who allows you to know all of this about them and also actively wants your attention. The bonds we form with these animals are unimaginable and you will never be ready for the depth of emotion that comes with building a relationship with a killer whale.

CHAPTER TEN – LIVING THE DREAM

As I continued at Loro Parque, I cannot say that I was given no opportunities whatsoever. I needed to fight tooth and nail to be allowed the same progression that was freely handed to my male colleagues. I was required to speak out for what I deserved because I knew it would never come my way otherwise. All those years of grit and determination that saw me through university and internships was still coming in handy.

Once I had finally advanced to working Skyla steadily in sessions I saw a steady progression in what I was learning and, mostly thanks to Skyla herself, I grew confidence in my training abilities.

There was nothing more fun than sitting in the office planning creative, fun sessions that she would enjoy and then test them out on her and watch her reaction.

Underneath the pools at Loro Parque is a tunnel which housed the trainers changing rooms and several windows which offered underwater viewing of the whales.

One game in particular that the whales loved involved taking a blackout curtain and placing it over the whole window, completely obscuring the trainers' body from view. There were two small holes which allowed room for our hands to poke through, giving the whales the impression that our disembodied hands were floating in mid-air.

Every single time we did this within a session, the whales would start making excited whistles and clicks underwater and would go on to do behaviours with an incredible amount of energy.

In other words, they freaking loved it.

Organising sessions like this involved a lot of planning, a loud voice and a lot of running around. Taking the time to plan out which behaviours will be sent, placing trainers at different positions within the pools with some down in the tunnel, one at the glass beside the show pool and two others on either side of the slide out. Deciding which behaviours are better reinforced with primary or secondary reinforcement, and if the choice is secondary, which toys would this particular whale prefer?

No matter how much planning goes in to sessions like this, the end result will always be a mess.

Trainers screaming from down below trying to communicate to the trainers above what the whale understood under the water. Trainers on the other side of the pool throwing toys in for an overexcited whale willy-nilly. Other trainers completely forgetting the end of the plan because they got lost in just having fun with the animal. The only thing that is certain is that we would get swept up in the fun that the animal was having.

When the whales are happy. We are happy.

The nice thing about having the tunnel below the pools was that whenever we were changing up our sessions by adding in an underwater element, or sometimes we were just playing or chilling with the whales at the windows, the public got to interact more with the whales too.

We were able to explain a little more about their personalities, or about the sessions we were about to do. The groups would often ask us questions that we were usually able to answer in a more in-depth way than the tour guides.

By bringing the public closer to these animals it sparks a connection. The people who experience that connection are more likely to want to know more. By having trainers available to the visitors and able to answer their questions, these people leave with a much greater understanding and respect for killer whales and marine life.

People who are inspired one day will care for a lifetime.

These animals present us trainers with never-ending possibilities to get creative and challenge them.

However working as an orca trainer means that no matter how hard you try, you will undoubtedly make mistakes. A hazard of working with one of the smartest animals on the planet, they will undoubtedly make you look like a fool on a regular basis.

I would rehearse potential situations in my head to try and be ready for any scenario that would come my way, to limit the amount of mistakes that I might make, in order to avoid the verbal battering that would ensue during the post-show debrief.

Sometimes it worked, sometimes I just ended up making a different mistake.

Every time I took Skyla out into a show my aim was to connect with the audience. I wanted to bring every single person watching us into our relationship, I wanted them to see how much I loved Skyla, I wanted to inspire them in the exact same way I myself felt inspired when I was eight years old.

One of the last show segments that a trainer will learn is the fastest and final segment called a 'Romp' or a 'Speed' segment.

This segment usually involves the majority, if not all of the whales performing and so trainers are required not only to watch their whale but all of the other whales and trainers around them. You need to keep an eye on who is reinforcing and remember to reinforce your whale if she/he is more dominant than the other whale. Memorising which behaviours have already been sent by the others so you don't end up with a very repetitive show and keeping an eye on your timing, making sure that you send your behaviours at the right time so there are no big gaps between behaviours which ruins the flow of the show.

To be able to perform calmly in this segment of the show takes practice.

The first few times I did a Romp I was crapping my pants.

My hands were shaking and my mouth was dry. I had so many people and whales to watch, I needed to remember what behaviours had been sent so I could send Skyla on something different, but it had to be on the right position and it had to be sent at the right time. I was a mess.

Thinking back on it now I smile and realise how far I have come because here at Marineland the 'Speed' as we call it, is my favourite part of the show. Especially when you have a motivated animal. Every other thought leaves your mind and it is just you and your killer whale and you feel like you are on fire. It is an adrenaline rush.

One of the best things about being a killer whale trainer is that this never stops. No matter how long you spend with your animals you will always feel that bond and that connection deepen and strengthen over time. The animals themselves are always growing and changing and so you are constantly learning new things about them and watching them grow.

Even though performing a fast-paced show with six whales and trainers shouting over the top of each other may be overwhelming at the beginning, it is a pure adrenaline rush to an experienced trainer.

As amazing as it can be to perform in shows with your animal, there are many more important things to train.

Being able to have enough trust between animal and trainer to perform necessary and sometimes uncomfortable husbandry behaviours is incredible. To be able to ask a killer whale to give you their tail when they see the vet standing right beside you and they know they will be about to feel a pinprick as the needle goes in, uncomfortable but not painful, and they give you their tail anyway?

Relationship goals right there.

The first husbandry behaviours I learned were the ones that were the easiest for Skyla to do. Things like an ultrasound.

Ultrasounds were performed on all three of the females at Loro Parque periodically to check their reproductive health. Because all of them were on and off Regumate, the hormone we used for birth control, we needed to keep an eye on their ovaries to be sure they were cycling normally. Now birth control can have the same negative effects in killer whales as it can in humans, so it was wise to take the three females off of it periodically, usually once every 12 to 18 months. During the period where they were off of Regumate, we would do ultrasounds daily to track the progress of their cycles. If they had a follicle present (meaning they were fertile) we would separate them from the males to avoid any unwanted pregnancies.

In order to get an ultrasound reading, something we trainers actually started performing for ourselves since we were doing so many of them daily, all the animal is required to do is lay out calmly on their side.

Unfortunately someone somewhere messed up the readings of the ultrasound one day because Morgan ended up pregnant.

Needless to say, this caused immediate uproar within the anti-captivity movement who were still celebrating their victory over the breeding ban. They began to write articles and make statements claiming that Loro Parque had timed the change of ownership of the animals perfectly in order to impregnate Morgan.

This is a perfect example of how much activists do not know, and exactly how many of their claims are based on speculation.

Even before I left Loro Parque, there were rumours floating around that SeaWorld was going to transfer the whales officially within a few months. One of the SeaWorld higher-ups who regularly visited Loro Parque all but confirmed it to us. Considering how long legal agreements like this can take to process, we can be assured that the two companies had been discussing it long before anything was finalised.

And although when the news of Morgan's pregnancy was announced I was already employed at Marineland Antibes, I immediately contacted my old friends and co-workers on the orca team at Loro Parque to find out how it had happened. In fact, Morgan had gotten pregnant while I was still working there. At that moment in time Morgan had been taken off birth control, not in order to breed her, but to allow her body to cycle naturally before putting her back on birth control a couple of months later. This is done with all female orcas in order to protect their reproductive health.

There was absolutely no plan in place to breed Morgan before she fell pregnant.

As far as any of the trainers or vets at Loro Parque know, she somehow managed to have sex with Keto naturally while she was ovulating and fell pregnant. This could have happened in a number of ways, either the ultrasound was read wrongly and the trainers and vets missed a period of ovulation, or she had sex through a gate with Keto. This has already resulted in the birth of one calf in SeaWorld where two orcas who were separated had sex through the gaps in a gate. An adult male orcas penis is around two meters in length and so is perfectly capable of reaching a female's reproductive tract through a gate.

During my two years at Loro Parque we discussed the possibility of breeding Morgan and how it would of course provide more genetic diversity. But there was never any action taken or plans made. In fact whenever mating behaviour was seen between Morgan and any of the three males, she was immediately separated from them and put with the females in order to prevent pregnancy.

The trainers and the company were worried that her hearing impairment would cause problems in her ability to raise a calf. They were also worried about the potential rejection of a calf, especially given their history with Kohana, who rejected both of her own.

Given all of these potential issues, the CEO of Loro Parque made his opinion quite clear. He wanted to focus on the well-being of the animals currently at the park and explore options of facility expansion to further improve their quality of life, before attempting to breed more orcas.

Accidents happen.

So when the trainers and vets finally figured out that Morgan was pregnant accidentally it was too late to do anything about it. They announced the news a week after SeaWorld announced that the four whales originally transferred in 2006 now belonged solely to Loro Parque.

Morgan was already seven months pregnant by that time. They definitely did not time the transfer and then immediately get Morgan pregnant. They simply waited to announce the pregnancy until all of the male whales were officially owned by Loro Parque and therefore no longer subject to the SeaWorld breeding ban.

In any case, ultrasounds are used not only during pregnancy, but to check the internal health and development of all of the animals. Ultrasounds are a relatively easy behaviour for the animal as all they have to do is lie calmly at the surface of the water and all the trainer has to do is hold their pec fin. This, along with a faecal sample, will usually be one of the first husbandry behaviours you learn as a trainer.

Faecal samples are similar, except the whale will be lying on their back as a small, flexible tube about 30cm in length is inserted into their anus in order to extract a small sample of uncontaminated faecal matter.

I remember the first time I was allowed to insert the tube.

I gloved up my hands and grasped it firmly, determined to prove that I was ready for this responsibility.

As the two trainers on the tail side of Skyla looped the supporting strap around her peduncle to keep her anus clear of the water to avoid contamination of the sample, I wiped any of the water left on the surface of her body gently away.

She was lying perfectly still and calm so I proceeded to slowly slide in the tube.

And it got stuck.

My brow furrowed in concentration as I pushed slightly harder.

It still wasn't going in!

I turned and looked to the senior trainer behind me who knelt down and showed me that if I angled my hand in a different way then tube would slide in more easily.

Once I had gotten the hang of it, the tube slid in with no problem and less than thirty seconds later, the tube was out and we had our sample!

Some trainers also like to either blow or suck into the other end of the tube in order to better extract the faeces. I have seen it done efficiently both ways, so I'm not entirely sure if one works better than the other, but I have definitely heard horror stories from trainers who have sucked a little too enthusiastically and ended up with a mouthful of orca poop.

Orca poop is liquid and dark green. If you learn nothing else from this book you have just learned the colour and consistency of orca poop. You're welcome.

The fact that orca and dolphin poop is liquid, is really nice for us cetacean trainers because we just let the filters do their job to clean the pools, unlike pinniped teams who spend hours scraping and hosing poo off of enclosure walls and often the animals themselves.

Graduating to doing blood samples is a nice milestone. It means that your supervisor is trusting you enough not to mess up your animals conditioning. A blood sample is probably one of the most crucial behaviours that we train. Because of our inability to anaesthetise cetaceans to perform operations, we rely largely on preventative measures, meaning that a monthly blood sample is mandatory.

When starting on a blood sample you will always be doing it when the animal is in perfect health and seems like they are in a good mood. This way you will be the most likely to get a good positive outcome. Out of all of the hundreds of blood draws I have seen taken on killer whales, only a handful have been failed (meaning that the animal split from control and refused to let the vet stick them). This was always because the animal was ill or in some kind of discomfort and they weren't staying in good control for the trainer before the vet came down anyway.

My first blood draw was early in the morning on a routine sample check.

I gave Skyla the hand signal to turn over onto her back and present her tail to me, which she did ever so slowly, as if to say 'you woke me up for this?'

I grabbed onto her massive flukes as they drifted past me and she allowed me to pull them up in front of my knees, so her tail was resting on the wall to give easy access to the vet.

I nodded to the vet that he could come on in and he swabbed down the area with alcohol and felt for her vein.

Cetacean veins are not like ours, they are concave not convex, and so they are relatively easy to see from the surface of their skin. Soon the vet had found a good spot and stuck the needle in. The needles used for blood draws on orcas and dolphin are actually even smaller than the needles we use for ourselves.

Soon the tubes were filling up with dark red blood and Skyla was lying on her back, so calm and relaxed, I started to wonder if she had gone back to sleep.

When the vet was done he took out the needle and passed me the gauze to hold to the tiny bead of blood to apply pressure and help it to clot, exactly the same as we would do at the doctors surgery.

A few seconds later Skyla was getting fed her entire first bucket, and getting her favourite toys thrown into the pool as a bonus, simply for lying calmly on her back.

That is the definition of successful positive reinforcement.

One of the most difficult husbandry behaviours are gastric samples. This involves passing a tube down an animals' throat to take a sample of gastric juices, usually done in the morning before an animal has eaten. Now I myself had an endoscopy done when I was eighteen years old and it was one of the most traumatic experiences of my life. I came out of that hospital swearing that I would never have one done again. They stuck a tube down my throat that was the width of a standard garden hose and twice as stiff and wiggled it around with a camera inside of it to have a good look around my stomach.

No thank you.

Now, with the whales we pass a flexible tube only three centimeters in diameter down their throat until we get to the stomach, we kink the end of the tube and take it straight back out again, the vacuum created by kinking the end allows the gastric juice to be sucked up and we get a sample. Passing a tube that small down the throat of an animal that can swallow over ten kilos of fish whole in one mouthful and that has no gag reflex is nowhere near as uncomfortable as what I experienced.

Even so, we would never force an animal to go through this procedure unless we had good reason to.

 We train it routinely so the animals are desensitised to it. Sometimes they just don't want to do it. They move their head back so the tube comes out and then they swim away. Very clearly telling us that they would rather do something else. Sometimes we will ask again immediately and other times we will just decide to try again the next day in the hopes the animal will be more willing. Of course there are videos on the internet and people have seen trainers holding down dolphins and attempting to hold down orcas to get tubes down their throats in order to do endoscopies. This is only done in life-threatening situations. As I have already stated several times, you cannot give cetacean's general anaesthetic. They are conscious breathers and so they need to think about every breath they take. If we put them completely to sleep they would die. Therefore if they are seriously ill or have swallowed a foreign object a guest has thrown into the pool (yes it happens) we need to hold them still while the vet gets the sample or the object out using an endoscopy probe.

It is not a nice thing to have to do and no trainer ever wants to see their animal in that position, but if we have the choice of high standard veterinary care or leaving our animal to die then we will do whatever we can to save them.

Just before my contract ended I was lucky enough to be able to perform a couple of gastric samples on Skyla. The most important, and awkward, thing was trying to angle the tube just right to allow it to pass down the throat while keeping my hand outside of her mouth.

In actual fact Skyla and Morgan were the best at gastric samples when I left. They were excellent at floating still with their mouths open and allowing the tube to be passed down into the first of their three stomachs.

We had even reached a level of training where we started to hydrate them too.

As I previously mentioned this is a great way to keep them hydrated, along with feeding unflavoured gelatin and ice cubes. The whales at Marineland love ice cubes the way my six year old cousin loves M&Ms.

For some reason a lot of activists have a problem with the fact that we give the whales extra water in this way, as well as the fact that we give them daily vitamins. They claim that orcas should be eating fresh live fish, even though in the wild they stun the fish before eating them. I would imagine it could be very uncomfortable to swallow a live, wriggling fish whole. They also misunderstand the word gelatin, claiming that we are feeding the whales pig parts. In actual fact, the gelatin we use is extracted from fish, no added sugar, colourings or flavours. Just extra water. I have no idea why the whales love ice cubes so much but they descend on a bucket of ice cubes like I descend on a box of Dunkin' Donuts so I will not be the one to deprive them of their treats.

In any case, we send away a sample of all of the fish we feed to the whales to an independent laboratory and we receive chemical analysis on each delivery so that the fish we feed our whales is of the highest quality.

A far cry from the wild population who are washing up on beaches with stomachs full of plastic. A terrifying statistic from my own country read that in the last year, every single marine mammal that washed up on a beach in Scotland was found with plastic inside of them.

Time to re-think using that straw.

I wonder how those same activists who don't agree with what we feed the animals would feel if I told them that the captive population of orcas at Loro Parque recently took part in a research study to try to save the endangered Southern Residents and other sub-groups of wild orca.

Loro Parque paired with a Spanish University a couple of years ago to provide blood samples from all six of the whales who were currently present at the park.

The scientists involved were attempting to manufacture some kind of vaccine or cure for the dangerous levels of PCB toxicity within the bodies of wild whales. Given that the whales born in captivity have virtually no toxicity residing in their blood, they are trying to find a way to use this 'clean' blood to rid the wild animals of the poison in their bodies which is slowly killing them.

PCB or polychlorinated biphenyl was widely used in industry until the late 1970s when it was banned because it was found to be carcinogenic and highly toxic. However before this date there had been so many poorly maintained hazardous waste sites, leaks, improper disposal of waste or even burning, that these chemicals have been absorbed into the marine environment.

Due to its incredibly long half-life, meaning that the compound takes a very long time to break down, it is still present in very large concentrations in the ocean. It is easily taken up into the bodies of small organisms such as krill or fish and because fish are at the bottom of the food chain, this toxicity multiplies the further up the food chain it goes.

Until it reaches wild killer whales, the undisputed top predator of the oceans who are so saturated with PCB toxicity that their bodies simply cannot function naturally any longer.

As a direct result of this pollution the whales are becoming increasingly infertile, or calves are being born dead or dying within their first few years of life. It is thought that the mother's body attempts to rid itself of the toxins by 'dumping' them all into her calf.

We are incredibly lucky that we have a very healthy population of captive orcas, not only to act as ambassadors to inspire people to play more of an active role in conservation, but also to safeguard the future of wild killer whales.

Husbandry behaviours may not be the most comfortable thing for the whales, but there is no denying that they are necessary, especially when we make them as positive as possible for the animals. Being able to carry out procedures like this, with the voluntary participation from your animal, even if it means that they are peeing all over your hand, or that you end up with crap in your mouth, it still feels like a victory.

During my time at Loro Parque, the orca team were privileged enough to be able to learn more about the husbandry side of training from one of the best (if not the best) marine mammal veterinarians in the world. She was our consultant vet who would visit the park periodically to do overall check-ups on the whales, even though we had several in-house veterinarians for everything more routine.

Due to the relationships that we form with our whales and how close we are able to get to them, it simply made sense for her to teach us some simple veterinary techniques to be able to better care for, and better understand, the whales' health.

Because of this, the trainers on the team at Loro Parque are highly proficient in performing veterinary check-ups such as ultrasounds on all of the whales. Taking courses on reproductive health and the correct reading of an ultrasound in the classroom as well as being taught how to properly manipulate the ultrasound probe.

In this way the team were given the opportunity to literally know their animals inside and out.

When training techniques and veterinary medicine line up together like this, the standards of care for the animals skyrockets.

Not only are you eliminating stress on the animal by slowly desensitising them to a medical procedure over a period of weeks or months, you are also performing the procedure yourself.

Without having to introduce a person, or several people, the whale has never met before and does not necessarily trust.

Aside from medical husbandry behaviours, arguably some of the most important and interesting training sessions I observed were in-water desensitisation training sessions.

Every three months we would have a visit from a highly respected and experienced killer whale trainer from SeaWorld who now independently consults.

The aim of his trip was to observe how far we had come with the desensitisation training of Keto and Kohana and offer advice on the next steps we could take.

I remember him telling me that he was excited to watch the desensitisation sessions here because it had taken him so long to convince the team to do it.

SeaWorld had been training all of their killer whales on desensitisation for years, to the point where they were now confident that if a trainer was ever to fall into the water, the whales would simply ignore them.

Even though we develop very close relationships with the killer whales we work with, we can never forget that we are working with the top predator of the oceans. All of the orcas I have worked with personally have been born in captivity (with the exception of Morgan who was recused in the Netherlands), but we still keep a healthy level of respect. The safety and security of the trainers is of the utmost importance at all facilities and I can honestly say I have never felt unsafe at work in my career.

One of the most important safety practices at all facilities is the recall. A recall is used with a large number of species at a lot of different wildlife parks worldwide. It is a specific noise or stimulus that an animal associates with the most reinforcing scenario it can imagine. Therefore whenever it hears the noise it will theoretically drop whatever it is doing and go towards the sound.

The recall can be incredibly effective if a foreign object falls into the pool that would pose a danger to an animal if swallowed, in this case the recall can be pressed and the whale will immediately come to the recall point.

In theory, this can also be used if a trainer ever fell into the water. In Loro Parque the whales are not only trained on a sound recall, they are also trained on a light recall, which is when the lights quickly flash three times in a row. The light recall and bridge were both developed especially for Morgan, however with repetitive pairing of the light bridge and recall with the sound bridge and recall, all of the hearing animals began to associate the lights with the sounds and will now respond to either stimulus.

In fact during a previous visit, he had told us that in San Diego a trainer had been crossing a gate area with a bucket in his hand and fell into the pool, bucket included, with three killer whales.
Instead of panicking, the recall was sounded and all three whales ignored both the trainer and the buckets of fish now floating around the pool and came to control calmly.
This is excellent preventative training.
Even though we develop very close relationships with the killer whales we work with, we can never forget that we are working with the top predator of the oceans. All of the orcas I have worked with personally have been born in captivity (with the exception of Morgan who was recused in the Netherlands), but we still keep a healthy level of respect. The safety and security of the trainers is of the utmost importance at all facilities and I can honestly say I have never felt unsafe at work in my career.
One of the most important safety practices at all facilities is the recall. A recall is used with a large number of species at a lot of different wildlife parks worldwide. It is a specific noise or stimulus that an animal associates with the most reinforcing scenario it can imagine. Therefore whenever it hears the noise it will theoretically drop whatever it is doing and go towards the sound.
The recall can be incredibly effective if a foreign object falls into the pool that would pose a danger to an animal if swallowed, in this case the recall can be pressed and the whale will immediately come to the recall point.
In theory, this can also be used if a trainer ever fell into the water. In Loro Parque the whales are not only trained on a sound recall, they are also trained on a light recall, which is when the lights quickly flash three times in a row. The light recall and bridge were both developed especially for Morgan, however with repetitive pairing of the light bridge and recall with the sound bridge and recall, all of the hearing animals began to associate the lights with the sounds and will now respond to either stimulus.
The argument for desensitisation is that it gives you something to fall back on if a trainer was ever to fall into the pool.
Without it, that whale is going to react to the drastic change in its environment and you definitely do not want to be in the water when a 3000kg orca gets excited.

Because it simply isn't a case of a trainer falling into the water and a whale deciding to attack them. They don't attack us on land so why would they do it simply because we are in the water with them?

It is about teaching them to control their body and movements around us.

They are so much bigger and stronger than us that even the simplest movement of their tail has the capacity to really do us some damage. So if I ever had the choice to accidentally fall in a pool with a whale who had been desensitised to in-water interaction or a whale who hadn't, I know which one I would choose.

Unfortunately the team at Loro Parque didn't quite see it that way. They were more of the opinion that putting yourself voluntarily into the water with a killer whale was inviting in more risk. They would prefer not to do desensitisation training and simply hope that no-one ever fell into the water.

I did understand their point of view but I did not agree with it.

I would rather unload a gun than shoot a bulletproof vest.

At Loro Parque, in order to open three of the six hydraulic gates, we were required to walk across the gates themselves, slippery metal less than two feet wide.

The risk of falling into one of the pools on either side (flashback to me falling down the stairs and breaking my toe as an intern) was high.

Every twelve weeks when he came to visit he would sit the team down in the office and show us example videos of the training taking place at the SeaWorld parks. He would break it down step-by-step for us and thoroughly explain why it was safer for us to have the whales used to human presence in the water. During each meeting he would invite questions from the team and ask if we had any reservations. The team would always either remain silent or ask simple questions about the training steps involved.

But every single time without fail as soon as he left the office the team would descend into a heated discussion in rapid-fire Spanish about how dangerous and unnecessarily stupid the whole idea was. I couldn't listen to it.

I got into this world because of my love for killer whales. I watched the Believe show and saw with my own eyes the magic that can be created when trainer and whale enter the water together. There is absolutely no reason why a well-trained killer whale should be more dangerous in the water than a well-trained dolphin or sea lion.

The team attitude towards the animals was disheartening.

The same experienced trainers who preached the values of building a relationship with an animal and having trust form between both of you, were scared to get into the water with the same animals they professed to have a good relationship with.

I was frequently ridiculed and made fun of by the team at Loro Parque for making no secret of my desire to swim with a killer whale.

Being in the water with a whale you have a relationship with should not be something that terrifies you. It should be something that actively increases that bond between you and deepens the trust in one another when done in a safe and controlled manner.

It made me sad to see the anxious glances around the pool whenever someone started a desense session. I longed for people to whoop and cheer when the whales were succeeding but instead the most they could manage were relieved sighs and tense smiles.

I remember one particular session very clearly.

We gathered around the side of the medical pool and Keto was already static at the surface observing us.

He knew exactly what was going on.

A male bull orca weighing 4000kg with a generally sweet disposition but incidentally also the whale involved in the death of a trainer in 2009.

A huge animal with massive pectoral flippers, his dorsal fin completely collapsed and a head so big I wouldn't have been able to wrap both of my arms around it if I tried.

The SeaWorld consultant, Charlie asked us to lower the rising floor to waist-deep level, meaning that Keto was still unable to move freely but our supervisor could get in beside him in a reasonably deep body of water.

Keto was perfectly calm, he was smart, he knew that all that was required from him was to remain still, ignore the trainer in the water and he would get maximum reinforcement for minimal effort.

Easiest session in the world.

As our supervisor paddled around in the water beside Keto, up and down on both sides, Charlie asked if he was comfortable having the floor lowered more.

He agreed.

The control trainer still had two full buckets of fish and multiple secondary reinforcers in order to reward Keto for his cooperation and the trainer was looking comfortable in the water.

But I could sense the tensions rising in the other trainers around me.

This would be the closest Keto had been allowed to get to someone while the platform was lowered enough to allow him free range of movement.

Our supervisor sat down on the ledge to enter the water beside Keto and swim up and down his side, all while Keto was held in strict control by the trainer at the side of the pool.

Keto didn't even blink.

He was an animal who was always extremely motivated by primary reinforcement and one of the laziest killer whales I have ever seen.

He knew that if he simply lay still for less than five minutes he would be fed a third of his daily diet in one go.

That's like telling a human if they go and take a nap for an hour someone will pay them £1000.

It's a no brainer.

Our supervisor came out of the water, slightly out of breath from exertion and nerves. Even though he seemed comfortable, it is a big deal getting neck-deep into the water with an animal weighing almost four tonnes even with a strong relationship.

But he had enjoyed it.

A thoroughly nice man, although admittedly without the force of personality required to direct a team of extremely strong minded Canarian men. He was a people-pleaser who just wanted everyone to get along and for the day to be stress-free.

He was definitely working on the wrong team.

Charlie, began by congratulating us on the progress we had made with Keto's training over the past few months before he went on to outline our next steps.

I should mention that Charlie spoke no Spanish, meaning that all of our meetings were held in English, with him drawling away in his thick American accent. The majority of trainers on the team had only limited English, so he always made sure to speak as clearly as possible and tried to ensure that everybody had understood him before he finished.

He began to explain that the next step would be to ask Keto to do his perimeter swim around the pool with the bottom completely down, something he had already been trained on. He then explained how he wanted the same trainer, or another manager, to then enter the water directly behind Keto as he was swimming.

This was the first step in training Keto to ignore a trainer potentially falling into the pool from the side. By jumping in directly behind him, even if he failed at the behaviour and turned his head or body to check out the trainer, it was going to take Keto a lot longer to manoeuvre his 3600kg bulk around than it would for the trainer to safely exit the water.

Essentially working up from this first step, the trainer would then jump in to the pool when Keto was at any other point, building up to him being able to ignore a trainer no matter where they fell in. Charlie clearly outlined all of the steps involved in this next stage of the desense training and as far as he was aware the team was happy and eager to continue.

However as soon as he left I realised there had been a misunderstanding.

Some members of the team thought that the next step was to jump in front of Keto, not behind him and they soon began agitatedly discussing this between themselves.

The mistranslation was soon resolved but the sheer panic on the faces of the other members of my team at the thought of being so close to the whales in the water broke my heart.

Every time I looked at a whale and trainer in the water together, my heart soared.

It was, and always will be, the epitome of human-animal connection to me.

Having that magic dampened by the reservations of the rest of the team was slowly putting out the flames that had fuelled my desire to become a killer whale trainer in the first place.

I think that was the first time that I decided that I needed to try and find somewhere that my dream could continue to grow.

That evening as I walked down into the tunnel under the pools towards our locker room, the blinding Tenerife sun still blazing behind my eyelids as I descended into the dull light below. The puff and gasp of a killer whale breathing in C pool to my left was the only sound I registered before I left for the evening.

As I unzipped my wetsuit, the lining of the neoprene leaving deep grooves down my biceps, I walked past framed photographs of the park since its creation, the day the whales arrived.

Skyla and Tekoa when they were little.

A picture of Adan being bottle-fed.

Morgan's introduction.

The vocalisations of the whales in all three pools echoed through the walls of the tunnel.

At the end of the corridor I pushed open the squeaky white plastic door and realised that with my two-year contract coming to an end, it was time for a change.

CHAPTER ELEVEN – DREAM VS. REALITY

With the world of marine mammal training being relatively small, everyone knows everyone. When I decided that I wasn't going to inquire into renewing my contract at Loro Parque after two years, even though the majority of orca trainers' contracts were renewed due to the amount of time and effort it took to train each of us from scratch, I knew I needed to explore my other options.

In my heart I knew that I did not want to give up working with killer whales and go back to dolphins. As much as I loved being in the water with the dolphins I had worked with previously, and as much as I missed that, I was addicted to the complexity of killer whales.

I reached out to the head killer whale trainer at Marineland to simply ask if I could send him my CV and cover letter if there were any future possibilities.

A few months later he contacted me to ask if I could fly to France for a trial day and an interview.

The morning of my trial day at Marineland dawned rainy, cold and miserable. Not a good sign. Waiting at the information desk for Duncan to come and collect me, I was a bundle of nerves. I knew that this was my only other option to work with killer whales in Europe and I desperately wanted it to work out.

As he walked me over towards the killer whale area, he did a brilliant job of putting me at ease, chatting about little things and adding no pressure to the day.

When I arrived at the office I was introduced to the girls on the team, they had very kindly laid me out a second-hand wetsuit and some boots for me to wear so I would fit in. The team was smaller, but the way they interacted with each other already felt different to me than the team at Loro Parque. They already seemed eager to get down to the whales and get to work.

I was impressed by the sheer size of the pools at Marineland, with the show pool being the biggest in the world to house killer whales. As I walked down from the office I watched four killer whales start to pester the trainers who were already around the pool for attention. I had spent two years getting to know the complex personalities of the six killer whales at Loro Parque, I was excited to find out what these four strangers were like.

As I joined the team for the morning meeting, I struggled to follow along in my terrible high-school French and my cheeks had already started to ache from smiling. You can only make a first impression once and I was determined to make a good one! Luckily, several of the other trainers spoke very good English and were more than happy to translate, the benefits of having a very international team. Throughout the morning I shadowed some of the trainers, mucking in where I could by scrubbing buckets and hosing down enclosure areas just like everyone else. While watching sessions I hung back to observe and must have asked a hundred questions.

Even though I was aware that I needed to seem capable and with some level of experience, most of the questions came from natural interest.

There were so many similarities between the two facilities but equally as many differences.

I found myself grilling not only Duncan, but other trainers on the training techniques they used, their criteria for certain behaviours, even their safety and husbandry protocols.

I was so enjoying debating the pros and cons of a certain training technique with a trainer who would later become one of my best friends, that I had completely forgotten about my interview.

I soon found myself hurrying along behind Duncan, my nerves back in full force, as we went to meet with the person who would decide if I was a viable candidate for the position or not.

Sat down officially in front of her desk I gave the standard humble brag summary of my total experience and why they should pick me to be a trainer on their team.

I thought it was all going well, we were laughing and she was nodding along and seemed impressed at the things I had been able to learn at Loro Parque, when suddenly the conversation stopped.

"We have no positions available at the moment"

For the first time in my life I had to ask someone to repeat what they said. Not because I hadn't heard her properly, but because simply I could not comprehend the words that had just come out of her mouth.

"We have no positions available at the moment"

I remember trying to swallow even though my throat felt like it was filled with sand as I looked over at Duncan for an explanation but he wouldn't meet my eye.

It is quite funny now looking back, I wish someone could have filmed my reaction because I bet it was quite comical, but at the time I felt like someone had tipped a bucket of ice cold water over me.

I was so confused. I had been told that there was a position available which was why I had flown seven hours on two separate planes to get here for one trial day to prove myself.

I couldn't hear the end of the conversation for the ringing in my ears and as I walked out of her office with Duncan just behind me, I remember him telling me how he could see that I was very disappointed.

Disappointed? I was crushed. Obliterated. Finished.

I wanted to cry, I wanted to slam that office door and storm out. I wanted to run back to the hotel to my long-distance boyfriend and tell him that not only had I failed in relocating to be closer to him but that I had also lost my only other opportunity to continue to work with orcas. The suffocating thought of having to go back to the team at Loro Parque was enough to bring tears to my eyes. But I couldn't show any of that.

I hastily attempted to gather my thoughts and gain control of my facial expressions before we made it back to the whale pool.

I had exactly four and a half minutes to get my shit together.

Apparently there had been a last-minute decision by the company not to fill the vacant position immediately. This was decided in a meeting that took place as I was flying over the coast of Africa. Something that had been completely out of Duncan's control.

I knew that my only hope of continuing to work with killer whales was to continue to make a good enough impression on Duncan and the rest of the team, so that they had no choice but to hire me when the company finally decided to fill that position.

We are not defined by how we react to our successes, but how we react to our failures.

I needed to get over the crushing disappointment and decide to kick-ass for the rest of the day.

As we arrived back at the whale pool, my smile was firmly back in place and I was ready to prove my worth to the team.

What I was exposed to during the following six hours was the team I had always dreamed of being a part of. A group of individuals as passionate and dedicated as I could only hope to be myself.

Almost all of them noticed how disappointed I was, even though I was putting on a very good show, yet they all offered me words of encouragement and positivity despite them only having known me for half a day.

Watching how they interacted with the whales throughout the day only made me even more desperate to become a part of the team.

They were allowed to get closer to the whales than we were at Loro Parque, in some cases because the pool layout was different and allowed better access, and in others because the trainers were trusted to make smart decisions about their own safety.

And the whales were so responsive because of it.

Throughout the entirety of the day, trainers were running around at the side of the pool, messing about with the animals, making sure they were having the best time possible.

The whales were constantly seeking attention, either squeaking adorably at us to beg for an ice cube or offering their backs for a rubdown.

This overwhelmingly obvious love between trainers and whales, combined with the intelligent and thought-provoking conversations I had with several trainers throughout the day, convinced me by the time it came for me to leave, that I undoubtedly wanted to be a part of this team.

Not one of the trainers on that day really understood how hard I took the rejection from the earlier interview. It went far beyond disappointment.

At that time I didn't know how I was going to go back to Tenerife alone and face what had become a suffocating environment for me personally on the team there. For weeks before my trial date, the only thing that had been getting me up in the morning had been the thought that there was light at the end of the tunnel. That soon I might be able to leave with another job as a killer whale trainer. Now I faced going back there, devastated at the thought of not knowing when I would see my boyfriend again or when we would ever be able to live in the same country, as well as the possibility of having to finish my contract in Loro Parque without a job at all. On the way back to Tenerife, I had a six hour layover in Barcelona airport. I remember standing in front of the screens looking at all of the flight listings, thinking that I would rather fly anywhere in the world than back to the Canary Islands.

My family was in Scotland and I hadn't seen them in months. My boyfriend was in Holland and after a year of doing the long distance thing we were still no closer to being together.

I had no job secured behind me in France, only a team who made me feel worthless ahead of me in Tenerife.

I think it would be fair to say that it was one of the lowest moments of my life.

As much as I loved Skyla, and the other whales of the pod at Loro Parque, the dynamics of the orca team were becoming too much for me to justify staying.

When I first started out pursuing my goal of becoming a killer whale trainer, I dreamed of the day where I would put on my wetsuit, trot out in a single file line beside the other trainers to the roar of the crowd in the packed-out stadium.

I'm not going to lie I wanted people to look at me as an orca trainer and be impressed.

I longed for the miracle day, the first day I would be allowed to get into the water beside my killer whale. I wanted to know what it would feel like to have her swim beside me in the water, how her body would move under me, how I would eventually learn to move my body with hers while performing difficult behaviours together. I wanted to feel my stomach drop as she threw me into the air in a hydro behaviour so I could feel what it was like to fly.

That is the dream I had.

Unfortunately the reality was anything but.

I still pulled on the wetsuit and wore the whistle around my neck, but I was viewed differently. Constantly judged by online trolls and even by my peers. The majesty of waterworks were but a distant memory, the only hope left was the thought of one day being allowed to do a water-desense session. Something I knew I would never be allowed to do at Loro Parque.

Once the shows were finished, the endless fun of play sessions over and we left the whales to rest for the night, I found myself painfully alone in my life.

Killer whale training was all that I had.

That may have been enough when I was in directly in front of Skyla, but when all of your colleagues have been friends with each other for years, you are always an outsider on the team.

With the job itself becoming more challenging than ever from constant criticism and backlash from anti-captivity activists, I felt like I was rowing myself upstream in a boat that kept filling with water.

I was going nowhere.

With the release of *Blackfish* came the anti-captivity movement and after the two fatal accidents in 2009 and 2010, all waterworks with all whales at all facilities stopped.

Killer whale trainers stopped being revered and envied and instead became slandered and degraded.

The modern day is without a doubt the hardest time to be an orca trainer.

Back in the heyday of killer whale training throughout the 70s 80s and even 90s, if you told people what you did for a living, you were a superstar. We continually hear stories of trainers who would talk about their job at a bar and they would drink for free the rest of the night. Guys (and I'm sure girls) would use it as a pick up line, and it worked. I think these days we might be more likely to get the drink thrown back in our face.

Unfortunately, all of the incredible things we still get to experience in our jobs nowadays is marred by how we are viewed by the public.

Social media has become a minefield. We have to be careful with who we let follow us and we usually cannot have a public Instagram account because of the amount of negative comments we will receive on a photo of us with our animals. Even though my own Instagram is public and I am incredibly lucky with the community we have built where people who love the whales can come together and really celebrate our shared passion, I need to do a lot of deleting, reporting and blocking to keep it a somewhat hate-free space.

You couldn't imagine the language some people use.

They come to some kind of snap judgement about who I am as a person just from looking at one photo of me in a wetsuit. Even though I am careful to scroll through the comments and try to delete anything negative before it is seen by anyone else, I still read it and it always hurts.

Every single time I am called an animal abuser I wince.

I think my particular favourite was when I woke up one morning to, 'you aren't a whale trainer you are a whale torturer'. It was just so uninspired and lacking in creativity as a sentence that it made me laugh, I made sure to ask Wikie later on that day during her eleven thirty backrub if she felt like she had been tortured enough that day.

These people who criticise and condemn us don't know the first thing about the orcas we work with or their day-to-day lives. They like to think that they love them more than we trainers do and that the best thing for them is to be 'free' but the truth is that they are sadly misinformed.

It is easy to sit behind a keyboard and criticise, but it is much harder to drag yourself out of bed at five in the morning to go and gut fish for the whales or spend your weekends volunteering at dog shelters and organising beach cleans.

All of the personal effort that trainers make to eat less meat, consume only sustainably caught seafood, say no to single-use plastics, take their bikes to work instead of their cars, drink out of re-usable water bottles and limit their electricity consumption. All of the professional effort to educate the public about conservation, staying up all night with a sick animal, being the first on the scene to help a stranded animal with a rescue team that has been funded by the park's profits, providing comfort to your animal as they go through a hard labour.

This effort behind the scenes is what goes unnoticed by these internet trolls.

They do not feel the deep aches and pains in our muscles and joints because we spend more time taking care of the animals than we do taking care of ourselves. They do not understand that these animals are an extension of our own family.

They want to hurt you, they want to tear you down and they want to get a reaction out of you.

To all of the trainers and zookeepers who are also subject to online abuse and personal attacks every single day, wear your wetsuit like armour. Zip it up and let all of those hate-filled messages bounce off the neoprene.

You know why you do the hard work. You know that your facility is playing an important role in the conservation of species. You know that you can truly make a difference to your animals' lives. You know that you have the power to educate and inspire.

I salute all animal care professionals who are standing up for what they believe in, because it is no longer an easy thing to do.

For those people who are not trainers, but rather people who have come to an informed decision about what they believe in. Thank you for being open minded and for taking the time to see both sides of the story.

Perhaps you are completely for captivity and believe in everything we do. Maybe you agree that captivity is necessary but that there are things that can be improved. Even if you don't agree with captivity at all, you have the right to your opinion just as we have the right to ours. None of us can attack other people online just because they don't think the same way as you do.

Personally, I have no problem eating an animal that has been raised healthy and happy in a field, and enjoyed a good life, before it ended up on my plate. But I don't go around harassing people who buy inexpensive meat that came from a questionable source simply because they cannot afford free-range organic produce to feed their family. But there will always be people who are extreme in their views and who become hateful towards people whose opinions differ from their own.

Now that is not to say that all vegans or all anti captivity activists are spending their nights online hunting down meat-eaters and trainers (I hope they never find the photo of me in a wetsuit chowing down on a slice of meat lovers' pizza). Some do keep their opinion to themselves and simply choose not to visit zoos and aquariums or quietly abstain from eating meat because of their personal views. That I completely respect.

Caring for animals in a zoological setting brings no harm to any animals.

The animals are given the highest standard of veterinary care, restaurant quality fish, unending love and attention from their trainers, plenty of sessions and research projects to mentally stimulate them with a bonus of inspiring millions of park visitors which helps their wild counterparts.

I was once accused of being unable to see the bigger picture because my judgement was clouded by the profit I was making off of the whales. I think I spat out my cereal when I came across that trolling comment over my breakfast. If only that person could see my pay check at the end of each month. There's a reason my entire outfit came from Primark.

It is laughable to think that trainers would be in this for the money when in actual fact we do our jobs in spite of the miserable salary we are offered.

Our personalities, our reason for getting up in the morning, our very existence is so woven into our animals that we take every attack on our profession as a personal assault.

It is incredible that in such a short space of time, keeping animals in captivity has gone from being something that was widely accepted and normal to being taboo.

There seems to be a lot of discrimination these days depending on the species in question and their captive environment. Usually if it is a marine mammal, most particularly a whale or a dolphin, people will say it should be set free and should not be held in human care.

For some reason people don't seem to worry so much about the seals, sea lions and otters that are housed in marine parks.

There are people who say that orcas specifically should not be housed in a captive environment because of their intelligence or their size, but then post funny videos of captive panda bears falling out of trees on Facebook with a laughing face emoji. Or they follow so-called big cat 'sanctuaries' where the cubs are hand-raised by humans and filmed running around houses for reasons unknown.

There cannot be a double standard which discriminates based on species.

If you are a person who disagrees with the keeping of captive killer whales but you ride horses or bet on horse racing then you are being hypocritical.

Instead of running wild and free, that horse is being kept in a small stable alone or allowed to roam in a small field for a certain number of hours a day. Horses in human care are often asked to run races or jump jumps with a rider on its back. Something a wild horse would never naturally do.

If that horse has a clean stable, is groomed twice a day, given the absolute best nutrition and seems to genuinely enjoy jumping? Would you then say that the horse should be set free when it is perfectly contended living the only life it has ever known?

Yes, it is a very different life to a wild horse, but not necessarily worse.

You can argue that horses have been domesticated by man for thousands of years which is true, but orcas who have been born and bred in captivity are not completely wild, they are far from domesticated, but they are not wild animals.

Like I mentioned previously, captive killer whales when presented with a live salmon, cowered in a corner as far from the fish as possible instead of hunting it, showing that their instincts lie buried deep down beneath the surface.

That is not to say that those instincts are not there, however as demonstrated through the failed release of Keiko, those 'instincts' took years of re-training, without any proof of success once he was eventually on his own in the open ocean. Additionally, Keiko was born in the ocean, while our whales have been cared for in a zoological setting their entire lives.

I have even heard other zookeepers condemn marine parks for keeping cetaceans in human care. This is something that completely baffles me.

Why is a captive setting different for a tiger or hippo or chimp than it is for an orca or dolphin?

Is it because we train our animals for shows?

As I previously explained, our shows and training behaviours mentally and physically stimulate the animals. Therefore improving their quality of life with a benefit of entertaining the public which in turn inspires them to care for marine life.

Our shows are not merely 'circus tricks' as people like to refer to them as. Doing a front flip may not a natural behaviour for a killer whale, but as an animal who spends the majority of its time in the wild travelling to find food, they must be exercised in more imaginative ways in captivity because they cannot physically swim long distances.

Wild horses can travel hundreds of kilometres in a day but a captive horse is taught to jump twelve interchanging jumps in a small arena which is just as physically challenging. This allows them to expel that energy in a way the majority of horse riders would argue that the horse finds enjoyable.

If our whales were left with nothing to do all day, if we decided just to come around the pool to feed them and then leave again, they would be crying out at us to do something with them.

Because they would be bored!

Anyone and any animal would be bored if it had to sit around and do nothing all day!

In marine parks, for the ten hours a day that trainers are at work, the whales solve puzzles, perform in shows, have massages, exercise, socialise, learn something new, play socially with each other and with us trainers.

This gives them a very balanced life. It is our job to make sure that they are completely mentally and physically okay.

Just because part of that day includes a show, does not mean that they are worse off than animals in a 'typical' zoological setting.

Even if there was no audience, we would still be training and playing with the whales, a show just incorporates the best of that and sticks some music over the top.

The people who are inspired by our shows are the ones who will choose to leave the park and make a real difference. From listening to guest feedback, the majority of people miss the old theatrical shows because they feel that nowadays our educational presentations are too boring. Especially for children. Just because something is entertaining, does not mean that it cannot also be educational.

We need to find the balance.

To the keyboard trolls who try to worm their way under our skin or to the very blunt guests who have the audacity to say the foulest things to our faces, we will not let your words diminish us. We will continue to show up for our animals in the wind, rain and snow.

We will move away from our loved ones and work insane hours in order to make these animals' lives the absolute best they can be. Somewhere down the line people began to come up with this idea that trainers don't really care about the animals and that instead, we are actively hurting them.

That could not be further from the truth.

We spend every minute of every day thinking about their wellbeing because they mean everything to us.

It has gotten to the stage where most of the people I work with don't want to tell people what they do for a living because it always ends up in an argument or heated debate. Whether you are on a plane and the person next to you happens to see your screensaver and now you are stuck next to them for four hours with no escape from the same repetitive argument you have had a hundred times before. Some trainers have been about to sign a lease on a new apartment when the landlord has rejected them after seeing their job title on their work contract. I even know of some vet surgeries that refuse to treat trainers' sick pets.

Blatant discrimination which seriously impacts our lives is the reason why we are reluctant to tell people about the very thing we are most passionate about.

I myself have felt the same way but I am too stubborn to give in to it.

I am proud of what I do, I feel no shame in it and I have worked too damn hard to get to where I am now to pretend that I do something else.

Even if that means people laugh in my face, or look disgusted and proceed to reel of the same list of 'facts' that I hear on an almost daily basis.

A favourite 'fact' people like to present us with is that 'they swim thousands of miles a day in the wild'. In actual fact, killer whales in the wild are so varied that they have all adapted to whichever environment they exist in. There are some sub-groups that stay within the same shallow coastal area for their entire lives, this region will span hundreds of kilometres but they are certainly not swimming the length and breadth of it every single day. There are however other sub-groups that swim thousands of miles over a period of weeks or months in order to find food.

However, the original population of orcas that were captured whom our whales are descended from, were Resident orcas. Meaning that they typically stayed in the same area where they knew food would always be readily available.

With the main reason for swimming so far being the need to search for food, this necessity does not apply to killer whales in zoological settings, considering they always have food readily available to them. Humans operate in the same way, it's the reason Uber Eats was invented.

Activists also like to berate us because we keep orcas in 'tiny bathtub sized' pools.

Taking this metaphor literally we can easily see that the pools are much bigger than the word 'bathtub' suggests. Instead the tank size would be comparable to me living in a comfortably large four bedroomed house when in actual fact I live in a tiny studio. This is clearly because I make such a huge profit from exploiting the animals.

The fashionable term to use these days by activists is that we trainers and the companies we are working for 'exploit' our whales for profit.

Yes, the company makes a profit from the sale of tickets, but the majority of that profit goes right back into the animals themselves. But speaking realistically, what trainer would not love to have bigger pools?

I never understand why activists seem so obsessed with the size of the tanks.

Killer whales are enormous animals, of course we would love more space for them.

So why do we not have bigger pools or any plans in place to update them?

Because when activists campaigned to boycott SeaWorld after the release of *Blackfish* and their profits dropped as a result, they realised that people were losing interest in killer whales and so stopped investing in them.

Thanks to anti-captivity activists, the killer whales in zoological settings will not experience the benefit of larger enclosures. Aside from the unfortunate ruin of the Blue World Project due to boycotting, expanding the pools is also much more complicated than people think.

Where is the money going to come from to pay the construction workers and for the materials? Can our filtration system support more water and more animals or does that need re-modelling? Is it worth all of the stress the construction work is going to cause the animals?

It is all so much more delicate than people believe.

Another lovely accusation is that we deprive the animals of fish when they don't do what we want them to do. This may have been true back in the 1970's before trainers realised that it simply wasn't working and turned to more modern training methods.

Killer whales have huge fat reserves and they can refuse to eat for an extremely long time. In the wild they can go up to three weeks without eating, so they definitely do not care about the bucket of fish behind us. There are so many times that a trainer has been unable to do a session with a killer whale because they tried to rely on those 20lbs of herring instead of using what the whale actually wanted.

These are only some examples of the 'facts' that people like to present to us. They have been subjected to the misinformation and activist propaganda that has become increasingly popular over the internet. Thankfully, when people present these 'facts' to us, we can set the record straight.

And we can hope that they listen.

Because we are so tired of the same argument all of the time. We don't want to have to be continually defending ourselves and our work. We would not be here if we didn't believe the animals were happy and given the best possible care. But people don't like to believe that.

People like to believe it is as simple as picking up an orca and dropping them off 'home' in the ocean.

Potentially the only reasonable solution could be to create some kind of futuristic barrier system that would allow the whales to explore a large expanse of ocean in whichever naturally occurring pod structure they choose. Something that could potentially mirror wildlife reserves in Africa, where animals are free to roam while still being offered some level of protection. But this is somewhere that should be reserved for the wild marine animals who are already struggling to survive, instead of putting unnecessary stress on a whale born in a zoological park.

If activists spent less time decorating fancy cars and billboards with slogans like 'empty the tanks' and less hours protesting captivity with homemade placards outside of a marine park, and instead went out and did a beach clean or volunteered to help wild animals in distress or donated their money to wildlife charities then all animals would be better off.

I have already mentioned Ingrid Visser and her fruitless campaigning for the release of Morgan. Doesn't anyone think that the money donated to her Foundation could do so much more good if it was directed somewhere else? Instead of buying fancy camera equipment and booking court dates and flying herself to Tenerife, maybe she could donate that money instead to wild killer whales who actually need her help.

There are wild orcas dying right now, not only from plastic infested oceans but from genetic conditions, from starvation, from a million different human-related causes.

It is time the activists learned that to actually be an activist you need to create worthwhile change. If they want to do some serious good then they should go and help the animals that need it and not waste their time trying to free orcas that are living perfectly happy lives right where they are.

It is easy to stand in front of a park and hold a sign for a few hours. It is easy to sit behind your screen and type hateful messages to a stranger online.

But it is damn hard to be out there actually doing something. Giving up your free time to rid your local beach of plastic. Being a part of a rescue that takes more than sixteen hours so you are exhausted, sunburned and starving by the time the poor stranded turtle dies in your arms from being entangled in fishing line for too long.

Considering we are all people who feel passionately about animals, we should not be enemies, but for some reason, people like to have something to hate. Because we are so emotionally and personally involved with our animals, trainers become easy targets.

Whether it is the gut wrenching feeling of driving past yet another line of placards screaming 'captivity kills' while you are on your way to work. Or the trolling attacks on social media. Or the disappointment and devastation you feel when a celebrity you have loved for years suddenly comes out with a Peta campaign or writes a disparaging open letter to SeaWorld about their treatment of orcas (I'm looking at you Pink).

Trainers are the ones on the ground every damn day, in the freezing wind, in the rain, in the early hours of the morning hustling for the good of the animals. We are the ones who put in the dedicated hours to make their lives better. We are the ones who know them. So shouldn't we be the ones who are best qualified to decide their futures?

Yes there are ex-trainers out there who left the companies they worked for and have changed their opinions. They are usually very vocal on social media, some have even gone so far as to write books on the subject, but just think about how much money they made from selling their stories at a time when all the media wanted to hear was that captivity, and SeaWorld in particular, was slowly killing their killer whales.

Taking things to an even more extreme level than simple online trolling, some of the more potentially dangerous anti-captivity demonstrations have been occurring within zoological facilities themselves.

When a group of animal rights activists jumped into the dolphin pool at Marineland before a show in order to 'protest the cruelty', all they effectively did was terrify all of the dolphins. These animals were not used to multiple strangers jumping suddenly and aggressively into their home, towing large flapping banners behind them.

It would be the equivalent to having a group of rowdy strangers barge in through your front door, leaving muddy footprints on your cream carpet and smashing up your expensive furniture.

These activists manage to drop things like sunglasses and earrings into the pool while they jumped, meaning that divers had to be sent in to check the pool and remove all foreign objects. Being incredibly curious animals, any dolphin could have swallowed one of these loose items and died as a result. Not only did these activists terrify and endanger the animals, they also had the audacity to ask to be allowed to pet the dolphins before they were arrested.

This is where it gets even more unbelievably hypocritical.

A lot of people who are against captivity still want to be able to get up close to the animals and have some kind of interaction with them. I have had numerous people in dolphin swim programs who lectured me about how they thought captivity was wrong and how they had only agreed to swim so they didn't upset their family by refusing, only to demand that their kiss photo be re-shot three times because the angle was wrong.

I have seen so many people posting photos of themselves at places like SeaWorld on social media with captions like 'trying to figure out how to free the animals' and 'I know it's cruel but when you're in Orlando you have to right?'. These people have paid money to get into the park, actively contributed to SeaWorld's Rescue Team by giving a percentage of their ticket sale, spent a day in the park learning about these animals and being educated on how to conserve them for future generations. Then they simply turn around and pretend that they hated every minute so that they can fit in with popular opinion.

However, thankfully, not all of the people in the world who are anti-captivity act like this. The best people out there are the ones who don't agree with captivity but understand what we are trying to do. The ones who are open minded enough to recognise that the animals are contented and well cared for and simply decide that they won't visit the park.

These are the people who keep their opinions to themselves but instead make an extra effort to recycle, use their car less often and switch off lights in their house.

For anyone who doesn't quite know what to think about captivity since there are so many opinions out there, it is perfectly okay to question absolutely everything about it.

It is more than okay to say that you want better quality lives for the animals.

It is okay to want more space for them. It is okay to want a more enriching life for them. And it is okay to want them to be happy.

Because let me tell you a secret- trainers want all of those things too and together we have the opportunity to actually make them happen.

The changing attitudes towards captivity now means that we are no longer allowed to simply enjoy our jobs and the time we get to spend with the animals. Instead, we have to be ready to defend ourselves and our morals to anyone who questions it.

We need to know all of the facts to be able to accurately answer guest questions. I know several trainers, myself included who have had guests try to secretly record their voices or film them answering questions, hoping that we will slip up and say something damaging in order to release it onto the internet.

Our whole lives have become about defending our right to work with these animals and to have these animals in zoological facilities. People should not be making assumptions about what is best for animals simply because they would prefer them to live a certain way.

Of course it is a good thing that people are caring more about the animals, but not to the point where they are going to kill them with kindness.

*

When I was finishing up my second internship with dolphins in the Florida Keys, I remember watching the trailer for a movie called *Blackfish* on the computer in the office.

All of the trainers were gathered in the room, speculating about what kind of impact this movie could have.

I remember thinking that it was a movie with a silly name, low budget, and that there wouldn't be very many people interested in watching that kind of documentary, at least not outside of Florida. It seemed very niche. I ignorantly thought it wouldn't have much of an impact at all.

How wrong I was.

I finished my internship and went back home to Scotland and started seeing reviews of the movie that had been posted online. Newspapers and magazines were covering the story with people outside of the field talking about captivity and Tilikum like they were suddenly animal behaviour experts.

Suddenly, it was open season on marine mammal trainers. Social media became a minefield.

If your profile photo or description contained any information about your job then you were receiving hate messages daily.

You couldn't 'like' or comment on SeaWorld's page positively without someone asking if you had watched *Blackfish*, and if you engaged with them and tried to explain, they couldn't seem to understand how you could still support SeaWorld after watching it. Clearly this movie was having much more of an impact that I had first thought.

At the time, because I knew I wanted to be a killer whale trainer and was actively working towards that goal, I knew I would need to watch the movie myself. I knew that eventually I would be getting asked questions about it and I wanted to be in possession of all the facts to be in the right place to answer those questions.

The first time I watched it, it was being broadcast on channel 4 television and I watched it alone. It made me furious. From the opening credits of the movie, the outright lies and twisted truths sunk their teeth into my skin, they gnawed away at me until I felt like I had run a 10k race. My heart was pounding and I was shaking from anger and frustration by the time the end credits rolled.

I simply couldn't believe how they had turned something I so firmly believed in, into something despicable.

Everything I had been working towards for the last six years, everything I had been promoting and believing in, they had twisted it around in a warped ninety-minute film.

The second time I watched it was with my Mum because she wanted to see it for herself. I remember being worried about how the movie might change her mind about my chosen career path. I was scared that even though she had been the one to first expose me to SeaWorld and had taken me there multiple times, that this one film would completely change her opinion.

Because *Blackfish* is cleverly constructed.

Every scene is scored over with dramatic music. Video clips are interspersed with loosely based facts given by individuals who appear to have credibility, and so are made more believable to the viewer. The use of emotive language and shocking video clips are married together in a partnership designed to evoke a strong emotional response from those watching.

For me the movie is less of a documentary and more of a psychological thriller.

By definition, a documentary has to be a film or television piece that provides a factual report on a particular subject. However *Blackfish* took facts and transformed them into what they wanted those facts to represent.

Language is an incredibly powerful thing.

If I was to say 'Raped, impregnated and confined to a concrete cell', which in actual fact is a direct quote from an anti-captivity website, will evoke a much more emotional response than a simple 'artificially inseminated in zoological enclosure'.

It is all in the delivery and how the reader or viewer chooses to perceive what is said.

Unfortunately *Blackfish* is skewed in such an anti-captivity direction that almost all of the language and imagery used within the movie is designed to persuade the viewer that the whales in captivity are unhappy and abused.

Luckily, as a trainer I know that is far from the truth.

But I am all too aware that there are many people out there who take it at face value.

I was worried when my Mum first watched it, that she would turn around and tell me she didn't want me to continue to pursue a career with killer whales. I should have given her more credit for knowing her own mind. For the first twenty minutes or so I paused the movie continually in an attempt to explain what was actually happening until she took the remote away from me and forced me to sit in silence until it was over.

After it was finished I waited with baited breath to hear what she was going to say to me. I am still to this day so incredibly proud of what she said.

She told me 'Your dream has always been to work with these animals and we both know that they have the potential to be dangerous. But neither you, nor anyone else working with them is stupid enough to think that they are not. If you ever achieve your dream then I will be happy knowing that you spend every day doing what you love. People die every day just crossing the street. Go and inspire people to love these animals like you do'.

Ladies and gentlemen, the award for Best Supportive Mother goes to…

I will always be so thankful that my Mum completely understands exactly how I feel about killer whales and this job.

Unfortunately not everyone has the same understanding

In the early days after the movie was released I was really just answering questions from friends and family, or other people who didn't really know much about the subject. Thankfully, I was there to be able to answer their questions and they trusted my answers when I debunked the facts for them. Hopefully they are still of the same opinion these days.

When I started working as a dolphin trainer in 2014, the year after the movie was released, I began to get asked slightly more pointed questions about the topics covered within the movie and my about my line of work. I would always give the same reply, explaining that I would happily give my opinion and views on captivity but because I had never worked with killer whales or for SeaWorld then there were obviously going to be some gaps in my knowledge concerning some of the more complex issues.

Once, I was coming back from my lunch break onto the dock to take the next dolphin program into the water when a woman pulled me aside to ask me a couple of questions. She asked about what types of fish were living in the lagoons with the dolphins and how many animals we had in each lagoon. I explained how we kept the males and females separated to limit reproduction and inbreeding because, at that time, there were a total of thirty one dolphins at the facility. However there were twelve females in the large lagoon together, nine juvenile males in the lagoon at the back and several dolphin pairs in holding lagoons, either because they had calves or because they had been put together for potential breeding.

She breathed a sigh of relief and gushed about how much better this facility was than SeaWorld.

What she was unable to see was that even though those dolphins were in the ocean, the fish were attacking them, the company was running hundreds of dolphin programs per day solely to line their own pockets and giving nothing back to conservation efforts or the dolphins themselves. While SeaWorld has an entire separate rescue team that works tirelessly night and day in order to save as many animals as possible, something that is only made possible because of their profits. SeaWorld actively loses money on their rescue efforts but they continue to put so much into it because they genuinely believe in conservation.

33,000 animals have been rescued by SeaWorld and counting. When I first became a killer whale trainer I was presented with huge protocol binders that I had to read and sign, along with safety orientations and detailed animal profile histories that I had to learn and memorise.

The movie *Blackfish* centres around Tilikum and the fatal accident that resulted in the death of one of the best trainers our world has ever seen, Dawn Brancheau.

They present the idea that captivity causes whales to go insane, causing them to lash out at their trainers.

In reality, when whales get frustrated, either by training sessions or other whales, then they can get aggressive, just like a horse will attempt to kick or unseat its rider if he or she keeps jerking on the reins. However the extreme aggressions shown within the film are few and far between. Just as a well-cared for horse may attempt to unseat his rider if he is having a bad day, a killer whale may lash out if he or she is feeling particularly frustrated in that moment. However, the important thing to remember is that it is momentary. The whales are not spending their entire lives in a never-ending state of frustration and crazed anger, although the film does heavily suggest that this is the case.

Instead the whales act and react to their environment. Changes that we trainers make, and changes within their pod. Their feelings and emotions fluctuate and change in a similar way to ours. Sometimes they get frustrated, but other times they are perfectly content to lie back and let us give them a belly rub.

The picture *Blackfish* paints of captive orcas and our reality is very different.

There are numerous video clips and narrations of killer whales aggressing trainers in the movie. One of the most visually striking and dangerous was a long aggression on Ken Peters during a show. In this video, Kasatka grabs his ankle and drags him under the water several times.

One of the things I want to point out is that when killer whales aggress each other it can get incredibly violent, in captivity or in the wild. They are large predators with sharp teeth and they will rake each other or ram each other until they have worked their frustrations out.

In comparison to this, Kasatka taking Ken Peter's ankle and holding him under the water but each time bringing him back up to the surface to breathe is relatively calm. Obviously the whale wanted to make a point. She was frustrated with him and she wanted him to know it. Luckily, Ken Peters is an excellent trainer who had worked with that whale for years and is in fact still working there to this day.

He stayed calm.

During the video you see him controlling his breathing and stroking Kasatka's back. Relationship. He had a great relationship with her, probably what kept the accident from becoming so much worse.

Yes, you see him swimming as fast as he possibly could to the slide out at the end of the video. Of course he did, he was being forcibly held under the water by the largest predator in the ocean, of course he took his opportunity to get out of there as fast as he could.

The important thing to note here is that she could easily have swam after him but she chose not to, net or no net. Killer whales can swim up to 30mph (50kmph).

No one gets out of an orca pool unless the orca lets you.

Unless you were Ken Peters himself, Kasatka or even a trainer around the pool that day, you have absolutely no idea what exactly was going on during that aggressive incident and you have no right to give your opinion as fact. Even the explanation I just offered is subjective, from talking to fellow trainers who observed the footage we formed our own idea of what was going on.

People like to put thoughts and feelings into the whale's heads without knowing anything about the situation and make generic statements like 'he did it because he wanted to escape captivity'.

If you just look at the basic facts, these whales are huge and we are tiny in comparison. Even if they use less than half of the force they are capable of generating, just hitting us with a pec fin could kill us.

During the majority of aggressive incidents, all the animal wants to do is communicate to us how they are feeling in the only way they know how.

Speaking to numerous trainers who have had in-water accidents with killer whales, the majority of them will always say that it was trainer error that led to the whale becoming frustrated, possessive or that the whale had an excess of energy which caused them to act inappropriately in the water.

Some trainers who have had accidents with their animals continue to work with and love that animal unconditionally for years afterwards. Because they understand that the whale didn't have a personal vendetta against the trainer for selfishly holding them captive for years.

It was a moment of frustration which both trainer and whale should hopefully be able to move on from.

All of our safety training is aimed at stopping these kind of incidents from occurring and were all in place even before waterwork was stopped.

We were face to face, literally neck deep in the water with them, completely submerged in their world, trusting them with our lives and in over thirty years of swimming with killer whales there have only been three fatal accidents involving trainers.

If you compare this with the amount of deaths and accidents that occur on a yearly basis from keepers working with big cats or other large mammals despite being in completely protected contact situations where there should be a barrier between animal and trainer at all times, or with the number of people killed yearly from horse riding accidents.

Killer whale trainer mortality statistics are definitely on the low side.

Of course, we never want any accident to happen with any animal, but no trainer puts on that wetsuit and walks around the pool, or dives into the water, without knowing that they are working with a top predator.

Even so, I have never once come into work and felt unsafe.

I have always trusted in my team to know what to do if something were to go wrong, and trusted in my relationship with my whale. So that if anything were to go wrong we could work our way out of it.

I cannot offer my opinion on the accident involving Dawn Brancheau and Tilikum. I wasn't there, I have never worked for SeaWorld, I never knew her or her colleagues or family members and so nothing I say with regards to that incident has any value.

All I know is that I was lucky enough to see her in person performing waterwork in the Believe show, and I am always left in awe at her obvious connection with the whales whenever I re-watch my Believe DVD. She looked completely at home in the water with the whales, it was like she was meant to be there and she made it look effortless.

She was exactly what we all aspire to be.

An incredibly passionate and dedicated trainer who was one of the best in the field.

My own Mother knows that it is more likely for me to die at work by tripping over my own clumsy two feet and smacking my head on the concrete than it is for me to be killed by one of the animals. But she still knows that if it were ever to happen, then I chose to follow my dreams and pursue my passion regardless of the risks because I love what I do.

I would rather die tomorrow than live my whole life never having been a killer whale trainer.

But what I do know is how disrespectful and cruel it was for the makers of *Blackfish* to profit from and exploit her death. I once heard a trainer who worked in Orlando tell me that the day after the accident happened there were anti-captivity protesters at the gate screaming in trainers faces, brandishing placards as they came into work.

To have some basic human understanding and compassion, even if you are completely convinced that captivity is the worst thing for the whales, you still need to understand that on that day people lost a friend, a daughter and a role model. People should be allowed to grieve and remember her in peace without activists jumping on the opportunity less than 24 hours later.

I have the utmost respect and compassion for the family of Dawn Brancheau in the face of what the media tried to twist her death into. Despite the fact that they tried to make her a faceless name to further their vendetta against our industry, they managed to create something for the good of others out of their tragedy.

They started the Dawn Brancheau Foundation which is dedicated to helping children and animals in need and inspires people to follow their dreams just like Dawn did.

Every year they hold the 'Dream Big 5k' in memory of Dawn that is run at SeaWorld and all of the money raised is given to several local organisations, from youth clubs in need of new facilities to children's shelters. They, and all of us trainers, will forever remember her for her giant smile and her commitment and dedication to the whales.

Only two months before Dawn's accident, there had been another fatal accident between whale and trainer, this time at Loro Parque where Keto killed his trainer Alexis during a morning training session.

When I first listened to the story of how he died from the lips of a trainer had been his good friend, it was incredibly emotional. None of us had asked to hear the story, he just started talking about it organically but you could have heard a pin drop in that office. He explained to us the small errors in judgement that had led to Keto becoming frustrated. He told us how, in hindsight, he could see different things they could have tried which would have reduced Keto's frustration to a level where he could have safely exited the pool. He described the suddenness of how it happened, how quickly life can be taken away, one hit from an orca is all it takes. When you hear someone who knew him talk about the incident, Alexis no longer becomes 'that trainer who was killed' as guests like to refer to him, he becomes a person who was just like me. Who once sat in that same room, who worked with the same whales as I did, who hung up his wetsuit on the same rack. And that is when it becomes personal.

So now whenever a guest asks me a typically insensitive question about either Alexis or Dawn, instead of answering their morbid questions I ty to remind them that they were real people.

People deserving of respect.

People that trainers still light candles for in the office and hang memorial photos of on the walls so they are never forgotten.

I am happy that the guests chose to ask me and not one of my colleagues who knew Alexei well, because I could not imagine losing my best friend and having to stand there and answer prying and often insensitive questions about the details of their death.

Not only did it exploit the grief and memory of two brilliant trainers and their families, *Blackfish* stole so much more from us. It stole our credibility when it twisted video footage showing emergency husbandry procedures and training sessions to make it look like we were fighting against our animals. The slyness of the commentary insinuated that we had something to hide and in doing so it generated a great deal of mistrust in marine parks amongst the general public.

Blackfish stole one of the most important and special moments of a trainer's career from a beautiful and talented woman called Holly Byrd.

SeaWorld had filmed her first in-water training session with a whale called Katina for their 'Believe' DVD and it shows her incredibly emotional and touching reaction to taking that leap of faith with her whale. *Blackfish* inserted those video clips during a narration by an ex-trainer who was talking about her own first moment in the water with a whale. This made it look as if it was that trainer in the video and not Holly. They not only used that footage of Holly without her permission, but by putting it into a movie that attempts to discredit our whole industry and the work we do, they effectively ruined that moment for her.

Blackfish was essentially the catalyst that sparked the surge in popularity in the anti-captivity movement. It was the spark that activists had been waiting for to bring their argument to the public eye and allow them to influence the masses.

Now, trainers are surrounded by criticism no matter where we go, and it is always personal.

We don't clock out at 6pm and leave our work at work. We take it home with us.

When our animals and our integrity is being attacked online or through movies like *Blackfish* it has a profound effect on our emotions.

When people find out that I am a killer whale trainer, one of the first things they will ask me is if I have watched *Blackfish*. It is becoming increasingly difficult not to roll my eyes in response to this question.

Even if I hadn't seen it, do people really think that the movie producers know better than trainers who are living it every single day? Why do people trust a movie, over the opinion of people who have studied animal behaviour for years and know these whales better than anyone else? Do they really think that all it would take for an orca trainer to suddenly change their views about what they have dedicated their lives to, is to watch a 90 minute movie? That after the end credits rolled I would be happy to burn my wetsuit, cast off my bridge, turn my back on a lifetime of work and skip off to join the anti-captivity protesters?

Surely if everything *Blackfish* said was completely true, there would be no more killer whale trainers. There would be no more competition in our field because every single person who wants to be a killer whale trainer, or is one currently, loves the whales.

It would be impossible to love your whales and do the job in the way the movie paints it to be.

Therefore there must be more inconsistencies than the average person knows about.

A slightly older but no less emotional documentary that people who are against captivity like to reference is *The Cove*. This documentary still needs to be taken with a pinch of salt since it is incredibly biased but it did expose the Taiji drive hunts in Japan to the world.

For anyone who doesn't know, from September to January every year fishermen off the coast of Taiji Japan are given a quota of cetaceans to herd into the infamous cove and slaughter.

Species of cetaceans include bottlenose dolphins, pilot whales and false killer whales among others. Exposing this barbaric practice and trying to gain support to end drive hunts like this one, and others that take place around the world to this day, was a great positive for the movie. However the movie insinuates that western facilities, such as SeaWorld, profit from these drive hunts by purchasing animals before they are slaughtered.

It is true that some facilities do purchase animals from these drive hunts, but none of them have IMATA accreditation and the majority are located in Asia or Eastern Europe. The people who buy these animals like to say that they are saving at least a few of these animals from their inevitable death and are at least giving them some kind of life in human care.

But essentially all they are doing is keeping these drive hunts in business by allowing the people who run them to make profit.

In fact SeaWorld is actually one of the organisations actively donating to the cause and front-running the campaign to stop the drive hunts entirely. However the movie implies that SeaWorld purchases dolphins caught in the drive hunts by playing video clips from old SeaWorld shows. Further confusing the general public and twisting the truth to serve their own agenda.

In the Western world there are strict laws regarding the purchase or transport of animals into or out of the country, and the Marine Mammal Protection Act in the United States bans the capture of marine mammals from the wild entirely, so it would be impossible to import any animal captured from a drive hunt.

One of the most distressing things I heard after the release of *Blackfish* was that some teachers were asking children in their classes to watch the movie and write reports on why captivity was bad for animals. The idea that so many young impressionable children were being taught that animals living in a zoological setting is something negative is shocking to me.

Children should be allowed to form their own opinions on the subject and instead be taught about things like conservation and the threat of extinction, things that are actively taught and explored within marine parks themselves.

It made me think about my own potential future children.

Will I raise them around these whales, understanding that they are happy and well cared for, for them to go into school and be bullied for having a killer whale trainer as a parent?

Will my child go into the world believing that their mother is someone who cares for animals and does everything she can for them, only to be told by others that she is a jailor, a monster, an animal abuser and other horrible things people have called me over the years without even knowing me?

Will my children be subjected to the same hate and abuse that I myself am?

For this reason, and for so many others, this book needed to be written and it is also why people need to keep coming to the parks to see for themselves that there are always two sides to every story.

Captivity is definitely not one hundred percent perfect and there are still so many things we can do to improve and enrich the animals' lives, but just because it is a different life to the wild, does not mean it is inherently bad.

Unfortunately, especially nowadays, the wild is not the safe haven people imagine it to be for any animal.

The world is changing and public opinion is changing with it. Gone are the days where trainers were hailed as superheroes and people watched in envy as we danced in the water with our killer whales. We may need to adapt and change with the times, but there is no reason why that cannot be a positive thing.

*

The majority of people who are against captivity are concerned about the well-being of the animals.

There are a few in the minority who think that our whales would be better off dead than in our care. People who can see animals washed up on beaches and condemn organisations like SeaWorld for rescuing them, because even if they manage to rehabilitate the majority of the animals, some may never be fully healed enough to be released. These people would prefer that all of these animals were simply left to die on a beach or entangled in fishing line instead of living out the remainder of their lives comfortable, but in a zoological facility.

It is disgusting and shocking that there are people out there who would rather see Skyla and Wikie dead than playing happily with their favourite toys, something that is incomprehensible to me. Some people are firmly of the belief that it is impossible for a killer whale to have a happy life while under human care.

I have actually had multiple people send me messages telling me that our whales are 'better dead than fed' or that they would be happier if I 'put a bullet in their heads and put them out of their misery'.

It shocks me to think that some people genuinely believe that our whales would be begging for death. When I look at little Keijo come up to greet us in the morning squeaking excitedly or Inouk gazing up at us with his big dark eyes to ask for some ice cubes and a head scratch, or when Skyla would be physically shaking from excitement before a show. I don't understand where people get that impression from.

Do people really think captivity is as black as it is painted? When the whales are all together spending hours playing with their favourite toy, quite literally jumping for joy, I cannot fathom why people would choose to believe that they are anything other than happy in that moment.

This is what happens when people jump on a bandwagon and start proclaiming that everyone should boycott marine parks simply because they watched a movie. These are the people who can end up doing more harm than good.

Due to *Blackfish* portraying marine parks as places ruled by corporate greed, the general public have the feeling we are hiding some back-alley secrets that we don't want anyone to see. Some of the video footage within *Blackfish* was shocking but it was specifically edited to appear that way.

Of course watching a sick animal being forcibly held down for an emergency endoscopy is not nice to see, and for a trainer it is not a nice thing to do, but it is necessary if you want to give that animal potentially life-saving treatment.

For the same reason teeth cleaning was never shown to the public before because it looks bad.

It is widely known that captive killer whales have terrible teeth. The less well-known fact is that so do wild killer whales.

Cetaceans only have one set of teeth for their entire lifetime, their teeth aren't easily replaced like sharks and neither do they have a set of 'baby' teeth that fall out after a few years like humans.

The teeth that they do have are all long and conically shaped, adapted over the years to effectively catch fish and swallow them whole, rendering molars for chewing completely unnecessary.

Because they never have a need to chew tough food, their teeth are incredibly fragile.

The whales in human care are fed so much fish that their stomachs are always comfortably full, meaning that they usually like to regurgitate some of their fish to play with it. Cetaceans have no gag reflex so passing fish up and down their gullet like this is no problem for them. The problem is that gastric juice will come up into their mouth along with the fish, and as is seen commonly in bulimics, the acidity of the gastric juice will wear down the enamel of their teeth, leaving them even weaker than before.

With these weak teeth they gnaw on and play with a number of hard plastic toys which can easily result in broken teeth. The whales also chew on walls, gates and each other's fins, not necessarily out of boredom as people like to claim, but because cetaceans use their mouths to explore everything in their environment, so whenever they are curious about something they will use their mouths to figure it out.

In this way the teeth of captive whales will begin to get worn down. When the teeth get worn down to the point where we can see the nerve, that tooth is becoming painful for the animal. This is where we will step in.

The area is numbed and the nerve inside the tooth is deadened so the whale will feel no more pain while using their teeth for any activity. However, if the tooth continues to get worn down further or breaks and exposes the pulp, we need to drill the tooth.

Similarly to a human visiting the dentist and having an infected tooth drilled, we use a small hand-held drill to get rid of any pulp that is already infected or could become infected in the future. However, there is no solution to be able to 'fill in' a broken tooth to protect the exposed pulp and dead nerve that still reside within the tooth itself like we can with humans. Instead, to prevent any possible future infection, we clean the teeth inside and out twice a day.

There is nothing at all about this procedure that is so out of the ordinary that would shock someone. You break a tooth, dentist drills it, you keep it clean, end of story.

But it looks bad and is easy to twist into something much darker and more dramatic.

Activists like to twist anything they can get their hands on to make us look like the bad guys, and this is something they can always latch onto as a fail-safe.

In the wild, especially in killer whales who feed on large mammals or sharks, the tooth wear that is shown is often even worse than you see in the captive population.

There was one whale in particular that was known to a group of villagers off the coast of Australia. He would aid the villagers in the hunting of grey whales and he later died within their bay with his body being removed for research purposes.

On examination of his skeleton, the majority of his teeth were either completely worn down to the gum line or broken. One tooth in particular had become so badly infected that it had eroded away a large section of his upper jaw. This infection had made its way so far through his head that visible damage was seen on the top of his skull. Scientists were in agreement that this infection could easily have been his primary cause of death.

Because we need to show the public that we have absolutely no need to hide things like this, nowadays facilities are opening their gates, posting more on social media, allowing visitors to see more medical procedures and removing some of the 'mystery' that once surrounded the world of orca training, purely to show the masses that we are doing nothing wrong.

Blackfish opened the floodgates holding back the tide of criticism against captive orcas but now it is time for us to let the tide come in and show everyone that the truth is on our side.

CHAPTER TWELVE – COMING HOME

Returning to Tenerife after my trial day for an undetermined amount of time, with the possibility of a future job at Marineland looking uncertain, I decided just to focus all of my attention and energy on the whales.

In my last months at Loro Parque, I barely remember anything else that went on that was not to do with the whales. I spent hours playing with Skyla and the other whales at the windows and around the pool in my spare time. I lingered at the end of the day as the sun set, just watching the pod wind down for the night, their breathing getting calmer and their backs relaxing as they settled into an easy rhythm. I tried my best to commit Skyla's face and expressions to memory. Her tiny freckles. The exact colour of her eyes. The strange little lines she has on her upper lip. Her special personality quirks.

Sometimes I worry that I am forgetting her. Or that she has forgotten me.

As difficult as it was for me to leave Skyla, I knew that I was making the right decision.

Thanks to a lot of convincing on the part of my current supervisor, I was offered a permanent position on the orca team at Marineland two months after my trial day. I don't think I will ever be able to repay Duncan for quite literally giving me back my dream job.

It was a horrible feeling to have my dream job at Loro Parque, but have it feel nothing like I imagined it would because of issues beyond my control.

When I received my contract from Marineland, the very next day I sat down with my supervisor at Loro Parque and explained why I was leaving. He was very sweet and completely understood why I was leaving, I don't think it came as a surprise to anyone, he said he was sorry that they were losing yet another international trainer for the same reasons and he wished me the best of luck. I walked down to human resources, handed in my resignation and felt like I could breathe again.

When I came back up to the office I announced to the team that in two weeks I would be leaving. I was grateful that a few of them genuinely wished me luck. I think everyone knew I would be happier somewhere else.

For my last show with Skyla, I had asked to be allowed to do the Quiet segment, in order for me to be able to showcase our relationship to the public one last time.

The music we were performing to at that moment was incredibly emotional- Leona Lewis' 'Footprints in the Sand' and when the music hit its crescendo and I asked Skyla to come up onto the slide out to the gasps of amazement from the crowd, I wrapped my arms around her as far as they would go and buried my face into her, allowing my tears to mix with the salt water running off her back. On what I knew was to be my last session with her, I made sure to grab her bucket before anyone else could reach for it, just in case, and asked if I could do a relate session with her. I took her over to the slide out and mucked about with her, playing with a leaf, generally being silly and then gave her as many cuddles as I was allowed to.

Strangely, I didn't cry.

Again, the same way as when I left Dali and Vicente, I felt numb. The emotion had come earlier.

For Christmas a few months later, my Mum gifted me an exact replica of her tail flukes in real silver that I wear around my neck every single day so a part of her is always with me. Even though I work with other whales now, she will always hold a special place in my heart for being my first.

Here at Marineland, this job is everything I expected it to be and more.

The team I am working on is filled with like-minded, equally passionate people who are as dedicated to the animals as I am myself. We frequently stick around at work after hours chatting about research or our day in general because we simply aren't in a rush to get home. We love our jobs so why would we be desperate to leave?

The thing I am most blessed about is that my team understands and supports me.

I'm pretty sure that if you interviewed people at Loro Parque about my personality and then people at Marineland, you would think they were talking about two completely different trainers.

Here, my passion is appreciated and my dedication to the job is seen as career drive instead of pushiness. Here, when trainers ask for more time with the animals, that time is made available to them for whatever reason.

Every single person on this team has a voice and is heard.

Of course no team is one hundred percent perfect and there will be days where there are arguments and tensions within the group, especially because we are passionate about our jobs, but for the majority of the time we spend our days smiling and laughing.

A day here at Marineland will typically start with some of us grabbing the first session buckets out of the fish kitchen. One trainer from any of the animal departments will prepare the entire daily diet for the penguins, sea lions, seals, dolphins and orcas with the help of the interns.

The trainer in the kitchen starts an hour earlier than everyone else, so the first bucket of the day is usually ready for us when we arrive. We will grab the whales' buckets, a green tag for Inouk, red for Wikie, yellow for Moana and purple for Keijo, along with a massive container we will fill to the brim with ice cubes. Even though it is great to hydrate them this way, for some reason the four whales love eating ice cubes more than they like fish.

If only my favourite treats had as little calories.

The buckets are then taken around the pool and one trainer will stuff the fish with the whales' daily dose of vitamins. The whales can get all of the nutrients they need from the fish that we feed them, but just like my mum used to feed me a multivitamin every morning when I was growing up, we just like to make sure they are getting everything they need.

We were previously using standard multivitamins, just like you or I would consume, but we recently switched to vitamins specifically designed to support the system of marine animals.

A lot of people have a misconception that the fish we feed our whales is somehow sub-standard to the fish in the ocean because we give vitamin supplements and hydrations. But these are just some of the many ways in which we try to provide the best healthcare possible for our animals.

Due to the fish being thawed from frozen, it does lose a little of its water content. In a similar way we are told about the benefits of eating fresh versus frozen vegetables from the supermarket. I have heard it suggested that in the wild the whales would have a better diet and be able to get all of the nutrients they need without supplements. However, when you consider the fact that the majority of fish species in the ocean are so polluted and filled with plastic and toxins like PCBs, with more and more marine life washing up on beaches as a result, you soon realise that the reality facing any captive marine mammal is very different.

The morning routine will always consist of a safety check-in of the pool area, meaning that we check the air pressure in all of the scuba tanks and spare-air bottles we have dotted around at various locations. We also have extra masks and fins, long-reach poles, buoys and ropes as well as the nets, in case they were ever needed in an emergency situation. If any of these items has been moved, is missing or broken, then it is reported and fixed within the course of the day.

If you aren't the trainer doing the check-in you will be doing the water test.

The pool water at Marineland and at Loro Parque is pumped into the facility directly from the ocean. However, in order to efficiently clean the water thoroughly enough, it passes first through the filters and then we need to add chlorine to the pools. This is where the rumours come flying in from all sides.

Yes we use chlorine in the pools, but the concentration is less than you or I would find in a glass of tap water. We use only the exact amount needed to rid the ocean water full of whale poop of any potentially harmful bacteria. We have a dedicated team of specialists who monitor the water throughout the whole park day in and day out. The animals' skin does not smell of chlorine. When I am swimming in the water I do not taste chlorine, only salt. When I swim in the water my eyes do not burn, meaning that the percentage of chlorine used is so minimal it has absolutely no effect on the animals whatsoever.

And the way we monitor the level of chlorine in the water to ensure it stays so low?

We test the water throughout the day.

First thing in the morning one trainer will go around and take a sample of water from each of the pools and then use a machine to accurately test the level of chlorine in the water in each pool. If the chlorine exceeds a certain amount for whatever reason then we immediately call our technicians who adjust it and move the animals out of that pool until we test the water a second time to ensure the levels are back to normal.

Once the check-in and water test are finished and the whale area is opened to the public we will all gather together to have our morning meeting.

During this quick ten minute meeting, every trainer is able to discuss what they would like to do during the day.

This is not always limited to training sessions. Yes each whale has a handful of behaviours that they are being trained on at any given time and those will usually always be on the board, but trainers can also suggest play sessions, relate sessions or essential husbandry sessions too.

In this way every trainer will have the opportunity to do their own sessions with the animals, and the animals will always have lots of variability in their day.

Ensuring that we create opportunities for different social interactions, pool configurations, session variety and trainer variability, each day is constructed to be positive and fun for every animal.

Additionally, because we never have the same team of trainers every single day due to vacations and days off, the whales are always seeing different trainers who work with them in different ways.

Each whale has a team of trainers dedicated to them.

In this way, whenever any trainer has days off or is on vacation, there is always someone there who knows that animal. For example I work primarily with Wikie and Keijo but my colleague Gwen works with Wikie and Moana.

Gwen is more than capable of taking Keijo for gatings or even sessions, but he is not her focus animal. The same goes for me with Moana. Moana and I don't have a relationship but he has seen me around the pool enough, has received thousands of ice cubes from my hand and been beside me in enough sessions to partner with me for small things.

For this reason, when a new trainer starts out they will be paired with one animal until the two get to know each other. That relationship keeps building until they grow in confidence around one another and step-by-step can start accomplishing more together. Really experienced trainers with strong relationships with their whales will be the ones doing the most challenging things like gastric samples and in-water work, simply because it takes a lot of trust. When you first start out you will spend most of your time in relate and play sessions, things the animal finds the most enjoyable.

Usually when we want to focus on training a new behaviour with a whale, we will separate that individual from the rest of the group into one pool to allow them to better focus on the session.

Due to the way that we plan out our days within that morning meeting, in the space of eight hours I might be able to train a new behaviour with Wikie, do a show with her, play around with a new enrichment device, as well as spend some quality time just chilling out together.

We are incredibly lucky that the whales at Marineland are so responsive to us trainers. Whatever amount of time and energy we give to them, they give right back to us and we can do entire sessions without giving a whale a single fish.

Some of my favourite moments to spend with the killer whales are the quiet times.

Usually last thing in the evening when everything is settled and we are about to finish the last bucket, or are clearing away for the night, when the sun is just passing behind the massive arch of the stadium. I like to finish with a rubdown, feeling the smoothness of Wikie's skin and watch the tracks my fingers make on her back as the water parts where they have passed by.

Some days I cannot believe it when I look down onto the mirror-like surface of her back and see my own face staring back at me, my reflection in an orca. Knowing that she knows I have no more fish to give her but she will lie there with me anyway, just two souls searching for a way to bridge the gap between us. Looking into her eyes, wishing I could talk to her.

There is something so profound and transcendent about being blessed enough to be allowed to be face to face with a killer whale and stare so deeply into their soul, and feel them staring right back. Wikie humbles me every day.

As well as making me feel like the dumbest, clumsiest, most ridiculous creature that ever walked the earth compared to her queen-like, composed, all-knowing demeanour.

Skyla may have taught me a lot about understanding killer whales and moulded me into the trainer I am today, but Wikie has had an incredibly profound effect on who I am as a person.

She is a much more difficult whale and infinitely unpredictable.

I think perhaps one of the reasons I feel like I developed a relationship with my two whales at Marineland much faster than I did with Skyla, is because we are allowed to get so much closer to the animals.

Of course, it could also be to do with the fact that I already understood the killer whale psyche and was better able to read their body language and anticipate changes than I was two years previously when I had been a complete beginner.

Being able to have close contact with the animals is something I really cherish here at Marineland and I feel it makes the animals' lives more enriching.

The orcas at Marineland behave very differently to the animals at Loro Parque, potentially due to the differences in how they experience interaction from their trainers. They are so much more affectionate, constantly asking for attention and interacting with the trainers as if we are simply an extension of their pod regardless of if we are in session or have reinforcement with us.

The strict security measures at Loro Parque make it a lot more difficult to get close to the animals and so it limits the amount of affection the trainers can show towards the whales.

As of right now, Marineland have four orcas that were all born at the park.

The dominant female Wikie is mother to the two young males Moana and Keijo and sister to the adult male Inouk. Previously, the group was led by the infamous dominant female Freya, and her son Valentin was another pod member, who unfortunately died from a stress related condition in 2016 after the floods that swept through Nice.

Having a real family pod of four individuals like this means that the social bonds are a lot stronger and as a result they are often easier to have together than the group at Loro Parque.

However, it also presents its own challenges.

Because they are so close as individuals, sometimes they would much rather swim together without interference from us trainers. That means that no matter how many times we call them over or how many buckets of fish we have, they can sometimes ignore us for hours.

Learning how to work with Wikie and Keijo gave me a greater appreciation of how very different each animal is, more so than I ever understood just working Skyla and watching other trainers work other animals around me.

With each animal you have to change your behaviour, how you act and react.

Something that Keijo would love could potentially make Wikie refuse to do anything else for you. Something Wikie would love could potentially make Skyla very uncomfortable.

One really good example is rubdowns.

Skyla found rubdowns tolerable, but you could only give her a rubdown on her terms and if she wasn't in the mood she would always try to move away from your hands. Even if she was in the mood she would never stay still for very long. She preferred to be active.

Wikie on the other hand will approach her trainers outside of a session, knowing full well that the trainer has absolutely zero reinforcement for her and still offer her tail for a scratch. In fact, she will often attempt to lie there even while the show starts, completely ignoring the intro music to try and prolong the rubdown. I couldn't even have tried to give Skyla a rubdown before a show, she would never have been calm enough!

A day with little Keijo can be great fun, because he is so young you spend the majority of your time playing, but it can also be challenging and at times frustrating. He can lose focus quickly due to his short attention span and occasionally he doesn't want to do sessions at all because he just wants to be with his Mum. You need to be ready to adapt to the situation and know how your whale is feeling.

A day spent with Wikie can be a nightmare if she is in a bad mood. If you make a mistake and you piss her off then you have pretty much ruined the day for every other whale and trainer around the pool. Pissing off the dominant female is a big mistake to make.

But a day spent with Wikie in a good mood can be the best day of your week. She can be the sweetest and most giving whale in the world, playing around with you so much that you don't even want to leave the pool and even when you eventually do, you have the biggest smile on your face.

Wikie is so intelligent that not only does she understand our training methods incredibly quickly, but she continually tries to guess at what we are asking her to do. So we can be halfway through our training plan, expecting to need at least five more small steps before the completed behaviour, and she will take off and do the full behaviour as if saying 'this is what you want right?' My experiences of training behaviours with Wikie have been so satisfying because she is so receptive to our communication, she makes me look like a really good trainer.

The first behaviour I trained on Wikie from start to finish, with the help of Duncan, was the breakspin. This is a behaviour where the whale slides up on a beaching on their side, pauses for a moment and then whips their tail in the water to give them the momentum they need to spin around 360 degrees. This is a commonplace behaviour at all three SeaWorlds and at Loro Parque because their beachings, or 'slide-outs', are completely flat. The breakspin had never been trained before at Marineland because the beachings are sloped, making it so much more difficult for the whales to stop themselves simply sliding back into the water halfway through their turn.

When we spotted Wikie sliding herself up and turning around on the beachings when we weren't around, Duncan started playing around with it. Since she was already doing something similar naturally by herself, we could conclude that she enjoyed it, therefore we finally decided to seriously train it.

Duncan asked me to train the behaviour with him since I had frequently seen and sent the behaviour with the whales at Loro Parque.

I was so excited to get started. This was an incredibly difficult behaviour to train, and neither of us had any idea of where to begin! We started off by bringing Wikie up on her side in different parts of the beaching to try and determine which place would give her the flattest surface on which to turn herself. We got the target out to try and bring her head around, we placed reinforcement in front of her, behind her, to the side of her. We had three trainers helping out, then one trainer, we even had a dolphin trainer come in one day because they had trained the behaviour on the dolphins. Myself, Duncan and Wikie basically spent five months figuring it out through trial and error. Eventually we learned that in order to let her spin, she had to bring both her head and her tail up properly. If her head was flat to the beaching she would glide into the water, even if she was keeping her tail in a good position. We took the target out and instead started running from reinforcement points, dodging her spinning tail each time as we ducked around the back to get to the other side before she finished spinning. For the first time I experienced what it must be like for the whales as they are being trained, each session is about figuring out what to do and waiting to see if it works.

In each session we were trying new things, new positions, new prompts, sending from a different place. Never knowing which one would give us the desired end result.

It was addictive, and I was so determined to see the behaviour through to the finish. Even when halfway through we thought that we might never be able to get a complete turn, suddenly Wikie started showing us how to do it.

In what seemed to be the space of a week, she started to push me further to the side each time she came out of the water. So instead of being in a straight line, she now faced the right side of the beaching with her body lying diagonally across. As this was not what I had asked of her, I stepped back ready to give her an LRS and wait for her to slide herself back down into the water. Instead she arched herself up and pushed with her powerful tail flukes and did her first complete 360 degree turn. She might not have slid up exactly how I asked her to but you can be damn sure that I gave her that whole bucket of fish after that! She had started to figure it out, and she knew that as she was a part of our team, she could also contribute her own ideas.

Which, as usual, was a much better idea than anything Duncan or I were suggesting.

After almost a year of working on the breakspin behaviour, Wikie can now do 540 degree turn, spinning one and a half rotations to finish with her head entering back into the water, without needing to use her tail to help her back around. This is something that I know the Loro Parque orcas cannot do, even on a flat beaching. Every single time I send her on a breakspin and I watch her do it perfectly, it solidifies my belief that we understand each other. I feel a sense of pride that I was able to gain the trust of an orca and have her willing to listen to me enough to be able to do something so incredibly complex.

Even if she did do the majority of the work.

Skyla used to anticipate what we wanted during training sessions too, but she made our job a lot more difficult. Skyla would wait patiently for three sessions, following our carefully planned out approximations and then suddenly on the fourth session, would guess the behaviour we were trying to train and then only stick with this guessed behaviour for six months. Like an over-eager Labrador not quite getting the right end of the stick, she was adorable but just missing the mark. Meaning not only did we have to keep trying to train the new behaviour, we also had to train the one she had gotten stuck in her head out of her.

Skyla's energy got in her own way sometimes.

But Wikie makes intelligent guesses.

When I was first starting out with her, Duncan would tell me to just let her try things without any help, to have a little more faith in her. When I was training her new porps behaviour, we had only finished a couple of sessions and I was very unsure that she had remembered the new positions. I thought there was no way she knew it already.

But when we let her do it by herself she got most of the behaviour right. Sometimes when we were near the end of a finished behaviour all I would have to do was point her in the right direction, something completely unrelated to the training process and she would get it.

Often killer whales will behave very differently depending on who their trainer is.

Killer whales are like the most popular kid in school who has the arrogance to believe that the world revolves around them. And the annoying thing is that they are right.

I have often waited at the side of the pool, having been assigned to Wikie for a session and watched as she swam to sit in front of my supervisor who was standing beside me and refuse to move because she wanted to stay with him. I mean I don't really blame her, he has worked with her since she was born, and I have been a mere blip on her radar compared to that.

I have also seen Wikie try to swim to any other trainer available instead of working for my supervisor after he came back from vacation because she was annoyed at him for leaving her for so long.

The dominant female before Wikie, Freya, would never let a trainer who wasn't on her team touch her. She could be lying out accepting a rubdown from four trainers on her team who she knew well but if a trainer she didn't know came along and tried to join in, she would immediately move whatever part of her body they were reaching for out of the way. Not every animal is as extreme as this but it is one of the reasons why relationship is so incredibly important.

In my opinion, being able to train an orca is an experience unlike training any other animal.

Due to their complexity, you have to be able to adapt your training approach and techniques depending on which animal you are working with.

It can take a long time to train certain behaviours and only minutes to train others because every behaviour is different and you never know what you are going to get. The first time I was allowed to train a behaviour by myself for the first time I was terrified. I felt so much pressure to prove to myself and to the rest of my team that I was a talented trainer. I had spent so many years striving towards this job, simply focused on getting there, that when I was stood there with a target pole in my hand I realised I had never given much thought to worrying about whether I would be any good at it.

Training an orca compared to a dolphin is an incredible experience. Sometimes you can spend half a day creating a multi-step training plan to make sure that you take 'baby steps' with your animal to maximise success and accept that you may need weeks before you get an approximation even close to what you want. Then your animal learns the whole behaviour in three sessions and skips 90% of the steps in your training plan. You always have to be able to jump one step ahead because they are so good at anticipating, if they do guess right, you have to be ready with what comes next.

But it can also work the opposite way too. When everything you have tried isn't working it begins to feel like a lost cause, so sometimes you need to take a break from the behaviour for a few months before trying again afresh.

Training is the fun part of the job, it is one of the ways we can really communicate with our animals and see how well we are able to bridge that gap between us to see if they understand what it is we want. And with orcas the majority of the time it is a two way street.

For example, sometimes whales offer random behaviours that they find enjoyable, or do naturally when they are contented. Some examples can be blowing bubble rings, various vocalisations and sticking their tongues out. Some of the ways the whales train their trainers is learning what kind of behaviour we find 'cute' or 'funny' that will ultimately result in us reinforcing them.

That is why we are followed around the pools by whales making funny squeaking noises or poking their tongues out or metaphorically batting their eyelashes at us until we throw them some ice cubes or a toy. Or when we stand up to finish a session and the whales turn around and stare at us with their big black eyes therefore making it impossible for us to stop giving them cuddles. A lot of the time our job is made easier because of their complex communication skills between each other. Usually if we want to train a baby on a new behaviour, most of the time we can send them on the behaviour with their mum and after a couple of tries the baby will usually copy the mother. We cannot say 100% that this is because she is telling her baby what to do or if the baby is simply copying what he or she sees but some level of communication is going on.

At Marineland we are able to interact with the public on an even closer level than before as we have opened up our orca encounter. This gives us trainers the ability to educate people on a more interactive level than we can during a show and it allows the guests to ask questions directly to us trainers and hopefully develop a greater appreciation for the animals.

The killer whales in captivity are ambassadors for their species in the wild and if people come to the parks, see our orcas and leave with a greater understanding and respect for marine life than we have done our jobs right.

When I became a killer whale trainer I was well aware that waterwork was a thing of the past, that it would never come back into shows and I would never be able to do it myself.

I had accepted that, and I had thought that I would never see it again with my own eyes. Working at Loro Parque I had observed numerous desensitisation sessions in the medical pool where Keto or Kohana would swim calmly around the perimeter and the trainer would either swim around or jump in and out.

However, one day after I had come to Marineland, people started throwing words around like 'waterwork' and 'swimming with Inouk' during the morning meeting.

I remember feeling a little glimmer of hope in my chest before quickly squashing it down and reminding myself that it didn't happen anymore, they were probably talking about desense training. So we started getting out the safety equipment and making sure it was easily available to us just like we did for any normal desensitisation session and I took up my position at the corner of the pool holding a spare air bottle.

And then Gianni got into the water with Inouk and they swam together.

It was that simple togetherness that took my breath away.

The whole point of desensitisation training is that the trainer and whale are completely separate and ignoring each other. But what I was seeing here was a flashback to the old days. I remember standing open-mouthed, my heart pounding, clutching that spare air bottle like it was my lifeline.

It is a little ridiculous when I think back to it now, they were only doing the most basic things, little A to B points, pec waves and small rubdowns. But I had such an emotional reaction to seeing trainer and killer whale together in the water again. it had been ten years since I had seen it in person and had somehow forgotten the undeniable magic of it.

When the session was over and we went to debrief in the office I started crying. I remember trying not to let anybody see, remembering how I had been bullied before for my opinions on water work. But to my absolute delight I was met instead with hugs and smiles from people who understood how amazing it is to watch trainer and whale in the water together.

I honestly didn't think I would have such an emotional reaction to seeing it again but it had the same effect on me as it had done back when I was eight years old and watching the Shamu Adventure for the first time.

When you can see such an obvious trusting relationship between trainer and killer whale, it takes your breath away. It makes me incredibly proud that I get to work at a facility that still believes in the power of the special bond that can occur between humans and orcas.

To be able to see how the whales react to it, how gentle they become, how responsive to every little touch by the trainer. From reading their body language you can see how much they enjoy having their trainers so close to them.

Nowadays we are constantly asking them to come into our world, how nice it must be for the whales to have us in theirs, if only for a short period of time.

*

To commit your life to caring for killer whales, or indeed any animal, is never going to be easy. It is a life filled with too many personal sacrifices. But when you have the privilege to look into the eyes of a killer whale and form a relationship with arguably one of the most intelligent beings on the planet, all you can think about is how lucky you are to share their world.

CONCLUSION- BELIEVE IN OUR FUTURE

The world we are living in is changing, rapidly. And we are changing with it.

But these changes happened long before the movie *Blackfish* was even an idea in someone's mind.

It is true that companies make a lot of money from having orcas, dolphins and other animals within the park. Visitors will pay to come and see these wonderful creatures, so it is beneficial to keep reproducing animals within zoological facilities, not only as a way to preserve endangered and vulnerable species but as a way to keep the visitors coming back again and again.

However, the majority of zoos and aquariums are taking the majority of their profits and putting them directly back into the welfare of the animals who live in their parks. Or they are using this revenue to donate money to conservation charities or setting up their own conservation foundations.

SeaWorld pours a huge amount of its profits into its rescue projects, paying for trainers and rescue team workers to be sent out in cars, planes and boats to help in the rescue of turtles, dolphins, whales and manatees to name but a few. A couple of years ago they even put a stop to all of their sea lion shows in California to send out every single trainer they had on staff to help rescue Californian sea lion pups during an epidemic along the Californian coastline due to unseasonably cold temperatures.

SeaWorld makes exactly zero profit off of their rescue programs but remains dedicated to saving as many needy animals as they possibly can, even if that means guests complaining about cancelled shows within the park.

The animals that they are rehabilitating remain behind the scenes, a constant drain on revenue and resources. From expert vet care to the thousands of kilos of food the animals consume per day and yet the company makes their rescue efforts a huge priority.

Over 33,000 animals have been rescued by SeaWorld to this day and this number is steadily growing.

Of course, people who are completely against SeaWorld will always say that the company is doing this because it gives them good advertising material and it is making them look better. However, SeaWorld has been rescuing animals like this for decades. They haven't managed to rescue 33,000 animals in need since *Blackfish* was released, they are simply giving the public more information about the other aspects of the company in an effort to show people that SeaWorld genuinely does care about the animals.

In actual fact, the majority of marine parks around the world would be better able to run research and rescue projects like the ones at SeaWorld if they were making more of a profit. Unfortunately, all the majority of parks can afford to do in reality is keep putting money back into the animals they already have at the parks and pay their staff.

The majority of marine parks and zoos do work for profit, but that is the reality of the world we live in. Not every company can work as a not-for-profit organization, and because businesses like SeaWorld are able to make such huge profits off of things like rollercoasters and entertainment, they can afford to put more money back into their rescue program.

I once heard a story about an anti-captivity campaigner protesting against the injustice of keeping endangered orangutans in captivity at a zoo in France. He was protesting that if the people who worked at the zoo had any morals then they should be over in Borneo trying to stop the production of palm oil instead.

Thankfully, someone stood up at this point and stated that the zoo had recently donated over 30,000 euros towards finding sustainable alternatives to palm oil. They had also sent five of their keepers over to Borneo to learn more about the plight facing wild orangutans and to volunteer at the orangutan rescue centre, providing invaluable information to the people over there about how to properly care for the primates.

I wish I could have been there to see the activists' face when he realized that in comparison to the incredible good the zoo was doing to help and save orangutans both now and in the future, he was doing absolutely nothing.

In fifty years the world will not look like it does now. Even in my own lifetime we have lost so many species, meaning the unfortunate reality is that soon we will only be able to see these animals in zoological settings. So what is the difference between having an orangutan or a rhino in captivity at a zoo and an orca or dolphin at a marine park?

Some people say that because the animals are not endangered then they shouldn't have to be in a zoo. Should we just wait until they all become endangered and then go out with capture boats again and round up the last few individuals to try and save the species? Doesn't it make more sense to keep the captive population healthy and diverse and conduct research studies, not only to learn more about them, but also possibly learn how to help their counterparts in the wild? The southern resident population of orcas are already endangered and the rest will not be far behind.

I for one would rather be a happy, comfortable orca that lived in a zoo, surrounded by my family with a full belly, a masseuse on demand and more toys than I knew what to do with, than a starving orca swimming endlessly day after day trying to find food in a sea full of more plastic than fish.

Back in the 1980s, once people learned how intelligent killer whales were and their apparent capacity for emotion, they began to care more about the animals which led to better standards of care for them.

Where orcas were once held in small dolphin pools, new bigger, deeper pools were constructed to house them with the space that they needed to thrive.

Trainers soon developed positive reinforcement techniques based on operant conditioning in order to properly communicate with the whales and they learned to develop relationships with the animals. With this change came new shows, gone were the basic circus-like tricks, and presentations soon became more educational and based on the ability of orcas to form close connections with man.

Nowadays we are going through an even bigger change.

Our shows are becoming even more educational, sometimes in danger of completely losing the entertainment factor. Some of the general public have begun to comment negatively on how the whales are being presented.

Even though there are a large majority of people who come to see the whales because they want to be educated and learn more about them, there are also a large percentage of the population who want to be entertained and sit back to watch a rousing demonstration of the power and capability of the orcas.

I have been asked hundreds of times why the trainers aren't allowed in the water during shows anymore and this is because people genuinely miss watching water work.

The struggle for marine parks everywhere now is to try and find the balance.

Have educational shows but still include an aspect of theatricality to be able to excite and entertain an audience to hold them enthralled. Capture the audiences' attention with fantastically powerful behaviours and leave them hanging on the edge of their seat, their hearts full of passion for what they are witnessing. Use emotive language to explain the plight facing wild killer whales and suggest what the individual person can do to help as they watch trainer and whale demonstrate their deep relationship right in front of their eyes.

That is how you inspire a generation to make a difference.

Nowadays, an orca trainer needs to be able to explain all of this, to constantly have the words ready to explain, to defend, to inspire. Because the future of a generation rests on our shoulders.

Not only the next generation of killer whale trainers, but the next generation of activists too.

Of course we need activists!

'Activist' shouldn't be viewed as a negative word, we should all be animal activists, ready to donate and devote our time and money to saving the animals most in need of our help.

But education should always come before activism.

I want my children to grow up in a world where they won't be picked on in school because of what their Mother does.

I want them to see animals in zoological settings and feel inspired, and use that inspiration to be a force for good in this world.

When I imagine the future I imagine myself standing on the stage, my killer whale in front of me and a packed audience in the stands behind her.

I want to look into her eyes and see that she is as ready for the show as I am. That she is ready to show these people exactly why we are a team. I want her to not only enjoy the life that we give her, but also to be a force for good in the world and give a voice to all of her voiceless struggling distant cousins out in the ocean.

She may be safe but they are not.

In the future when there is even more plastic in the ocean and things like over fishing and pollution have driven the wild killer whales to the brink of extinction, I want to be proud to work for a company that has been steadily donating a margin of its profits towards conservation efforts for decades. I want to spend evenings discussing the new research programs that we are implementing in order to help save wild killer whales. I want to look behind me at the back pool and see the new calf that has just been born as a result of a newly incorporated and strictly regulated breeding program that is focused on keeping the species alive and viable, hopefully indefinitely.

And for all of those people in the audience, I want them to feel the same inspiration that I felt sitting in Shamu Stadium as an eight year old child.

Because our world is changing and we need to change along with it.

Some of you may be wondering where our future lies, what is the point in fighting against the barrage of anti-captivity activism that seems to be slowly wearing us down?

The point is that there are animals in need of our help, and the only way we can save them is by putting aside our anger and hate and working together.

Regardless of who you are, where you are, or what you do. You can make a difference.

So before you form an opinion based on a documentary or on one sided arguments, come and visit our parks, speak to trainers and make an informed decision for yourself about what you choose to believe in.

Together, in spite of any differences of opinion we may have, we can make a difference to the lives of millions of animals all over the world.

Every day that I walk into work and am greeted by the four black and white faces before me, I want to know that myself and others like me are fighting for their future.

Because I want them to have a future.

Here at Marineland Antibes, I have found somewhere I can truly be myself and it feels like almost all of the pieces of my puzzle are clicking into place.

Every day when I pull on my wetsuit I feel like I am exactly where I am meant to be. When the whales greet me around the pool by offering me a pec fin or their back to run as their way of saying 'good morning', I count my blessings that I managed to make my impossible dream a reality.

When I am hanging out above the stage with this amazing group of trainers and watch the whales have the best time playing with a new enrichment device or ridiculously elaborate birthday cake we made them, I feel like I belong.

Five years into my career I have lived in three different countries, learned two new languages and each experience, whether good or bad, has made me into the trainer I am today.

I might be living in a very small apartment and praying that nothing major needs fixed on my car because there is no way I can afford a large bill in any month of the year.

I may not be able to get home to visit my family more than once a year and am always craving a well-cooked steak and ale pie and galaxy chocolate.

I may have been willing to go through a long distance relationship for almost three years because even though I love my boyfriend, the real loves of my life are here in the South of France.

Even though my job is an extension of who I am, unlike in Tenerife where all I had was the job, I have been able to make a life for myself outside of work here in Antibes.

I started singing again after almost seven years without performing.

I have terrible stage fright any time I have to go out and perform, my nerves get so bad I swear I feel like I am about to throw up and I get nervous butt sweat, even if I only need to provide some gentle background music for a hundred elderly ladies at their local charity gala.

In comparison, I can perform in a stadium that seats twelve thousand at Marineland with Wikie in front of me and feel no nerves at all.

This is because when I am with Wikie I am not alone. We are a team. No matter what happens out there, we are in it together. I trust her to take care of me and she trusts me to take care of her. So when we go out in front of those large summer crowds I don't even see the people in the stadium.

I only see her.

She, and the other whales by extension, are my world. They always have been, ever since I made the decision to pursue a career as a killer whale trainer aged fourteen.

I look at my friends and family who are buying gorgeous houses and getting married or settling down with their families close by and part of me does envy them.

I would love to come home every night to the man I believe is my soulmate and sit down in my lovingly decorated house with our five rescue dogs and earn enough money to go on exciting and adventurous vacations every year.

But that blissful future picture has one gaping hole inside of it, because it doesn't include killer whales.

I have sacrificed so much to get to where I am now, to be able to share my days by the side of four incredible orcas, and it is all because I believe in what I am doing here every single day.

I am able to get up out of bed every morning and look forward to what the day will bring. I get to challenge myself and the whales with new and innovative training techniques that explore our abilities to communicate. I am blessed enough to live in an incredible part of the world where I can go sunbathe at the beach in the morning and reach the snowy heights of the Alps by the afternoon.

I love being able to pop into the quaint little bakery beside my church in the morning before work and pick up the butteriest, most delicious croissant you have ever tasted.

I have felt myself truly flourish on the team at Marineland. Where I felt oppressed and inadequate on the team at Loro Parque, I now feel like I am in an environment where I can truly grow with the guidance of those around me.

Now, when I am training killer whales and making decisions, I do it with confidence in my abilities and I know my superiors have faith that I will make the right call.

At least I know that when I do mess up and make mistakes, they will have my back and explain what it is I can do to improve for the next time.

To walk out around the pool each morning and hear that glorious rush of an exhale followed by a deep inhale as the broad black back glides towards you in welcome is, for me, to feel truly complete.

Pursuing this dream job has given me so much. I will never forget the people I have met along the way and because of them I am so far away from the little girl I was when I first left my village in Scotland.

For any fellow trainers out there, your hard work and dedication is recognised and well worth it (but you all know that already).

For any aspiring trainers, know that with enough hard work and determination that you can make it happen and never stop believing that our industry has a bright and brilliant future.

For anyone who still isn't sure about captivity, remember that we can do so much more good for animals everywhere if we work together.

I always dreamed about becoming a killer whale trainer but I never imagined exactly how much my journey could give me along the way.

That journey isn't over yet, I have no idea what my future will bring me personally but I still believe that the zoological facilities are the hope for saving future species. I firmly believe that killer whales have an essential part to play in inspiring future generations to make necessary changes. I believe that we have a purpose and a future. I always have.

I always will.

ACKNOWLEDGMENTS

Mum, I owe you everything.

Gran, you were the one who turned me into a bookworm, I just wish you were able to check this book out of the library and cosy down to read it yourself.

A special thanks to my supervisor, Duncan, for taking me seriously when I presented him with my notes. Hastily scribbled in an angry scrawl across the back of some scrap office paper. You took my idea seriously and helped me to believe that I could actually make a difference.

Jonathan Kershaw, for all of the effort you put in to make the book cover great and for accepting my first proposal.

To everyone who has sent me warm well-wishes over social media or in person, you have kept my motivation up even when I started to doubt my credibility and it seemed like this book would never get finished.

Gwen, thanks for being there to tell me when my ideas sucked, as well as when they were great. Thanks to your insights this book was made better.

Dee, thanks for playing the part of my official editor so well.

To all of my fellow trainers out there, I hope that this book will bring you some relief and something positive to hold on to.

ABOUT THE AUTHOR

Hazel McBride was born in Glasgow, Scotland in 1993 and was raised by her single mother, Marie. She currently lives and works in Antibes, France at the marine park Marineland, where she hopes to continue to learn and grow within the team. Her growing passion is to be able to have a voice on behalf of her fellow trainers, and the animals themselves, in order to spark greater understanding within the general public.

Made in the USA
Coppell, TX
05 February 2021

49805682R00162